[handwritten at top:] five scenarios: see pg 10, weforum.org/en/initiatives/scenarios/...

[handwritten:] Typical design: 40 hrs over 4 mo p92

More Praise for *Scenario Planning in Organizations*

[handwritten:] Assessment Tools pg 97/see pg 199

"All CEOs, university presidents, leaders of national nonprofits, and politicians face the same problem: coping with uncertainty. Scenario planning addresses this central problem. One cannot attend a planning session in any large organization without the topic of scenario planning arising. Professor Chermack puts the various approaches to scenario planning in a highly readable and useful context. For those of us who have used a variant of scenario planning for many years, there is much to learn in this approach. Professor Chermack is well on his way to becoming a major resource for this important planning tool."

—**Vance Opperman, President and CEO, Key Investment, Inc.; Audit Committee Chair, Thomson Reuters; and former President, West Publishing Company**

"With extensive expertise, Tom Chermack spotlights scenario planning as a fundamental tool used by organizations to achieve long-term sustainability. This book helps me guide diverse management teams through strategic decision and problem-solving processes using a collaborative and forward-thinking approach."

—**Carla McCabe, Director of Human Resources, Technicolor**

"Scenario planning has benefitted our entire organization by helping us understand a volatile environment and how to move forward. Scenarios have helped us think through options, create insights, and spark innovative ideas. Chermack's approach held us accountable and emphasized creative thinking as well as assessing where and how the scenarios added value."

—**James Steven Beck, MBA, CPA, Vice President—Administration, Eltron Research & Development, Inc.**

"Professor Chermack has made the mysterious process of scenario planning available in a format accessible for both leaders of large corporations and small business owners. Creating a common working language about the future is essential for the long-term success of any enterprise. Tom's clear guidelines provide practical tools for organizations to create scenarios that will help them discover new ways of thinking, planning, and being."

—**Kim Cermak, President and COO, KDC Management, LLC**

[handwritten:] Garr Reynolds Presentation Zen .com

[barcode:] D0861942

...ee spend less than 10%
of their time on strat issues

Michaels ...ly...

testing → Experience →
obs + reflect
→ initial conclusions / abstracts

org performance: goals, design + mgt.
graphic on p 66 → scenario building + deployment
p 68 → scenario process

learning scenarios help w/ global, macros
then regional
then local or focused

cherry tree p 87
key questions: what can we do to ...

Data Gathering

(STEEP)
Social, Tech, Econ, Envir, Political

DeBono's Thinking Hats
White: neutral / analytical
Red: Emotional
Black: Devel's advoc
yellow: Positive, optimist
Green: Creative
Blue: overview, summary/synthe, conclu

(SWOT)

7 key interview questions p 113   <u>Capture</u>

Which problem might we think more deeply about
which opportunity " What if we took on ___?

SCENARIO PLANNING
IN ORGANIZATIONS

make cards to represent the <u>hats</u>

Drucker's theory of business: p115   <u>Capture</u>
    good for board work too
9 perf variables p121   (KL)
Swanson's perf variables p 122

Developing Scenarios
1) Describe the Predetermined Elements   4 types:
    Slow changing   Tease out the ones
    constrained   w/
    in the pipeline   highest relative impact
    inevitable   ↕
                                   highest relative ⌐Choose
2) Critical uncertainties   uncertainty   2

(Innovation: Slow down, step away, change
             location + reflect   p163)

Easiest:

Inducive → brainstorming — stickies 1 each, no talking

offical forecast: where might we be wrong? → interview question

A Publication in the Berrett-Koehler
Organizational Performance Series

Richard A. Swanson and Barbara L. Swanson,
Series Editors

good for experienced in strat + scen — less structured

8 steps p 131

first 4 in workshops → building the shared mental model

brainstorm — forces that impact the issue — then — predet vs truly uncertain

Rank —

1) Lay out left to right low to high impact on the strat agenda

2) Then high to low — Relative uncertainty ↓ to make a matrix

separate steps — no quadrants at first

high uncertainty

crit uncert.

low — high impact

what res here?

Low

3) Analysis

Predet. elements?

double check this

4) Choose 2 crit unces → relevant, plausible, challenging, meaningful

to lay out

1

2

p 142

Choose 2-4 scenarios → must be robust enough to generate "characters" & data.

Can use the "official future" as a safety net in 1 of 3 to 4.

SCENARIO PLANNING
IN ORGANIZATIONS

HOW TO CREATE, USE, AND ASSESS SCENARIOS

for each scenario - driving forces?
Uncertainties?
Inevitable?

Plot ideas p.148
guidelines for the scenario stories p152

THOMAS J. CHERMACK

Assessment (from Pink): Design, Story, Symphony, Empathy, Play, Meaning
Checklist p164

Berrett–Koehler Publishers, Inc.
San Francisco
a BK Business book

Berrett-Koehler Publishers, Inc.
235 Montgomery Street, Suite 650
San Francisco, CA 94104-2916
Tel: (415) 288-0260   Fax: (415) 362-2512   www.bkconnection.com

Ordering Information

Quantity sales. Special discounts are available on quantity purchases by corporations, associations, and others. For details, contact the "Special Sales Department" at the Berrett- Koehler address above.

Individual sales.   Berrett-Koehler publications are available through most bookstores. They can also be ordered directly from Berrett-Koehler: Tel: (800) 929-2929; Fax: (802) 864-7626; www.bkconnection.com

Orders for college textbook/course adoption use. Please contact Berrett-Koehler:
Tel: (800) 929-2929; Fax: (802) 864-7626.

Orders by U.S. trade bookstores and wholesalers. Please contact Ingram Publisher Services, Tel: (800) 509-4887; Fax: (800) 838-1149; E-mail: customer.service@ingram publisherservices.com; or visit www.ingrampublisherservices.com/Ordering for details about electronic ordering.

Berrett-Koehler and the BK logo are registered trademarks of Berrett-Koehler Publishers, Inc.

Printed in the United States of America

Berrett-Koehler books are printed on long-lasting acid-free paper. When it is available, we choose paper that has been manufactured by environmentally responsible processes. These may include using trees grown in sustainable forests, incorporating recycled paper, minimizing chlorine in bleaching, or recycling the energy produced at the paper mill.

Production Management: Michael Bass Associates

Cover Design: Irene Morris
Cover Photos: © Matthias Clamer/Stone+/Getty Images

Library of Congress Cataloging-in-Publication Data

Chermack, Thomas J.
Scenario planning in organizations : how to create, use, and assess scenarios /
    Thomas J. Chermack.
       p.   cm.
ISBN 978-1-60509-413-7 (pbk. : alk. paper)
1. Management—Simulation methods. 2. Strategic planning—Simulation methods. I. Title.
HD30.26.C48 2011
658.4'012—dc22

                                              2010030700
First Edition
16   15   14   13   12   11   10   9   8   7   6   5   4   3   2   1

Contents

List of Figures

Using the scenarios to explore the
 focal issue:
   questions p 174 or
   process on p 176   3 to 5 oppor
                      3 to 5 threats
   then id strategies — are any common across
   scenarios ??

Test current strat through the scenarios p 178
Id signals

Simple testing grid p 182
Strategic gains + Losses p 209

Foreword

Louis van der Merwe

IT COMES AS NO SURPRISE that in our world of discontinuities and volatility, the use of scenarios as part of strategic planning processes has taken off. According to the Bain & Company annual survey of the most-used management tools, scenario work has risen considerably. Scenario use has risen from 40 percent of those surveyed in 1999 to 70 percent in 2006 (*Economist*, 2006). *The Economist* goes on to say, "As a result of its scenario planning, the New York Board of Trade decided in the 1990s to build a second trading floor outside the World Trade Centre, a decision that kept it going after September 11th, 2001."

As the environment becomes more volatile, one wrong assumption about future conditions or markets could put you out of business or set your organization back years. Leaders of organizations and governments need to skillfully use state-of-the-art tools and methods in order to steer their organizations away from dangers and to identify new opportunities. Appreciating how a specific method works and its underpinning theory is important for practitioners and leaders alike.

Lewin's (1951) famous quote "There is nothing so practical as a good theory" (p. 169) is probably overused. However, it is particularly relevant for scenario planners, because the practical utility of theory has not yet been emphasized.

This book is aimed at the evolving community of practitioner-scholars involved in scenario work across the globe. Chermack's theory building, together with that of scholars such as Richard Swanson, Susan Lynham, and others, is based on traditional scientific inquiry (Swanson & Holton, 2005), naturalistic inquiry (Denzin & Lincoln 2000), as well as action research (Reason & Bradbury, 2001). Chermack has based this work on his own experience as a practitioner and researcher as well as what he has learned from the deep tradition of scenario practitioners. This book provides the emerging scenario builder with a practical and theoretical foundation on which to build a competent practice.

For the first time, the theoretical foundations of scenario planning have been put forth.

Providing the theoretical foundations for the scenario method for the first time through this book is important and essential for advancing practices. An example for thinking about scenario use can be illustrated by recalling what happened when you last purchased a car. What did you notice when you drove your car out onto the streets? You probably noticed how many people were driving the same car! It may have appeared as though there were many more cars like yours than you had noticed before, when in fact there is only one more of the same car on the road—yours! Becoming aware of your selective observation (which is a skill that develops when scenario work is done well) enables you as a decision maker to notice relevant dynamics more quickly than someone who has not explored the what-ifs.

A rigorous theory base stabilizes scenario practice and lays the foundations for establishing best practice. Chermack's work provides an excellent start to articulating this body of theory. *Theory* can be defined as "a scholarly description of what works best and why." This book provides that basis and will guide practitioners and leadership toward best practice. While it provides practical how-to's, it argues strongly for the theory underpinning this practice, as well as useful metrics for measuring the impact of scenario work.

Chermack's writing takes the reader onto the cutting edge of strategy making—namely, strategy making as strategic conversation. Here you will get the big picture of scenario-based strategy in a framework that allows you great freedom to bring in your own experiences as tools. Alternatively, if you are new to scenario planning, a high level of detail is shared. For example, a calibrated instrument for measuring the quality of strategic conversation is provided, as well as recommended tools for measuring other aspects of dynamic organizations. Chermack has contributed an emphasis on performance. It may be assumed that scenarios add value, but it is in the best interests of the art of scenario planning to create a tradition of documenting the actual results.

The discipline of scenario planning needs to establish a track record of its contributions. Assessing scenario work is overdue, and, like the establishment of underlying theory, doing so will stabilize scenario practice and boost quality. Chermack has described an elegant approach to assessment that provides the practitioner with many different tools for pinning down scenario impact. The invitation is for scholar-practitioners to add to this body of knowledge, through their action research, reflection, and inquiry. A comprehensive, theory-based practice that emphasizes assessment will create a professional cadre of competent practitioners for scenario work.

We have learned from MIT's Peter Senge and the community of practitioners building learning organizations that learning faster than competitors is the ultimate competitive advantage. Scenario-based strategy is in essence a learning and unlearning methodology. Pioneers such as the late Don Michael (1973) in his book *Learning to Plan and Planning to Learn* and Arie de Geus (1988) in his popular *Harvard Business Review* article "Planning as Learning," first drew attention to the fundamental role of learning in organizations as the basis for competitive advantage.

While developing the scenario method in Royal/Dutch Shell, Group Planning, Pierre Wack aimed scenario work at shifting the assumptions in the minds of decision makers. This process enabled them to notice emergent dynamics in the environment, before competitors, as they had visited and studied them during the scenario-building process. This capacity of aligned assumptions with the capability to self-correct early provided Royal/Dutch Shell with a significant competitive advantage when oil prices were volatile in the 1970s. The assumptions on which they had based their decisions were influenced by the scenario development process and therefore held a wider view of their world.

Because scenarios can be powerful tools, they have been used in widely differing application areas. Herman Kahn used them to shift attention onto the impending dangers of a nuclear holocaust, and Royal/Dutch Shell leaders used scenarios for decision-making. In South Africa, scenarios were used to push people toward "the high road" and away from "the low road" of racial conflict and economic destruction. Engaging the emerging South African national leadership in a conversation about the future scenarios they might be confronted with resulted in avoiding populist policies that compromised the future of the economy. The list of application areas grows.

Initially, scenario practice was learned via an apprenticeship model. If you were fortunate enough to be a member of the Royal/Dutch Shell Group Planning, you could learn from the masters, such as Pierre Wack, Ted Newland, Arie de Geus, Kees van der Heijden, and Peter Schwartz. The first public courses for learning the craft of scenario development emerged in the early 1990s. Early teaching was based on simulating a typical scenario project providing practice and coaching in the essentials of the various phases of developing a set of scenarios.

The recently established Scenario Planning Institute at Colorado State University is destined to provide a home for scholar-practitioners and capacity building for scenario-based strategy. It promises to become a center for high-quality scenario work, training of skilled scenario practitioners, and the dissemination of performance-based scenario planning.

I wish you all the success with the scenarios you develop. May you grow with other practitioners in the field and use this book and scenarios to make the world a better place.

Louis van der Merwe
Centre for Innovative Leadership
June 2010

Preface

THE FUTURE OFTEN ACTS like a drunken monkey stung by a bee—it is confused and disturbing, and its behavior is completely unpredictable. Organization leaders are struggling with an uncertain and fast-changing environment. Many are frustrated by the promise of tools for managing the future that come up short. A variety of terms has been used to describe the environment, such as *whitewater, the rapids, VUCA* (volatile, uncertain, complex, and ambiguous), and *turbulent*. These terms all emphasize that business decision making is an activity that has reached high levels of frustration and confusion. Signs point to increasing complexity and uncertainty. This means choosing among options will become even more challenging, and carving a path into the future will require more diligent use of better tools.

Traditional approaches to business planning have had their day. Linear approaches to strategic planning worked in the 1950s and 1960s because the environment was relatively stable. Linear approaches only lead to disappointment in today's environment because they cannot account for uncertainty—they assume that the environment of tomorrow will be the same as today's. Scenario planning is a revolutionary alternative to traditional strategic planning because it recognizes the unpredictable nature of the future. Early scenario planners helped organization leaders see that the future was not going to consist of historic trends, projected forward. Instead, recognizing their problematic assumptions of a stable environment, decision makers found a way to think about alternatives in scenario planning. Scenario planning makes uncertainty a part of the plan. Many companies have been able to avoid major strategic losses due to the alternative way of thinking found in scenario planning.

The most valuable advantage of creating and using scenarios is the recognition that uncertainty is a basic feature of organizational environments. By accepting the reality of uncertainty—and making it a part of how planning happens—decision makers can widen the scope of what is assumed to be true about what the future might hold. A more open view of what is possible allows decision makers to be more prepared and adjust with minimal delay and disruption. An expanded view of the terrain is developed by changing perceptions among key people in organizations. A primary outcome of scenario planning is to shift perceptions. Scenario planning is a tool for helping decision makers reperceive the potential future in alternative ways. Having these alternative ways of seeing helps decision makers avoid surprises and prepare for a variety of plausible futures.

Over the last thirty years, scenario planning has been used in a variety of contexts and organizations (Ogilvy, 1995, 2002; Ogilvy & Schwartz, 2000). For example, scenarios have been employed with great success in anticipating the oil shocks in the 1970s, potential outcomes of Hurricane Katrina, the events of September 11, 2001, and developing responses to bridge collapses and other emergencies. Certainly, each of these events had numerous management issues, and some were more effectively directed than others. In each case, scenarios were developed that told stories quite similar to how reality unfolded (D'arcy, O'Hanlong, Orszag, Shapiro, & Steinberg, 2006; Hoffman, 2002; Lynch, 2005). Although there are many anecdotes of scenario use, few have rigorously studied scenario planning, and the process has been modified and changed as needed. As a result, scenario planning means different things to different people, and the reported approaches are incomplete.

The purpose of this book is to provide a complete approach to scenario planning that includes key pieces missing from existing literature. These missing pieces are the theoretical foundations of scenario planning, a detailed guide to using scenarios once they have been developed, and a structure for assessing the impact of scenario projects. The theoretical foundations of scenario planning are important for understanding how scenario planning works. Such an understanding is critical for anyone serious about using scenario planning to steer an organization into the future. Precisely how to use scenarios is not well covered in the literature, either. This book provides detailed suggestions for putting scenarios into practice and using them to support organizational change. Finally, not a single text on the topic deals with how to assess the impact of scenario projects. This book provides a clear, concise guide to assessing the benefits of scenario planning in organizations. These three contributions make a complete scenario planning system that is the focus of this book.

AUDIENCES

This book is for thoughtful people trying to move their organizations forward—leaders, managers, decision makers, practitioners, consultants, and executives. This book provides the tools for facilitating scenario planning in organizations and is therefore a guide. This book is also a text for university courses focused on organization and business planning. Although this suggestion may indicate two separate audiences, I argue that they are one and the same. Students in business planning courses are usually also managers, decision makers, practitioners, consultants, or executives. Again, these are people struggling to move their organizations forward amid a great deal of chaos and uncertainty.

STRUCTURE OF THE BOOK

This book features three parts: (1) Foundations of Scenario Planning, (2) Phases of the Performance-Based Scenario System, and (3) Leading Scenario Projects.

Part One is focused on the foundations of scenario planning. These chapters review scenario planning, its history, development, and influential figures. Performance-based scenario planning—the contribution of this book—is described and explained. Chapter 1 describes the development and evolution of scenario planning. Key definitions, outcomes, and major approaches are reviewed. Chapter 2 is a synthesis of the theoretical foundations of scenario planning, and is a comprehensive review of the major content disciplines that inform the practice of scenario planning. Chapter 3 situates scenario planning in the organization system, and Chapter 4 presents a case study. Part One provides a sense of the context in which scenario planning was developed as a strategic tool, as well as an understanding of the position of scenario planning inside organizations.

Part Two presents the phases of the scenario system. These are Chapters 5 through 9, covering the major phases of scenario planning: (1) project preparation, (2) scenario exploration, (3) scenario development, (4) scenario implementation, and (5) project assessment. These are the chapters that become a guide for using the scenario system. Detailed examples are provided, and the core case study that is presented in Chapter 4 is expanded further in each subsequent chapter. The examples illustrate key outcomes of each phase.

Part Three presents tips for managing and leading scenario projects. Chapter 10 describes several pitfalls in scenario planning and how they can be avoided or overcome. Chapter 11 summarizes some cutting-edge neurology research and how it relates to cognitive activity and human perceptions in the scenario process. Finally, Chapter 12 offers suggestions for getting started on your own scenario projects, followed by a summary of the book.

MY OWN FASCINATION WITH SCENARIO PLANNING

What continues to fascinate me about scenario planning is its potential application to almost any context, problem, issue, or situation, and its evolving nature. There are many nuances throughout the facilitation of scenario projects. As a result, there are always opportunities for improving scenario planning and finding ways to increase its effectiveness. For timely examples, Noah Raford is studying how to maintain dialogue over electronic media such as Twitter, Facebook, and other Web 2.0 technologies in scenario planning (see http://news.noahraford.com/?p=129). Others are working on how scenario planning is used in nonprofit organizations, communities, and nations. As the world's problems evolve in their complexity, there is only increasing utility for scenario planning.

Scenario planning is a decision-making tool that can be used to explore and understand a variety of issues in a variety of organizations and issues. For example, scenarios can be used to consider the future of global climate change, global water supply, natural resources, as well as business and community decisions (such as in the Mont Fleur scenarios that explored the end of apartheid in South Africa). These are all issues that involve complex dynamics including diverse sets of stakeholders and varying knowledge bases, and they are likely to require interdisciplinary collaboration to address. Any situation in which a group of people is trying to work out how to create aligned movement toward a common goal can consider scenario planning a potentially useful tool.

Human perceptions in scenario planning are another fascinating topic for me. As I continue to witness strategic insights among participants in scenario projects, I wonder why some participants have them and some don't. What are the characteristics of individuals that lend them to thinking deeply about problems? What are the characteristics of scenarios that help people open up their thinking? These questions pose challenges to what is known about scenario planning and how to maximize its impact. Neuroscience research is getting close to helping us understand how the brain learns and what happens physiologically during these strategic insights, but there is still a long way to go.

A lot about scenario planning remains unknown. Each scenario project I work on reveals more about how to do it better next time. This book introduces scenario planning and its foundations, explains how to do it, and describes how to tell whether it produces benefits. This is a book for people who want to improve the way their organizations prepare for the future. Readers are encouraged to access the latest research on scenarios from my website (www.thomaschermack.com) and to e-mail me reports of their experiences. I have also recently established the Scenario Planning Institute at Colorado State University, and readers who want to get more involved can engage at www.scenarioplanning.colostate.edu.

Finally, scenario planning is a lot of fun! Scenario planning is a blend of creative and analytical activities. There's nothing like arranging complex variables into stories that make sense, are rigorously researched, and can move an audience. Seeing the moment when new understanding comes together for a participant is exciting and rewarding. Indeed, helping people think in new and interesting ways has immediate impact that can be applied in a variety of situations. Wack (1984) may have put it best when he wrote, "In our times of rapid change and discontinuity, crises of perception—the inability to see a novel reality emerging by being locked inside obsolete assumptions—have become the main cause of strategic failures" (p. 95). Scenario planning is a way to avoid such crises of perception by learning how to see the environment differently and perhaps a little more completely.

ACKNOWLEDGMENTS

Some people say that writing a book is an inherently personal endeavor. Mine has been a humbling experience. This book is the result of thousands of interactions, conversations, scholarly debates, e-mails, and other exchanges with a variety of people over the last ten years. So, while it has been a personal experience, I could not have written this book by myself.

Richard A. Swanson's name should appear as the second author of this book. I offered it to him, but he would not accept it. He read, critiqued, edited, moved, improved, shifted, guided, and reviewed every word on these pages. His contributions made the final product much more useful than it would have been without his generosity. Thanks are not enough to cover my appreciation for his direction and guidance, but it is all I can do in this preface. Thank you, Dick.

Thanks to Susan A. Lynham and Louis van der Merwe for their mentorship and guidance. Many conversations, experiences, and stories from Susan and Louis have been foundational to my thinking about scenario planning. I am grateful for the guidance and advice of two such accomplished professionals. Thank you, Susan and Louis.

Thanks to Evie Chenhall, Janet Colvin, Jennifer Fullerton, Maggie Glick, Lea Hanson, Chris Harper, Stacey Herr, Martin Kollasch, Kyle Stone, and Joy Wagner. Their contributions appear in some of the materials for the Technology Corporation case, and their comments, suggestions, and reviews have improved this book.

Thanks to Ziad Labban, Dave Peck, John Weatherburn, Paul Grimmer, Steve Beck, Joanne Provo, and Monica Danielson. Writing a book about scenario planning requires experience in using its tools. These individuals all provided learning opportunities and gave me access to situations in which to learn how to apply scenario techniques.

Thanks to Kees van der Heijden, Art Kleiner, Peter Schwartz, Napier Collyns, George Burt, George Wright, Paul Schoemaker, and Louis van der Merwe. These individuals have influenced and inspired me, and their efforts have established the scenario planning discipline. Thank you.

Thanks to the late Pierre Wack and Ted Newland. These two visionary thinkers sought a way to think differently about the future. Their work has inspired many and is certainly the foundation of my own thinking about scenario planning in organizations.

Finally, thank you to the outstanding team at Berrett-Koehler and, in particular, Steve Piersanti and Jeevan Sivasubramaniam.

Thomas J. Chermack
December 2010
Fort Collins, Colorado
www.thomaschermack.com
www.scenarioplanning.colostate.edu

FOUNDATIONS OF SCENARIO PLANNING

IF WE LOOK BACK over the history of planning in organizations, we can see a fundamental illusion that is beginning to come to light. The illusion is that planning can function like a machine, that the steps of organizational planning need only be carried out. The basis of that illusion is an assumption that things more or less stay the same. Today, our rhetoric would indicate we have realized our erroneous assumption, but actions indicate otherwise. The world is changing faster than ever, yet many planners and decision makers behave in opposition to what they know is true about the world—they seek the answer, as if there is only one correct answer and their job is to find it.

A key premise of this book is that things are ever-changing. Planning therefore needs to take a different approach, one that assumes tomorrow's world will be fundamentally different from today's. Scenario planning explores a variety of outcomes, a variety of potential answers, and uses them to create awareness and readiness. The hardest part of scenario planning is recognizing our desperate clinging to a single answer and consciously shifting toward an open future of vast potential—both positive and negative. This book asks its readers to take a journey. To interact with their environment. To ask difficult questions that lead to more difficult questions. To become comfortable with ambiguity.

Part One consists of Chapters 1 through 4. These chapters provide a working knowledge of scenario planning.

Chapter 1, "Introduction to Performance-Based Scenario Planning," establishes the nature of the business environment, describes why traditional approaches to strategy are no longer effective, and lays out the development of scenario planning as a major evolution in planning under uncertain conditions. This is an extensive chapter that provides a comprehensive background of the need for scenario planning, and the critical breakdowns of existing approaches to scenario planning. Unlike existing approaches, performance-based scenario planning provokes conversations about expectations, delivers a variety of options for putting scenarios to use, and makes assessment a required part of the project.

Chapter 2, "Theoretical Foundations of Performance-Based Scenario Planning," presents the major disciplines that form the theoretical basis for scenario planning. This chapter examines the connections between scenario planning and learning theory, mental model theory, decision-making theory, and performance improvement theory, among others. This chapter is a comprehensive treatment of the knowledge required for effective scenario planning. While not required for immediate application, this chapter reveals many nuances about what scenario planning is and how it works.

Chapter 3, "The Performance-Based Scenario System," situates scenario planning within the organization. Drawing on system theory concepts, this chapter generally outlines the position of scenario planning as a subsystem in organizations. This chapter also presents the performance-based scenario system, which is the focus of Part Two.

Finally, Chapter 4, the "Scenario Case Study," presents a short description of a real organization (disguised for the purposes of confidentiality). The case illustrates the phases of the performance-based scenario system described throughout Part Two.

1

Introduction to Performance-Based Scenario Planning

This book describes a method for including the realities of uncertainty in the planning process. Uncertainty and ambiguity are basic structural features of today's business environment. They can best be managed by including them in planning activities as standard features that must be considered in any significant decision.

This book focuses on avoiding crises of perception. Scenario planning is a tool for surfacing assumptions so that changes can be made in how decision makers see the environment. It is also a tool for changing and improving the quality of people's perceptions. Uncertainty is not a new problem, but the degree of uncertainty and the effects of unanticipated outcomes are unprecedented. Learning how to see a situation—complete with its uncertainties—is an important ability in today's world.

This chapter presents some of the challenges posed by today's fast-changing environment. A tool for dealing with those challenges has traditionally been strategic planning. Basic approaches to strategic planning are described; however, the rate and depth of change have increased over time to the point that those methods are no longer useful. Scenario planning emerged as an effective solution in the 1970s, and the ensuing history of scenario planning is discussed here. This chapter also describes a variety of major approaches to scenario planning, including their shortcomings. The fundamental problem with existing approaches to scenario planning is that they are not performance based. Evidence of this critical oversight is presented by reviewing the definitions and outcomes of scenario planning as they are described by major scenario planning authors. The outcomes they promote are generally vague and unclear. Finally, this chapter introduces performance-based scenario planning—which is the contribution of this book.

DILEMMAS

Some authors prefer to use the term *dilemma* instead of *problem* because the term *problem* can imply that there is a single solution (Cascio, 2009; Johansen, 2008). Most often, strategic decision making involves ambiguity and a realization that numerous solutions are possible. Each usually comes with its own caveats and difficult elements that must be considered. Hampden-Turner (1990) saw dilemmas as a dialectic and used the description "horns of the dilemma" to describe this way of observing specific dynamics in the environment. This way of describing complex dynamics takes a first step into looking for underlying systemic structure.

This book focuses on *complex problems or dilemmas* with *unknown solutions*. Therefore, its intent is to develop the understanding and expertise required to explore difficult, ambiguous problems and consider a variety of solutions in a wildly unpredictable and turbulent environment. Because there are no clear answers to questions of strategy and uncertainty, decision makers are compelled to do the best they can. These types of problems are the most complex, most ambiguous, and often the most deeply rooted. Experienced scenario planning practitioners have demonstrated their capacity to detect blind spots, avoid surprises, and increase the capacity to adjust when needed. Most important, modern-day dilemmas take place in an environment the likes of which we have never seen before.

THE ENVIRONMENT

Organizations operate in environmental contexts. These contexts include and are shaped by social, technological, economic, environmental, and political forces. The external environment has received much attention in literature from a variety of disciplines. Emery and Trist published a seminal work on the importance of the external environment in 1965. They suggested a four-step typology of the "causal texture" of the external environment:

Step 1—a placid, randomized environment
Step 2—a placid, clustered environment

Step 3—a disturbed, reactive environment
Step 4—a turbulent field

Few would disagree that most contemporary organizations are heavily steeped in turbulent fields. *Turbulent fields* are worlds in which dynamic processes create significant variance. These turbulent fields embody a serious rise in uncertainty, and the consequences of actions therein become increasingly unpredictable (Emery & Trist, 1965). These four different types of environments have existed over time, but today we are dealing with turbulent fields beyond the original conceptualization.

Reminding readers of Emery and Trist's classification, Ramirez, Selsky, and van der Heijden (2008) use the ideas of turbulence and complexity to frame their edited book *Business Planning for Turbulent Times*. They make their case that turbulence and environmental complexity are undeniable features of the business environment by citing research showing significant increases in published material focused on turbulence and uncertainty. It could be argued that these descriptors are more relevant today than they were in 1965.

Another description of the external environment uses the terms *volatility, uncertainty, complexity*, and *ambiguity* for the acronym VUCA (Johansen, 2007). VUCA originated at the U.S. Army War College, which has since become known as VUCA University. Indeed, the elements of volatility, uncertainty, complexity and ambiguity are undeniably present in the operating environment of any organization—the only question is the degree to which each element may be in play.

These external environment elements have equal and opposite forces that must be understood and emphasized. For example, to overcome volatility, one must use *vision*; to address uncertainty, one must develop *understanding*; complexity yields to *clarity*; and ambiguity can be addressed with *agility*. Each of these solutions is based on an open-ended, continuous learning orientation (Johansen, 2007).

The general societal environment and organizations within it continue to evolve to new heights of complexity, turbulence, volatility, uncertainty, and ambiguity. The rate of change is not likely to slow, and most decision makers are simply trying to keep up. Timelines for strategic thinking are short. Organizations operating on a minimum of resources will find that eventually something must be given up. For many, the time to think strategically is sacrificed. Logically, this reaction is just the opposite of what is required if decision makers are to have any chance at navigating a chaotic environment that is challenging them.

A BRIEF EVOLUTION OF STRATEGIC PLANNING

Military planning has long concentrated on strategy principles dating back to early Chinese philosophers such as Sun Tzu and Japanese philosophers such as Miyamoto Musashi, as well as ancient scholars like Niccolò Machiavelli. These early opinions about battle positioning have heavily influenced modern thinking about strategy (Cleary, 1988; Greene, 1998). Through several world and national wars, the notion of planning for strategic warfare positioning has evolved dramatically (Frentzell, Bryson, & Crosby, 2000). While the history of military planning is extensive and has evolved in many ways completely on its own, military strategy has borrowed and contributed concepts from and to corporate planning over the years (Frentzel et al., 2000).

Alfred Sloan advanced corporate planning practices at General Motors in the 1930s. The concept of planning as a central organizational activity was further advanced by Igor Ansoff and Alfred Chandler. These strategy thinkers spent their time in the 1950s and 1960s trying to convince managers that their companies needed strategies. During this period, frequent links and parallels were drawn with military strategy and the events of the era. Economic forecasting was the key tool in the strategist's arsenal of weapons for blasting a path to the desired future. This approach to planning continued through the 1960s and generally involved three phases—namely, defining the desired future, creating the plan (or steps to achieve the desired future), and then implementing the plan (Micklethwait & Woolridge, 1996). These phases also denoted the initial division between strategy formation and implementation, with the formation being a process reserved for senior executives and the CEO, and implementation being the job of managers. Strategic planning became increasingly complex over the next decade with the introduction of several levels of planning. A notable contribution of this time period was the Boston Consulting Group's Growth Share Matrix. The matrix was intended to indicate a general strategy to executives and managers based on templates of opportunities and strategies in any industry.

In response to the demands of World War II, planning became a top priority for most industries. The military also heightened its connection to the research coming out of the RAND Corporation that was headed by Herman Kahn (Kahn & Weiner, 1967; Ringland, 1998). The developments in Kahn's "future-now thinking" quickly translated into military efforts to predict the future (Kahn & Weiner, 1967), and military planning groups added physicists and mathematicians specializing in modeling (Ringland, 1998). Although much of the planning strategies used by the military were classified, it seems clear that the thinking going on in Stanford Research Institute's Futures Group, and that of Herman Kahn himself at the Hudson Institute, provoked what became more widely known as simulations, or events that positioned participants in hypothetical situations.

Later, Forrester's (1961) work at the Massachusetts Institute of Technology also contributed greatly to the development of simulations, and his expertise was sought for military operations on several occasions. One of the applications of Forrester's systems dynamics modeling was to uncover counterintuitive possibilities in the future. The essence of the Forrester systems dynamics models is to develop the underlying causal relationships that drive a specific dynamic. Through a process of identifying and modeling the size of stocks and the strength of flows, complex dynamics could be captured. These models also enabled an evidence-based argument about how specific dynamics might unfold in the future.

Military groups began using simulations to allow individuals to experience situations without the implications of their actions in those situations translating into reality (Frentzel et al., 2000). The emphasis on war games, the advent of computer modeling, and other technology produced by the military and industry in the 1950s and 1960s have led to elaborate training strategies involving virtual reality and devices such as flight simulators. Military planning has incorporated some of the early scenario planning concepts, but the core point of differentiation has been a lasting focus on prediction in military planning (Frentzel et al., 2000).

Michael Porter's work on business strategy took a cue from some of the military planning concepts and applied them to business organizations. His work concentrated on the idea that there can be both unique solutions to strategic problems and general solutions that may be examined for relevance to any strategic situation (Porter, 1985). Porter's work then shifted to the idea of competitive advantage and that, indeed, generic paths for achieving competitive advantage are freely available to any corporation and its planning analysts (Porter, 1985). Porter also stressed the idea that organizations should think of themselves as value chains of separate activities. Planning took a serious turn to focus on analysis until Japanese companies were performing as anomalies in Porter's planning framework. Lengthy, formal, and involved approaches to planning came under tough scrutiny by overseas business leaders; eventually, even the Harvard Business School explored more simplified approaches to strategy.

The shift in thinking toward simplicity had an effect on most organizations. Many corporations ridded themselves of their planning departments as the concept of reengineering took center stage in the 1990s. Strategy consulting firms like McKinsey and the Boston Consulting Group shifted their expertise to reengineering to capture the rising demand. Planning practices in the 1990s and early 2000s became hybrids of everything from formalized annual retreats that attempted to re-create the days of planning, to simple strategies that could be communicated and rolled out to employees on business cards.

In light of the negative and devastating effects of many reengineering efforts, some companies have attempted to revive practices of strategic thinking in their organizations, and some companies have managed to hold onto their formal planning processes. The 1990s also brought about a concentration on developing strategic vision. Jim Collins, in his best-selling book *Good to Great* (2001), demonstrated how vision-led organizations are sustainably more profitable than others. He combined this point with a leadership theory called Level Five leadership that he described as a combination of fierce resolve and humility. This approach was thought to be the solution—somewhere between the bureaucratic formalized planning that was deemed a failure in the past and a strategy written on a cocktail napkin.

PHILOSOPHICAL VIEWS ON STRATEGY

There are three overarching paradigms of strategy (van der Heijden, 1997, 2005b). These philosophies are critical to understanding the context in which planning takes place. Although it is tempting to "choose" one of these philosophies with which one finds alignment, it is important to realize that all three of these views are valid. To place scenario planning in context, we must consider the backgrounds of each of these views: rationalist, evolutionary, and processual.

The Rationalist School

The rationalist school features a tacit and underlying assumption that there is indeed one best solution. The job of the strategist becomes one of producing that one best solution or the closest possible thing to it. Classic rationalists include Igor Ansoff, Alfred Chandler, Frederick Taylor, and Alfred Sloan (Micklethwait & Woolridge, 1996). The rationalist approach to strategy dictates that an elite few of the organization's top managers convene, approximately once each year, and formulate a strategic plan. Mintzberg (1990) lists other assumptions underlying the rationalist school:

- Predictability; no interference from outside
- Clear intentions
- Implementation follows formulation
- Full understanding throughout the organization
- The belief that reasonable people will do reasonable things

The majority of practitioners and available literature on strategy is of the rationalist perspective (van der Heijden, 1997, 2005b). Although it is becoming clear that this view is limited, and as the belief in one correct solution wanes, the rationalist perspective is still alive and well, and fully embedded in many organizational planning cycles.

The Evolutionary School

With an emphasis on the complex nature of organizational behavior, the evolutionary school suggests that a winning strategy can only be articulated in retrospect (Mintzberg, 1990). Followers of this theory believe that systems can develop a memory of successful previous strategies. In this case, strategy is thought to be a "process of random experimentation and filtering out of the unsuccessful" (van der Heijden, 1997, p. 24). Organizations with strong cultures and identities often have trouble seriously thinking about alternative futures because the company brand is so influential.

The issue with this perspective is that it is of little value when considering alternative futures. This view can sometimes reduce organization members to characters of chance, influenced by random circumstances.

The Processual School

The processual school asserts that although it is not possible to deliver optimal strategies through rational thinking alone, organization members can instill and create processes within organizations that make it a more adaptive, whole system, capable of learning from its mistakes (van der Heijden, 1997, 2000). Incorporating change management concepts to influence processes, the processual school supports that successful evolutionary behavior can be analyzed and used to create alternative futures. Van der Heijden (1997, 2000) offers the following examples of metaphors for explaining the three strategic schools:

- The rationalistic paradigm suggests a machine metaphor for the organization.
- The evolutionary school suggests an ecology.
- The processual school suggests a living organism.

Because van der Heijden views scenarios as a tool for organizational learning, he advocates the integration of these three strategic perspectives. "Organizational learning represents a way in which we can integrate these three perspectives, all three playing a key role in describing reality, and therefore demanding consideration" (van der Heijden, 1997, p. 49). It is widely accepted that effective scenario building incorporates all three of these perspectives (Georgantzas & Acar, 1995; Ringland, 1998; Schwartz, 1991).

HISTORY OF SCENARIO PLANNING

Scenario planning is a participative approach to strategy that features diverse thinking and conversation. Diverse thinking and conversation are used to shift how the external environment is perceived (Selin, 2007; Wack, 1984, 1985a, 1985b). The intended outcomes of scenario planning include individual and team learning, integrated decision making, understanding of how the organization can achieve its goals amid chaos, and increased dialogue among organization members (Chermack 2004, 2005). These outcomes collectively prepare individuals and organizations for a variety of alternative futures. When used effectively, scenario planning functions as an organizational "radar," scanning the environment for signals of potential discontinuities.

Scenario planning first emerged for application to businesses in a company set up for researching new forms of weapons technology in the RAND Corporation. Kahn (1967) of RAND pioneered a technique he titled "future-now thinking." The intent of this approach was to combine detailed analyses with imagination and produce reports as though people might write them in the future. Kahn adopted the name "scenario" when Hollywood determined the original term outdated and switched to the label "screenplay." In the mid-1960s, Kahn founded the Hudson Institute, which specialized in writing stories about the future to help people consider the "unthinkable." He gained the most notoriety around the idea that the best way to prevent nuclear war was to examine the possible consequences of nuclear war and widely publish the results (Kahn & Weiner, 1967).

Around the same time, the Stanford Research Institute (SRI) began offering long-range planning for businesses that considered political, economic, and research forces as primary drivers of business development. The work of organizations such as the SRI began shifting toward planning for massive societal changes (Ringland, 1998). When military spending increased to support the Vietnam War, an interest began to grow in finding ways to look into the future and plan for changes in society. These changing views were largely a result of the societal shifts of the time.

The Hudson Institute also began to seek corporate sponsors, which exposed companies such as Shell, Corning, IBM, and General Motors to this line of thinking. Kahn and Weiner (1967) then published *The Year 2000,* "which clearly demonstrates how one man's thinking was driving a trend in corporate planning" (Ringland, 1998, p. 13). Ted Newland of Shell, one of the early corporate sponsors of scenario planning, encouraged Shell to start thinking about the future.

The SRI "futures group" was using a variety of methods in 1968–1969 to create scenarios for the U.S. education system reaching to the year 2000. Five scenarios were created; one entitled "Status Quo Extended" was selected as the official future (*official future* is a generic term to denote a desired future that has been "selected" by senior management). This scenario suggested that issues such as population growth, ecological destruction, and dissent would resolve themselves. The other scenarios were given little attention once the official future was selected. The official future reached the sponsors, staff at the U.S. Office of Education, at a time when President Richard Nixon's administration was in full swing in 1969. The selected scenario was quickly deemed impossible because it was in no way compatible with the values that Nixon was advocating then (Ringland, 1998). The official future provided little insight into major issues of the time, and it failed to do more than present a report of present trends playing out into the future as they were expected to. The SRI went on to do work for the Environmental Protection Agency, with Willis Harman, Peter Schwartz, Thomas Mandel, and Richard Carlson constructing the scenarios.

Earlier, Jay Forrester (1981) of MIT was using similar concepts to describe supply-and-demand chains. The use of scenario concepts in his project was specifically aimed at stirring up public debate rather than solving a dilemma or issue. In other words, he used scenarios as tools for entertaining multiple sides of an issue and exploring the various viewpoints. The results were published by Meadows, Meadows, and Randers in 1992.

Scenario planning at Shell was well on its way. Ted Newland suggested in 1967 that thinking six years ahead was not allowing enough lead time to effectively consider future forces in their industry (Wack, 1985a). Shell began planning for 2000. Newland was joined by Pierre Wack, Napier Collyns, and others. When the Yom Kippur War broke out in 1973 and oil prices rose sixfold, Shell was prepared. The ability to act quickly has been credited as the primary reason behind the company's lead in the oil industry over the years.

Shell's success with the scenario planning process encouraged numerous other organizations to begin thinking about the future in this different way. Because the oil shock was so devastating to views of a stable future, by the late 1970s the majority of the Fortune 100 corporations had adopted scenario planning in one form or another (Linneman & Klein, 1979, 1983; Ringland, 1998).

The success of scenario use was short-lived. Caused by the major recession and corporate staffing reductions of the 1980s, scenario use was on the decline. It is also speculated that planners oversimplified the use of scenarios, confusing the nature of storytelling with forecasting (Godet & Roubelat, 1996; Ringland, 1998; Sharpe, 2007; Wright, van der Heijden, Burt, Bradfield, & Cairns, 2008). According to Kleiner (1996, 2008), the time had come for managers to realize that they did not have the answers to the future. Porter (1985) led a "back to the basics" approach suggesting that corporations use external forces as a platform for planning. In this time of evaluating how planning happens, many consulting firms began developing scenario planning methodologies. Huss and Honton (1987) described three approaches of the time: (1) intuitive logics, introduced by Pierre Wack; (2) trend-impact analysis, the favorite of the Futures Group; and (3) cross-impact analysis, implemented by Battelle. Royal Dutch/Shell continued to have success with scenario planning through two more oil incidents in the 1980s, and slowly, corporations cautiously began to reintegrate the application of scenarios in planning situations. Scenario planning has been adopted at a national level in some cases, and its methods have been successful in bringing diverse groups of people together (Kahane, 1992; van der Merwe, 1994). For example, scenarios were used to explore the potential transformation of South Africa at the end of apartheid (Kahane, 1992). Scenarios have also been used as tools for community building and dialogue (van der Merwe, 1994).

PUBLICATION ACTIVITY IN FUTURES AND SCENARIO PLANNING

As the world has become more uncertain, the need and therefore the popularity of scenario planning have increased. Scenario planning has seen considerable growth as a topic of publication in academic journals since the mid-1990s (Ramirez et al., 2008). In addition, scenario planning as a specific strategic management tool has also seen a rise in use, according to Bain & Company's annual Management Tools Survey (Ramirez et al., 2008).

DEFINITIONS OF SCENARIO PLANNING

Scenario planning is still a relatively young discipline, and many variations have been developed. The diversity of thought concerning scenario planning is an asset in that it has brought about a variety of interpretations about what scenario planning is. However, the use of a variety of methods mandates close and careful study to determine what is effective and what is not. Variety can also be found in the available definitions and stated outcomes of scenario planning. Figure 1.1 provides a list of definitions in the scenario planning literature.

OUTCOMES OF SCENARIO PLANNING

Many of the definitions examined here do not explicitly state the outcome variables of scenario planning, which indicates that some authors may be unclear about the aims of their definitions. This also suggests that scenario planning professionals are just beginning to consider the importance of

FIGURE 1.1   Scenario Planning Definitions and Outcome Variables

Author	Date	Definition	Dependent Variables
Porter	1985	"An internally consistent view of what the future might turn out to be—not a forecast, but one possible future outcome" (p. 63)	A view of one possible future outcome
Schwartz	1991	"A tool for ordering one's perceptions about alternative future environments in which one's decisions might be played out" (p. 45)	Ordered perceptions about alternative future decision-making environments
Simpson	1992	"The process of constructing alternate futures of a business' external environment" (p. 10)	Constructed alternate futures
Bloom and Menefee	1994	"A description of a possible or probable future" (p. 223)	A described possible or probable future
Collyns	1994	"An imaginative leap into the future" (p. 275)	An imagined future
Thomas	1994	"Scenario planning is inherently a learning process that challenges the comfortable conventional wisdoms of the organization by focusing attention on how the future may be different from the present" (p. 6)	Challenged comfortable conventional wisdoms about the future
Schoemaker	1995	"A disciplined methodology for imagining possible futures in which organizational decisions may be played out" (p. 25)	Imagined possible decision-making futures
Van der Heijden	1997	(1) External scenarios are "internally consistent and challenging descriptions of possible futures"; (2) an internal scenario is "a causal line of argument, linking an action option with a goal," or "one path through a person's cognitive map" (p. 5)	Descriptions of possible futures; explicit cognitive maps
De Geus	1997	"Tools for foresight-discussions and documents whose purpose is not a prediction or a plan, but a change in the mind-set of the people who use them" (p. 46)	Changed mind-sets
Ringland	1998	"That part of strategic planning which relates to the tools and technologies for managing the uncertainties of the future" (p. 83)	Managed future uncertainties
Bawden	1998	"Scenario planning is one of a number of foresighting techniques used in the strategic development of organizations, which exploit the remarkable capacity of humans to both imagine and to learn from what is imagined"	Human imagination and learning made explicit

(continued)

FIGURE 1.1 Scenario Planning Definitions and Outcome Variables (*continued*)

Author	Date	Definition	Dependent Variables
Fahey and Randall	1998	"Scenarios are descriptive narratives of plausible alternative projections of a specific part of the future" (p. 6)	Plausible alternative projections of a specific part of the future
Alexander and Serfass	1998	"Scenario planning is an effective futuring tool that enables planners to examine what is likely and what is unlikely to happen, knowing well that unlikely elements in an organization are those that can determine its relative success" (p. 35)	Examined future likelihoods and unlikelihoods
Tucker	1999	"Creating stories of equally plausible futures and planning as though any one could move forward" (p. 70)	Stories of equally plausible futures that inform planning
Kahane	1999	"A series of imaginative but plausible and well-focused stories of the future" (p. 511)	Plausible stories of the future
Kloss	1999	"Scenarios are literally stories about the future that are plausible and based on analysis of the interaction of a number of environmental variables" (p. 73)	Informed, plausible stories about the future
Wilson	2000	"Scenarios are a management tool used to improve the quality of executive decision making and help executives make better, more resilient strategic decisions" (p. 24)	Improved executive strategic decision making
Godet	2001	"A scenario is simply a means to represent a future reality in order to shed light on current action in view of possible and desirable futures" (p. 63)	A represented future reality

defining what they do and explicitly stating what they intend to achieve by doing it.

Figure 1.1 shows that almost half of the available definitions date from 1997 to the present. Such a surge of publication activity related to scenario planning suggests a recent increased use of this strategic tool. Of interest is that the first available definition of scenario planning is offered in 1985, yet the process has been applied in practice since the 1960s. The increase in recent scholarly literature around scenario planning suggests that the process is developing and maturing with the help of professionals concerned that scenario planning does not suffer the same inadequacies and criticisms that have been leveled against general strategic planning processes (Fahey & Randall, 1998; Mintzberg, 1994).

The dependent variables of Figure 1.1 can be synthesized into four major outcome categories of scenario planning:

- changed thinking,
- informed narratives or stories about possible or plausible futures,
- improved decision making about the future, and
- enhanced human and organization learning and imagination.

Of significant note is that none of the available definitions of scenario planning includes an outcome of performance improvement. Due to the depth of expertise and high costs usually associated with the practice of scenario planning, it is surprising that performance improvement has not been an explicit outcome of this strategic process. Some may simply assume that scenario planning will result in performance improvement. However, although such an assumption may be logical or known based on practical experience, there is little evidence that the practice of scenario planning actually results in performance improvement. Building this evidence can only help bolster the practice of scenario planning as a strategic activity. The lack of focus on performance improvement may be attributed to general difficulties in measuring the effects of scenario planning projects. Performance must be included and developed as a critical outcome expectation of scenario planning and as part of the definition of scenario planning. One approach to linking scenario planning to performance is described in detail in Chapter 9.

In an attempt to construct an integrative definition of scenario planning, it is important to include the outcomes stated in the available definitions highlighted in the next chapter in Figure 2.4. The following definition of performance-based scenario planning synthesizes the outcomes in Figure 2.4 and adds the performance orientation:

Performance-based scenario planning is a discipline of building a set of internally consistent and imagined futures in which decisions about the future can be played out, for the purpose of changing thinking, improving decision making, fostering human and organization learning and improving performance.

The performance orientation changes the game for scenario planning. An expectation of performance improvement forces a conversation about outcomes, without diminishing the capacity to wonder about the future. Having a performance improvement perspective means that there will be a way of determining whether the scenario project produced any benefits for the organization. So far, this question has been infrequently asked, and answers are often vague and unrelated to the initial reason for engaging in scenario work. It is important to clarify that a performance orientation does not preclude additional unexpected outcomes from emerging. They often do, and they can be very powerful. The performance orientation defines targets, identifies areas of potential leverage, and works to shift the thinking inside the organization. Logically, a performance orientation mandates assessment of the project. As noted, Chapter 9 lays out a comprehensive approach to assessing scenario projects.

LEARNING

Scenario planning most certainly involves learning. Arie de Geus (1988, 1997) wrote the foundational treatise "Planning as Learning" and later a book titled *The Living Company* in which he compiled decades of research showing that the companies in history with the greatest longevity were those that framed planning as a learning process and used tools like scenario planning to keep learning about how to maintain fit in their environments. Most likely, de Geus's views were influenced by Pierre Wack and Ted Newland at Royal Dutch/Shell as Wack was famous for stressing, "Our real target was the microcosms of our decision-makers: unless we influenced the mental image, the picture of reality of critical decision-makers, our scenarios would be like water on stone" (Wack, 1984, p. 58).

Don Michael's (1995) view of strategic learning (detailed in his book *Learning to Plan and Planning to Learn*) is quite suitable to the purpose of scenario planning:

> It is imperative to free the idea of learning from its conventional semantic baggage. Learning used to mean (and for the most part still means) learning the answer—a static shift from one condition of knowledge and/or know-how to another. This definition of learning leads to organizational and stakeholder rigidification. But in the current and anticipated

conditions of dramatic unpredictability, learning must be a continuous process involving:

1. Learning to re-perceive or re-interpret a situation,
2. Learning how to apply that re-perception to the formulation of policy and the specification of action (including evaluation of policy and action),
3. Learning how to implement those policies and intended actions, and
4. Learning how to keep these three earlier requirements alive and open to continual revision. (p. 46)

APPROACHES TO SCENARIO PLANNING

There are varying approaches to scenario planning. Each has developed out of various schools of thought, and it is important to review the alternatives here before proceeding. The major approaches to scenario planning reviewed here include these:

- Royal Dutch/Shell and Global Business Network
- The French School
- The Futures Group
- Wilson and Ralston
- Lindgren and Bandhold
- Reference scenarios
- Decision Strategies International
- Procedural scenarios
- Industry scenarios
- Soft creative methods

These approaches to scenario planning have all developed in practice. No doubt, the different techniques have evolved under slightly different circumstances, and each contributes to the body of scenario planning knowledge.

ROYAL DUTCH/SHELL AND GLOBAL BUSINESS NETWORK

The overarching view utilized by the Global Business Network (GBN) was born out of Shell's application of scenario technology. GBN was founded by Peter Schwartz, Jay Ogilvy, Stewart Brand, Lawrence Wilkinson, and Napier Collyns. Pierre Wack first began applying Herman Kahn's concepts in the 1960s and refined them into a proprietary framework stressing the big picture first, then zooming in on the details. Wack believed that to begin with the details was to miss some key dimensions of the building process. Schwartz took over as the head of Shell's scenario division and eventually established a company, GBN, with a handful of other colleagues offering a variety of strategic business services worldwide. Schwartz (1991) gives a conceptual overview of the scenario building process in *The Art of the Long View*. At the center of GBN was a network of "remarkable people" (or RPs, as they became known) first used by Wack to challenge and shift the thinking and assumptions of decision makers within Royal Dutch/Shell.

Step 1 is to identify a focal issue or decision. Scenarios are built around a central issue outward toward the external environment. Scenarios based first on external environmental issues such as high versus low growth may fail to capture company-specific information that makes a difference in how the organization will deal with such issues (Schwartz, 1991). Accepted best practice is to engage the decision makers first in a conversation to uncover their current assumptions and concerns about the external environment and how they might unfold.

The second step is to identify and study the key forces in the local environment, which is logical after selecting a key focusing issue or question. Step 2 examines the factors that influence the success or failure of the decision or issue identified in the first step. Scenarios must be developed to shed light on the issue or question. Analyses of the internal environment and strengths and weaknesses are commonly conducted in this step as a way of identifying the internal dynamics that help or hinder strategy development.

Once the key factors have been identified, the third step involves brainstorming the driving forces in the macroenvironment. These include political, economic, technological, environmental, and social forces. Driving forces may also be considered the forces behind the key factors in Step 2 (Schwartz, 1991).

Step 4 consists of ranking the key factors (from Step 2) and the driving forces (from Step 3) on the basis of two criteria: (1) the degree of importance for success and (2) the degree of uncertainty surrounding the forces themselves. "Scenarios cannot differ over predetermined elements because predetermined elements are bound to be the same in all scenarios" (Schwartz, 1991, p. 167).

The results of the ranking exercise are to separate the important few from the unimportant many forces that are at play in the environment.

One method of developing distinctive story lines is to identify two axes along which the eventual scenarios will differ. Another method is to simply develop stories that can be contained within the key driving forces at work. Again, these stories are intended to shed light on the focusing issue or question. Step 5, then, is the development and selection of the general scenario logics according to the matrix resulting from the ranking exercise. The logic of a given scenario will be characterized by its location in the matrix. "It is more like playing with a set of issues until you have reshaped and regrouped them in such a way that a logic emerges and a story can be told" (Schwartz, 1991, p. 172).

Step 6, fleshing out the scenarios, returns to Steps 2 and 3. Each key factor and driving force is given attention and manipulated within the matrix developed in the scenario logics of step 4. Plausibility should be constantly checked from this point, for example, "if two scenarios differ over protectionist or non-protectionist policies, it makes intuitive sense to put a high inflation rate with the protectionist scenario and a low inflation rate with the non-protectionist scenario" (Schwartz, 1991, p. 178).

Step 7 examines the implications of the developed scenarios. The initial issue or decision is "wind tunneled" through the scenarios. It is important to examine the robustness of each scenario through questions such as these: What will we do if this is the reality? Does the decision look good across only one or two scenarios? What vulnerabilities have been revealed? Does a specific scenario require a high-risk strategy?

The final step is to select "leading indicators" that will signify that actual events may be unfolding according to a developed scenario. Once the scenarios have been developed, it's worth spending some time selecting identifiers that will assist planners in monitoring the course of unfolding events and how they might impact the organization.

THE FRENCH SCHOOL

When he took over the Department of Future Studies with SEMA group in 1974, Michel Godet began conducting scenario planning. His methodology was extended at the Conservatoire Nationale des Arts et Métiers with the support of several sponsors. Godet's work is based on the use of "perspective," advocated by the French philosopher Gaston Berger (Ringland, 1998). Godet's approach began by dividing scenarios into two categories: situational scenarios, which describe future situations; and development scenarios, which describe a sequence of events that lead to a future situation

(Georgantzas & Acar, 1995). Godet also identifies three types of scenarios that may exist in either category: trend-based scenarios follow what is most likely, contrasted scenarios explore purposefully extreme themes, and horizon/normative scenarios examine the feasibility of a desirable future by working backward from the future to the present. Godet's approach has evolved and now includes several computer-based tools that help highlight interdependencies between interrelated variables that may be ignored by more simple procedures (Ringland, 1998).

The French School approach is a structural analysis that is divided into three phases. Phase 1 begins the process by studying internal and external variables to create a system of interrelated elements. This approach focuses on a detailed and quantified study of the elements and compilation of data into a database. A cross-impact matrix is constructed to study the influence of each variable on the others.

Phase 2 scans the range of possibilities and reduces uncertainty through the identification of key variables and strategies. Future possibilities are listed through a set of hypotheses that may point to a trend in the data. Advanced software reduces uncertainty by estimating the subjective probabilities of different combinations of the variables.

Phase 3 is the development of the scenarios themselves. Scenarios are restricted to sets of hypotheses; and once the data have been compiled and analyzed, scenarios are built describing the route from the current situation to the future vision (Godet & Roubelat, 1996).

THE FUTURES GROUP

The Futures Group was a Connecticut-based consulting firm that developed a trend-impact analysis approach to scenario planning. This approach requires three phases: preparation, development, and reporting and utilizing (Ringland, 1998).

The preparation phase includes defining a focus, issue, or decision, and then charting the driving forces. Several questions should be answered in this phase: What possible future developments need to be probed? What variables need to be looked at for assistance in decision making? What forces and developments have the greatest ability to shape future characteristics of the organization?

The development phase includes constructing a scenario space, selecting alternative worlds to be detailed, and preparing scenario-contingent forecasts. Selecting a scenario space means examining the various future states that the drivers could produce. Illogical and nonplausible situations should be rejected. Selecting alternative worlds to be detailed involves limiting the number of future stories, since it would be impossible to explore every option. The key is to select plausible futures that will challenge current thinking. Preparing scenario-contingent forecasts is listing trends and events that would be required for the plausible future to exist. Depending on the assumptions of each alternative world, indicators are selected that might "signal" the direction in which the organization is heading.

Reporting and utilizing scenarios are covered briefly and quickly without enough detail for a user to apply. However, the futures group is one of a few approaches to even mention these activities.

Decision Strategies International

Paul Schoemaker has outlined an approach to scenario planning with many similarities to the methodology used by the Global Business Network, as might be expected since Schoemaker spent a bit of time in the planning department at Royal Dutch/Shell.

Step 1 defines the scope of the project. This includes setting a time frame, examining the past to identify rates of change, and roughly estimating the expected future rate of change. "The unstructured concerns and anxieties of managers are good places to start" (Schoemaker, 1995, p. 28).

Step 2 is to identify the key stakeholders. Obvious stakeholders include customers, suppliers, competitors, employees, shareholders, and government workers. The identification of the roles that each of these groups might play, how the roles have changed in past years, and the distribution of power according to the issue are all factors to be examined in this step.

Basic trends are identified in Step 3. The political, economic, societal, technological, legal, environmental, and industry trends are analyzed in connection with the issues from the first step. "Briefly explain the trend, including how and why it exerts its influence on your organization" (Schoemaker, 1995, p. 28). Trends can be charted in influence diagrams or matrices to help make relationships explicit. Examining trends can be useful, but remember that trends are put together by experts, and scenarios ask, "What if the experts are wrong?"

Step 4 considers the key uncertainties. What events, whose outcomes are uncertain, will significantly affect the issues of concern to the organization?

A further examination of political, societal, economic, environmental, legal, and industry forces emphasizing the most uncertain elements "will reveal the most turbulent areas" (Schoemaker, 1995, p. 28). Relationships among the uncertainties should also be identified. For example, "if one economic uncertainty is 'level of unemployment' and the other 'level of inflation,' then the combination of full employment and zero inflation may be ruled out as impossible" (Schoemaker, 1995, p. 29).

Once the trends and uncertainties have been identified, initial scenario construction can begin. A simple approach is to identify extreme worlds by putting all positive elements in one and all negatives in another. Alternatively, various strings of outcomes can be clustered around high or low continuity, finding themes, or the degree of uncertainty. The most common technique is to cross the top two uncertainties of a given issue.

Step 6 checks the initial scenarios for plausibility. Schoemaker identified three tests for internal consistency, dealing with the trends, the outcome combinations, and the reactions of major stakeholders. The trends must be compatible with the chosen time frame; scenarios must combine outcomes that fit (e.g., full employment and zero inflation do not fit); and the major stakeholders must not be placed in situations they do not like but have the power to change (e.g., OPEC will not tolerate low oil prices for very long) (Schoemaker, 1995).

From the process of developing initial scenarios and checking them for plausibility, general themes should emerge. Step 7 is to develop learning scenarios by manipulating plausible outcomes. The trends may be the same in each scenario, but the outcomes, once considered plausible, can be shifted and given more or less weight in different scenarios. These scenarios "are tools for research and study rather than for decision-making" (Schoemaker, 1995, p. 29).

After constructing learning scenarios, areas that require further research are identified. These are commonly referred to as "blind spots" (Georgantzas & Acar, 1995; Schoemaker, 1995; Schwartz, 1991; van der Heijden, 1997). Companies can use these scenarios to study other industries—for example, to consider plausible outcomes of advances in multimedia and then study current research in that area.

Step 9 reexamines the internal consistencies after completing additional research. Quantitative models are commonly developed in this stage. For example, Royal Dutch/Shell has developed a model that keeps oil prices, inflation, gross national product (GNP), growth, taxes, and interest rates in plausible balances. Formal models can be used to flesh out possible secondary effects and also to serve as another check for plausibility. The models can also help to quantify the consequences of various scenarios.

Step 10 is to determine the scenarios to be used for decisions. Trends will have arisen that may or may not affect or address the real issues of the organization. Schoemaker identified four criteria for effective decision scenarios. First, scenarios must have relevance to be effective but also challenge current thinking in the organization. Second, scenarios must be internally consistent and plausible. Third, scenarios must be archetypal, or they should describe fundamentally different futures, rather than simply vary on one theme. Finally, each scenario should describe an eventual state of equilibrium. "It does an organization little good to prepare for a plausible future that will be quite short" (Schoemaker, 1995, p. 32), yet many argue that planning cycles are getting shorter.

WILSON AND RALSTON

Perhaps the most detailed procedural account of scenario planning yet published, Ian Wilson and Bill Ralston based their 2006 book The *Scenario-Planning Handbook* on the Shell method but have made modifications throughout. Based on over fifteen years of experience as senior consultants at SRI, Ralston and Wilson have put their experience and knowledge to the test. This is a modern method that lays out an all-encompassing how-to manual for corporate executives. Wilson and Ralston's approach is detailed in Figure 1.2.

LINDGREN AND BANDHOLD

In 2003, Mats Lindgren and Hans Bandhold published *Scenario Planning: The Link between Future and Strategy*. The book details their interpretation of the scenario planning process in a model they call the TAIDA method. TAIDA stands for tracking, analyzing, imaging, deciding, and acting; and the method is a simplified version of the intuitive logics approach to scenario planning, which is based on the work led by Pierre Wack and Ted Newland at Shell. The book is essentially a practitioner's shorthand manual for exploring the basic concepts of scenario planning, with a useful appendix of methods that can be used in a variety of places throughout the scenario planning process.

FIGURE 1.2   Steps in Developing and Using Scenarios (summarized from Wilson and Ralston, 2006)

Step 1. Develop the case for scenarios.

Step 2. Gain executive understanding, support, and participation

Step 3. Define the decision focus.

Step 4. Design the process.

Step 5. Select the facilitator.

Step 6. Form the scenario team.

Step 7. Gather available data, views, and projections.

Step 8. Identify and assess key decision factors.

Step 9. Identify the critical forces and drivers.

Step 10. Conduct focused research on key issues, forces, and drivers.

Step 11. Assess the importance and uncertainty of forces and drivers.

Step 12. Identify key "axes of uncertainty."

Step 13. Select scenario logics to cover the "envelope of uncertainty."

Step 14. Write the story lines for the scenarios.

Step 15. Rehearse the future with scenarios.

Step 16. Get to the decision recommendations.

Step 17. Identify signposts to monitor.

Step 18. Communicate the results to the organization.

REFERENCE SCENARIOS

Ackoff (1970, 1978, 1981) identified four modes for organizations to cope with external change. *Inactivity* involves ignoring changes and continuing with business as usual. *Reactivity* waits for changes to happen and then developing a response. *Preactivity* involves trying to predict changes and establishing organizational position before they happen, and *proactivity* calls for interactive involvement with the external environment in order to "create the future for stakeholders" (Georgantzas & Acar, 1995, p. 364). Within these four modes, Ackoff uses the term *reference scenario* to mean the reference projections a firm would have if no significant changes occurred in the environment. Ackoff's call for strategic turnaround starts with an idealized scenario of a desirable future. To be effective, such a scenario should be interesting and provocative—it should show what to change to evade the mess of problems in an organization's given strategic situation.

PROCEDURAL SCENARIOS

Amara and Lipinski (1983) and Chandler and Cokle (1982) use very similar methods for constructing scenarios but prepare separate forecasts for each principal factor or variable. Chandler and Cokle (1982) "also define scenarios as the coherent pictures of different possible events in the environment whose effect on a set of businesses should be tested through linked models" (p. 132). The manipulation of macroeconomic models is a mechanism by which vague assumptions are translated into projected values of wholesale prices, gross domestic product (GDP), or consumer expenditures for an entire industry. The models used in these approaches are computer driven (Georgantzas & Acar, 1995) and provide a good example of procedural scenarios incorporating intuitive and quantitative techniques.

INDUSTRY SCENARIOS

Porter (1985) asserted that scenarios traditionally used in strategic planning have stressed macroeconomic and macropolitical issues. He further claimed that in competitive strategy the proper unit of analysis is the industry and defines industry scenarios as the primary, internally consistent views of how the world will look in the future (Porter, 1985). The essence of this view holds that there are two loops in building these industry scenarios. In this approach, industry analysis is within the larger unit of building industry scenarios. Industry-focused scenarios can help an organization in analyzing particular aspects of a business (Porter, 1985), but some have argued that beginning with a narrow focus will miss key dimensions (Wack, 1985a).

SOFT CREATIVE METHODS APPROACH

Brauers and Weber (1988) formulated an approach with three basic phases: analysis, descriptions of the future states, and synthesis. The analysis phase brings organization members to a common understanding of the problem. Based on this consensus, the problem can be further bounded and structured. Brauers and Weber recommend the use of soft creative methods for the analysis phase, including morphological analysis, brainstorming, brainwriting, and the Delphi technique. The second phase examines the possible development paths of the variables chosen in the analysis. The synthesis phase considers interdependencies among the variable factors to build different situations for the future states. These eventual scenarios are then fed through a complex computer program for linear programming and cluster analysis (Brauers & Weber, 1988).

WHERE EXISTING SCENARIO PLANNING METHODS HAVE FALLEN SHORT

This chapter has reviewed the major approaches to scenario planning available in published works. These approaches all have similarities, while some deviate largely from Pierre Wack's original method. Important similarities among the existing methods include a technique for identifying items that could potentially shift the organization and its focus, a structured way to think about the future that introduces multiple possibilities, and a craft of innovation and creativity. However, the existing methods lack some critical elements as well. Important pieces that are not found in available work on scenario planning are

- a presentation of the theoretical foundations,
- a clear guide for how to use scenarios, and
- a detailed guide for assessing the impact of scenario projects.

CONCLUSION

This book uses the scenario planning approach developed by Pierre Wack and Ted Newland at Royal Dutch/Shell and later documented by Peter Schwartz, Kees van der Heijden, and others at the Global Business Network as its key foundation. This approach features a qualitative, "intuitive logic" way of reasoning that separates organizational issues into things that are predetermined and things that are truly uncertain. When truly uncertain forces have been isolated, energy can be spent trying to understand those forces and how they might play out across a range of possible futures. Wack's primary goal was to shift the thinking and the mental models of managers inside Shell, and thus also the assumptions that framed their decision making. This book features an interpretation and extension of Wack's work with a focus on performance. The foundation set by Wack and Newland at Shell is solid and effective, yet it also provides opportunities for improvement.

No doubt there are myriad other scenario planning processes based on combining various elements of those described in this chapter. The point is simply that scenario planning has been developed in practice by numerous practitioners in various kinds of organizations and parts of the world. Clarifying the approach selected for any scenario project is helpful in eliminating confusion about the philosophies, steps, and theoretical basis on which the project will be built.

The unique contributions of this book are that it presents the underlying theory and research that explain scenario planning as an effective organizational intervention, detailed descriptions of what to do with scenarios once they have been developed, and ways to assess the performance contribution of a scenario project. None of the existing texts on scenario planning provide a theoretical explanation of how scenario planning works, and none provide detailed accounts of inquiry into what the outcomes of the experience really are. Nor do any cover a variety of methods for putting scenarios to use and checking to see that they were effective. As a result, this book targets reflective practitioners, executives, and academics who want to work through complex, ambiguous problems while at the same time understand how their actions affect the issues they are facing.

This chapter has described the state of the external environment that calls for scenarios and summarized the evolution of planning in organizations. A comprehensive list of scenario planning definitions has been provided, as well as the major approaches to scenario planning. The argument for performance-based scenario planning has been made.

Theoretical Foundations of Scenario Planning

Theory is a dirty word in some managerial quarters. That is rather curious, because all of us, managers especially, can no more get along without theories than libraries can get along without catalogs—and for the same reason: theories help us make sense of incoming information.

—MINTZBERG (2005, p. 249)

Pierre Wack told a story about approaching a cliff. He talked about how the odds of falling over the cliff increase as you walk closer to the edge. He asserted that the best way to avoid falling over a cliff is to help people see the characteristics of the cliff in advance. He helped them see how tall and steep the cliff is. He taught them to calculate how many different kinds of cliffs there are, how to recognize when a cliff is coming, and which kind it is. Pierre's story was an attempt to explain what a cliff was and how the cliff worked to prevent people from falling over it.

Most strategy and scenario planning texts provide readers with processes. Follow the steps and "do" your corporate strategy, they claim. Instead, this book provides a framework with numerous tools. The framework is designed to give the user a domain in which to exercise judgment. The tools described are aimed at helping decision makers decide their own specific course of action within the framework. Some have referred to scenario planning as more art than science. This chapter argues that scenario planning should remain artful, but it also must evolve into a theoretically and scientifically grounded art.

The purpose of this chapter is to present the theoretical foundations of scenario planning. These principles are critical to understanding what

29

scenario planning is and how it works (Torraco, 1997). The performance-based scenario system described in this book (presented in detail in Part Two) is based on the theories and theoretical principles outlined in this chapter. The tools and techniques provided in this book have been applied in the practice of scenario planning and have demonstrated results.

THE UTILITY OF THEORY IN SCENARIO PLANNING

A discussion of theory in the context of scenario planning is important for several reasons. First, the topic of theory is generally absent from the scenario literature. The only scenario planning text that includes a discussion of theory is *Scenario-Driven Planning* by Georgantzas and Acar (1995). However, their treatment of theory is limited to less than two pages. There are valuable insights to be gained from relevant theory domains that aid in understanding the practice of scenario planning. Scenario planning has grown as a practitioner's art and has received little academic attention. A responsible analysis of any phenomenon should cover the theoretical basis that makes the logic clear for understanding why practitioners take the actions that they do. This can work in reverse as well: insights gained from practicing a phenomenon can lead to a great depth of knowledge. To date, the majority of what is understood about scenario planning is based on knowledge gleaned from years of practice. This chapter suggests that much can be learned by studying related theory disciplines with an ultimate goal of integrating knowledge from practice and knowledge from close and careful study of the phenomenon.

A theory of scenario planning (Chermack, 2004, 2005) is used as an organizer for this chapter. The disciplines reviewed here provide support for this theory, as each discipline is reviewed in its relationship and contribution to the organizing theory.

THE SIX DOMAINS OF SCENARIO PLANNING THEORY

The proposed building blocks of a theory of scenario planning are based on extensive literature review (Chermack, Lynham, & Ruona, 2001; Georgantzas & Acar, 1995; Schwartz, 1991; van der Heijden, 1997; Wack 1985a,

1985b). The literature around scenario planning puts forth six key domains from which theories can be drawn to establish a theoretical foundation of scenario planning (see Figure 2.1):

- Dialogue, conversation quality, and engagement
- Learning
- Mental models
- Decision making
- Leadership
- Organization performance and change

These theoretical domains appear over and over again in the scenario literature. However, none of the current writings synthesize these elements in a comprehensive and clear manner. The use of these domains is intended to describe what the phenomenon of scenario planning is and how it works (Torraco, 1997). To be clear, this chapter presents a view of how scenario planning accomplishes its stated outcomes.

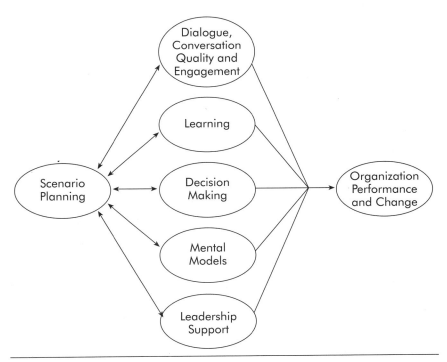

FIGURE 2.1   A Theory of Scenario Planning

Dialogue, Conversation Quality, and Engagement

Dialogue, conversation quality, and engagement are critical to the scenario planning process because they are the mechanism by which scenario planning happens. They are means for shifting the thinking inside the organization. As the chapters on scenario development and scenario implementation will describe in detail, dialogue, conversation, and engagement are the fundamental means for sharing mental models and developing a shared understanding of the organization and its external environment.

The specific work that informs how scenario planning involves dialogue, conversation, and engagement includes Rogers's communication theory; Nunnally, Miller, and Wackman's communication work; Argyris and Schon's work on advocacy and inquiry; and Lewin's theorizing on group dynamics. Each of these is described later, and the link to scenario planning is illustrated.

Definition

Dialogue and conversation are defined, respectively, as "conversation between two or more persons" (*Oxford English Dictionary*, 2001, p. 213) and "informal interchange of thoughts, information, etc., by spoken words; oral communication between persons; talk; colloquy" (*Oxford English Dictionary*, 2001, p. 187). Bohm's work (1989) sheds additional light on the subject:

> I give a meaning to the word "dialogue" that is somewhat different from what is commonly used. The derivations of words often help to suggest a deeper meaning. "Dialogue" comes from the Greek word *dialogos*. *Logos* means "the word" or in our case we would think of the "meaning of the word." And *dia* means "through"—it doesn't mean "two." A dialogue can be among any number of people, not just two. The picture or image that this derivation suggests is a *stream of meaning* flowing among and through us and between us. This will make possible a flow of meaning in the whole group, out of which may emerge some new understanding. (p. 6)

> Contrast this with the word "discussion," which has the same root as "percussion" and "concussion." It really means to break things up. It emphasizes the idea of analysis, where there may be many points of view, and where everybody is presenting a different one—analyzing

and breaking up. That obviously has value, but it is limited, and it will not get us very far beyond various points of view. (p. 7)

Description

Dialogue, conversation quality, and engagement, are the means by which ideas, experiences, knowledge, beliefs, assumptions, and tendencies are shared throughout the scenario project. Scenarios deal with the two worlds—the world of facts and data, and the world of ideas and perceptions (Wack, 1985a). Dialogue, conversation quality, and engagement allow people to experiment with ideas and perceptions by taking facts and data into imagined or speculative worlds.

Rogers's Work on Communication Theory

Carl Rogers spent much of his career focusing on individual experience. He eventually posited three conditions for health in relating to other people: (1) congruence, (2) unconditional positive regard, and (3) empathetic understanding. By congruence, Rogers (1957) means "a match or fit between an individual's feelings and outer display" (p. 97). Otherwise, individuals match their thoughts and actions. *Unconditional positive regard* is simply an attitude that one consciously tries to hold toward people; Rogers found that he experienced deeper levels of trust by doing so (Rogers, 1961; Rogers & Skinner, 1956). In addition, Rogers found that when people were reminded to use this attitude, they developed deeper levels of trust with others. Rogers's third condition, empathetic understanding, is focused on the benefits of listening. A willingness to explore what it is like to be another person is a skill that Rogers found to bring him closer to those he was trying to help (Rogers, 1961). Others have also drawn attention to empathy as a key skill for knowledge workers in the twenty-first century (Pink, 2006).

Miller, Nunnally, and Wackman's Work on Communication in Families

Nunnally developed a large body of work in the area of communication in interpersonal relationships and among family members. These works feature the self-awareness wheel as their primary contribution to understanding communication, dialogue, and conversation (Miller, 1971; Miller, Nunnally, & Wackman, 1976, 1979; Miller, Wackman, & Nunnally, 1982;

Nunnally, 1971; Nunnally & Moy, 1989). The self-awareness wheel helps individuals recognize their own sensations, feelings, intentions, and actions in the context of how they relate to others (Miller et al., 1979). The wheel can be used as an individual or a 360-degree assessment tool, when appropriate levels of trust have been established

While not specifically intended for use in scenario projects, the utility of the self-awareness wheel is to gain a better understanding of how any individual functions in relation to others. Linking to Rogers's work, the goal is to develop congruence among these five aspects around a given issue.

Argyris and Schon's Work on Advocacy and Inquiry

Argyris and Schon (1996) are well-known for their scholarship in balancing advocacy and inquiry in organizations. This balance is a combination of pushing for individual goals and respecting that humans are part of the larger organizational whole. They are most recognized for differentiating Model I and Model II learning loops. Argyris and Schon (1996) have proposed that a significant perceptual shift takes place when individuals begin to pay attention to their behavior and evaluate it as they would another person's behavior. The ability to reflect on one's own behavior is a uniquely human trait and constitutes Model II learning. When individuals focus on learning how they and others learn, a shift has taken place in terms of how that individual engages in learning activities. Emphasizing common goals, shared interests, and group efforts to achieve them, these understandings contribute to the idea of reflecting on the learning process. This reflection is known as Model II learning or double loop learning, and it contributes to the theoretical underpinnings of scenario planning.

Lewin's Work on Group Dynamics

Lewin's (1951) famous T-groups were a breakthrough in understanding communication among group members. The key contribution arose when researchers allowed a participant to be present for an analysis of her observed behavior earlier in the day (Lewin, 1948). The participant happened to be a woman, and she argued directly with Lewin about his inaccurate interpretations of things she did (Lewin, 1951). Conversation ensued, and a new method of intergroup skills training was born. Certainly, group interactions are critical in scenario planning. The importance of sharing insights, perceptions, and ideas will become clear as this book unfolds.

Linking These Theories to Scenario Planning

These theories explaining what communication is and how it works are relevant in scenario planning because they describe the mode for creating shared understandings of the internal and external environments. The engagement of multiple stakeholders participating in an ongoing dialogue about organization strategy has been called the *strategic conversation*.

Van der Heijden (1997) found that strategy is best approached as a conversation, rather than an activity bound as an annual event. The strategic conversation integrates all of the theories just described into a way of thinking and acting about the future. He believed both formal and informal aspects of strategy work together to form the strategic conversation. In other words, the informal, water-cooler conversations can be as important and influential as the strategy meetings that take place behind closed doors. The strategic conversation can take on a life of its own as organization members become involved in how their individual efforts link to the goals of the organization as a whole. The strategic conversation requires the kind of reflective thinking and respectful, empathetic communication that has been described earlier.

LEARNING THEORY

Learning theory is a critical foundational theory domain for scenario planning. In fact, several prominent scenario planning experts have described planning as essentially a learning activity (de Geus, 1988; Schwartz, 1991; van der Heijden, 1997), basing their argument on the logic that learning is a key driver of organizational performance (Swanson & Holton, 2001). The usefulness of learning in scenario planning is in the assumption that a core goal of any planning system is to reperceive (Wack, 1984) the organization and how it fits with the environment (Godet, 1987, 2000; Wilson, 1992, 2000).

Definition

Learning has been defined in many ways, and there are many specific philosophical orientations toward the learning process. Learning will be generally taken here to mean "the process of gaining knowledge or skill" (Oxford English Dictionary, 2001, p. 247). In the context of scenario planning, learning is defined specifically as a process of gaining knowledge about the internal and external environments and how they interact.

Description

The learning literature has identified five relevant meta-theories of learning—namely, behaviorism, cognitivism, humanism, social learning, and constructivism (Swanson & Holton, 2001). Each of these perspectives is distinctive in its purity, but it should be noted that in practice "they are usually adapted and blended to accomplish specific objectives" (Swanson & Holton, 2001, p. 150). Scenario planning seems to most effectively incorporate a blend of social learning, cognitivsm, and constructivism (Chermack & van der Merwe, 2003; de Geus, 1997; van der Heijden, 1997). Thus, principles of social, cognitive, and constructivist learning are presented here to explain how learning takes place in scenario building and planning systems.

The Individual Construction of Meaning

Piaget (1977) used examples of biological adaptation to illustrate his concepts of assimilation, accommodation, and equilibration. His early fascination centered on the variability of a snail's adaptation to the surrounding environments. Piaget adopted the view that new behavior changes the genes of the organism and thus results in new structures. He eventually arrived at the belief that behavior and the organism must be viewed as a whole system, and the goal is to achieve a balance between organism and environment. Piaget defined this concept of equilibration as a dynamic process of self-regulated behavior that balances two intrinsic polar behaviors, assimilation and accommodation. Equilibration is thought of as a dynamic process that is reached only occasionally as the learner is constantly taking in new information (assimilation), analyzing, and sometimes changing it (accommodation).

Similarly, De Geus viewed the organization as a living entity. "Like all organisms, the living company exists primarily for its own survival and improvement: to fulfill its own potential and to become as great as it can be" (1997, p. 4). Because a critical aim of scenario planning is to reveal assumptions and mental models, individuals interpret and construct meaning, or, more precisely, reinterpret and reconstruct meaning once their assumptions have been revealed to them. This is a classic example of Piaget's assimilation and accommodation. De Geus (1997) stated, "Corporations also have a form of learning by accommodation. . . . [L]ong-lived companies find ways to respond to signals of change in the business environment, by changing their own internal structure" (p. 18). Truly great companies have the foresight and innovation required to change the environment and set the pace for the industry.

Participants in scenario planning are continuously constructing individual meaning. They are taking in new information (assimilation) and modifying or changing it (accommodation) in attempts to reach equilibration (understanding). As information is processed, the mental models of the individuals change and result in new structures for understanding the business environment and how to negotiate within it.

There are two major aspects of scenario planning where construction of individual meaning takes place (Wack, 1985b). One is the analysis and research that takes place during the development of scenario stories. The step of ranking the driving forces in the environment in terms of relative impact on the future provokes a conversation during which the individuals developing the scenarios adjust their assumptions. These adjustments are a result of the assimilation and accommodation process. The second example of construction of meaning is when scenario thinking/assumptions are embedded in organizational decision making (Wack, 1985a).

Social Influences on Construction

Vygotsky (1962/1986) introduced three social influence concepts relevant in scenario planning: (1) the zone of proximal development, (2) the idea of "scaffolding," and (3) the cultural-historical approach.

The Zone of Proximal Development. The *zone of proximal development* is defined as "the distance between his actual development, determined with the help of independently solved tasks, and the level of the potential development of the [learner], determined with the help of tasks solved by the [learner] under the guidance of [experts] and in cooperation with his more intelligent partners" (Vygotsky, 1962/1986, p. 84). Through intelligence testing, Vygotsky determined that there were "optimal" periods within which to teach specific subjects. In brief, the zone of proximal development is the optimal period for almost any learning, that space between what we can accomplish on our own and what we can accomplish with some guidance.

Scenario planning targets the zone of proximal development, and the zone is often perceived as the learning capacity of the client. Vygotsky (1978) referred to the zone of proximal development as "the place where the client's newly acquired, but as yet disorganized concepts 'meet' the logic of experienced reasoning" (p. 24). The meeting of experienced reasoning with the disorganized concepts of the client often produces a novel insight into the strategic positioning of the organization (van der Heijden, 2005a)—what has been referred to as an "aha" experience (van der Merwe, 2002).

The Idea of Scaffolding. Vygotsky proposed that as learners struggle to formulate concepts, an inner dialogue occurs, and he argued that the most effective learning occurs when the learner and the expert jointly construct meaning (of an experience) through dialogue, thus drawing the learner out to the potential level of performance (Fosnot, 1996).

The notion of dialogue as a critical component of learning has been extended and developed into the concept of scaffolding. The famous example of this involves studying children and their mothers engaged in dialogues (Fosnot, 1996). Mothers often imitate babies, varying the response only slightly, but enough to provide an example for the child to imitate (Fosnot, 1996). The mother and child are thought of as constructing meaning together, the mother providing the "scaffolding," or the upper limit of the zone of proximal development.

The role of the scenario planning facilitator is to provide "scaffolding" for members of the organization. "Scaffolds need to be built around the existing knowledge structure to allow the client to relate new experiences to existing knowledge" (Vygotsky, 1978, p. 56). Thus, the planners provide the necessary scaffolding to draw up clients' thought-processing abilities to the limit of their zones of proximal development. Schwartz (1991) also emphasized the notion of drawing managers out to "think the unthinkable." Changing the mental models of managers is a necessary condition for successful scenario planning, and the scenario planner must be capable of providing the scaffolding required to do so.

Kolb's Learning Loop

Van der Heijden (1997, 2005a) supported a view of learning based on the idea of continuous development rather than seeking one right answer. In so doing, he incorporated Kolb and Rubin's (1991) learning loop into his description of effective strategic thinking. Kolb and Rubin's learning loop integrates many of the ideas advocated by Piaget and others. The learning loop features (1) concrete experience, (2) leading to observation and reflection, (3) fueling the formation of abstract concepts, (4) which are then tested in new situations. These elements are involved in a continuous, reinforcing feedback loop.

The learning loop integrates several distinguishing features, according to van der Heijden (1997, 2005b). Among these features are the notions that learning is a process that originates with a given experience. Reflection on the experience brings an awareness resulting in new patterns and trends that were not previously perceived. Mental models are shifted through an internal process of incorporating new patterns into old models, new actions are taken to test the implications of our new models, and all of this results in yet another new experience (Kolb & Rubin, 1991). "The learning loop describes the strategy development process in its integration of experience, sense-making, and action into one holistic phenomenon" (Kolb & Rubin, 1991, p. 34).

The Social Construction of Reality

The basic tenet of the social construction of reality is implied by the term: that reality is constructed by society, and it is constructed socially. The basic proposition set forth by the concept of the sociology of knowledge is from Marx (1953)—that human consciousness is determined by social being. Social constructionism also draws from Marx's concepts of ideology and false consciousness. The task for Berger and Luckmann (1966) was to address how the sociology of knowledge is concerned with what passes for knowledge in society. Berger and Luckmann approached reality from two perspectives, objective and subjective.

Objective Reality. In an examination of society as an objective reality, Berger and Luckmann (1966) posited that being fully human requires social interaction: "the process of becoming human takes place in an interrelationship with an environment . . . the developing human interrelates with a given natural environment and also with a specific cultural and social environment" (p. 21). Thus, social order is a product of human interactions and cannot be "derived from the laws of nature."

One critical element in formulating a social order is the natural tendency for humans to habitualize (Berger & Luckmann, 1966). As human beings, we tend to form habits to reduce options so that we don't have to think about *every* thing we do. Institutionalization occurs when there is a reciprocation of habitualization. For example, family roles are established through the reciprocal habitualization that a person will do X (Berger & Luckmann, 1966). Institutionalization implies control, and these reciprocal actions are built up "in the course of a shared history" (Berger &

Luckmann, 1966). Institutions become integrated through socially articulated and shared meanings established between individuals (Berger & Luckmann, 1966). The shared meanings that are stored in the human consciousness are referred to as *sedimented*. *Intersedimentation* takes place when several individuals share common experiences that are incorporated into the system of society.

The concept of legitimation refers to the "second-order objectivation of meaning," or the building from simple to complex social structures. Legitimation explains and justifies the institutional order by ascribing validity to meanings and designating normative characteristics to the meanings themselves (Berger & Luckmann, 1966). Legtimation occurs at several levels—incipient (signaled by the presence of linguistics), theoretical propositions (folk sayings, proverbs), explicit theories (the purpose of a department within an organization), and symbols (theories that connect the theoretical propositions, such as the purpose of the entire organization).

Subjective Reality. The individual is not a born member of society; rather, the individual is inducted into society by a process. This process is called *internalization*. Berger and Luckmann (1966) referred to *primary socialization* as "the first socialization an individual undergoes in childhood, through which he becomes a member of society" (p. 37). Through this process, objective reality becomes available and then is internalized into the individual consciousness. *Secondary socialization* is the internalization of institutional subworlds. "Secondary socialization requires the acquisition of role-specific knowledge" (Berger & Luckmann, 1966, p. 41)and refers to the process by which an individual is inducted into a further subgroup of a society. A ritual often signifies this process.

The maintenance of subjective reality is held within primary and secondary socialization. Socialization is an ongoing event; and although there are different levels of socialization, primary socialization is inevitable. Through each successive secondary socialization, reality moves further and further from the consciousness of the individual, as the meaning of reality is placed further into the social domain. "The most important vehicle of reality-maintenance is conversation" (Berger & Luckmann, 1966, p. 67). Speech takes place as the background of a world as it is taken for granted. It is through communicative interaction with other members of a society that meaning is derived and negotiated within a social structure.

DECISION-MAKING THEORY

Decision-making theory is critical to understanding what scenario planning is and how it works because decisions are often one of the outcomes of scenario planning (Wright & Goodwin, 2009).

Definition

A *decision* is "an act or process of reaching a conclusion or making up one's mind" (*Oxford English Dictionary*, 2001, p. 267).

Description

In the business context, decisions must have considerable forethought; however, one of the pitfalls of strategic planning has been in its inflexibility, causing planned decisions that do not account for changes within the environment (Mintzberg, 1994; Morecroft, 1983). Brehmer (1990, 1992) specified that decisions in applied contexts differ from the traditional cognitive decisions studied by psychologists in the following four ways:

- There is a series of decisions rather than a single decision.
- The decisions are interdependent—current decisions constrain future decisions.
- The environment changes autonomously and as a result of decisions made.
- It is insufficient for the correct decisions to be made in the correct order—they must also be made at a precise moment in real time.

Decision theory also clarifies four barriers to effective decision making:

- Bounded rationality
- Exogenous variables
- Knowledge stickiness and friction
- Policies and decision premises

Bounded Rationality. Bounded rationality is a main source of decision failure. Put simply, the mental abilities of human decision makers have limitations. Morecroft (1983) outlined the notion of bounded rationality as developed by the Carnegie School of Thought, a pioneering research foundation for decision making. *Bounded rationality* is defined as "the severe limitations on the information processing and computing abilities of human decision makers" (1983, p. 133). According to Simon (1957), bounded rationality is a property of decision making that inhibits objectively rational decisions because (1) all feasible alternative courses of action cannot be generated by the individual, (2) individuals cannot collect and process the information that would predict the consequences of an alternative, and (3) individuals cannot accurately assess the values of anticipated consequences. This simply means that humans cannot effectively cope with all of the available information and alternatives in making decisions. Furthermore, bounded rationality predicts that three main features will be present in human organizations:

- Factored decision making—decision making will be broken down into subdecisions for subgroups.
- Partial and certain information—research shows that ultimately, "decisions are made on relatively few sources of information that are readily available and low in uncertainty" (Morecroft, 1985, p. 133).
- Rules of thumb—rules of thumb, or heuristics, are built up over time that, through experience, make the gathering of information unnecessary.

Scenarios and Bounded Rationality. Scenarios appear to have utility in reducing bounded rationality. Scenarios communicate a vast amount of information in a story. Research has shown that scenarios are effective because they are highly memorable, conversational, and narrative in nature (Dorner, 1996; Martin, 1982; Morecroft, 1985). "Cognitive science research tells us that memorable information is more likely to be acted upon than is information that remains unconscious and not retrieved from memory. Therefore, anything that tends to make information more memorable will have a greater likelihood of assuming significance" (Martin, 1982, p. 103). This point explains the importance placed on the selection of titles for developed scenarios. Schwartz (1991) stated that "if the names are vivid and memorable, the scenarios will have a much better chance of making their way into the decision-making and decision-implementing process across the company" (p. 248). Important information about the future is often too imprecise and complex for display in tables and graphs (Brehmer, 1992), and thus, stories have several advantages: (1) they provoke an openness to multiple perspectives, (2) they aid in coping with complexity, and (3) they give meaning to events (Martin, 1982).

In an experiment testing consumer preferences, Stanford MBA students were asked to assess the persuasiveness of an advertisement from a California winery (Martin, 1982). Given a choice among numerical data from the winery's sales division, a policy statement about the winery's strict quality standards, and a story about the founder of the winery and his procedures for delivering a quality product, results showed an overwhelming preference for the story precisely because it contained the same, or very similar, data in a form that was easy to remember. Although the use of stories in this context varies slightly from the use of scenarios in a planning context, some parallels can be drawn. For example, this research demonstrates the availability heuristic that suggests an event made more available from memory will be more easily acted upon. In this sense, events made more available from memory through inclusion in a scenario can reduce the time required for managers or individuals to react to signals in the environment.

Scenarios might be helpful to decision makers in coping with their own bounded rationality by providing a vast amount of information in a detailed story exhibiting features that are easily remembered. Although scenarios can be helpful in addressing this core cause of decision failure, it should be acknowledged that bounded rationality, as a feature of being human, can never be completely solved. What is further required is a series of case studies, or research regarding the specific impact of scenario planning on individual habits of information gathering, synthesis, and decision making.

Exogenous and Endogenous Variables

Exogenous variables are variables that are external to the process under consideration and that come from outside the system. Decision makers have tended to think of all variables as exogenous, mainly because these variables are easily recognizable as external and are not often hidden by being coupled to the system. Forrester (1961, 1994) was among the first to take issue with a tendency for models (and therefore decisions) to incorporate only exogenous or external variables. Forrester argued that some variables are actually coupled to the system and are embedded in the information feedback loops. These were referred to as endogenous variables. *Endogenous variables* are internal variables that are often produced in the feedback within the system, and they then become coupled with the inputs to the system. Policies often have endogenous variables associated with them. Decisions that consider only exogenous variables, therefore, overlook critical inputs to the system, and decisions made without considering such variables have consequences that become magnified because of their association with feedback processes.

Scenarios and Exogenous Variables

There is a variety of scenario planning methods, and each of them differ slightly. However, all approaches advocate a systems view of the organization. The important link between scenario planning and systems theory has been outlined in detail (Senge, 1990, 1994), the implications of which include the examination of internal and external elements of the system. Van der Heijden's (1997, 2005b) approach to scenario planning begins with mapping the organization as a system in what he terms the business idea. Furthermore, he suggested the use of interviews, internal analysis, teams, and remarkable people as methods for avoiding a focus solely on external forces.

Senge (1990, 1994) has developed systems archetypes that are essentially common combinations of feedback loops that inhibit systems. The use of these archetypes as diagnosis tools forces scenario planners to consider system outputs that become system inputs—exogenous variables that become endogenous variables, addressing Forrester's (1961, 1994) concern. The systems view incorporates the consideration of internal and external variables and focuses on how they interact to change the system.

Stickiness and Friction

Stickiness and friction are characteristics of information and knowledge, respectively. Generally, the term stickiness refers to a characteristic of information and is associated with the cost of its transfer. Friction is a characteristic of knowledge that dampens motions in a social setting. Socialization itself causes a friction that catches minor errors before they can be magnified through feedback processes to a point at which they can cause a catastrophe. Stickiness, or the cost associated with transferring information, causes a problem for decision makers when expertise is needed. With automation threatening to replace humans in many work and decision-related settings (thus eliminating social friction), a concern has emerged about potential increases in minor errors that lead to drastic decision failures.

Stickiness. Organizations are increasingly relying on knowledge-intensive processes managed and operated by interdisciplinary teams (Ford & Sterman, 1998). *Stickiness* in this context refers to the difficulty in information transfer between or among people. Von Hippel (1998) defined *stickiness* as "the incremental expenditure required to transfer that unit of information to a specified locus in a form useable by a given information seeker. When this cost is low, information stickiness is low; when it is high, stickiness is high" (p. 629). Discussions of stickiness have included the simple recognition that a cost is associated with the transfer of information, as well as the distinction between stickiness and friction (Rochlin, 1998). That information becomes "sticky" is important in decision making because often expertise or knowledge of a specific domain is required for decisions. For example, McKinsey consultants who are on call and will fly anywhere in the world to make their expertise available are a result of the fact that knowledge becomes incredibly sticky and an example that the costs associated with transferring the information or knowledge can become quite high (Rochlin, 1998).

Friction. In social and political realms, "morals, ethics, knowledge, history and memory may all serve as the sources of 'social friction,' by which gross motions are damped, impetuous ones slowed and historical ones absorbed. Such friction is essential to prevent the persistence and multiplication of social and political movements once their driving force is removed" (Von Hippel, 1998, p. 132). Friction can be described as the nuances and double-checks that occur in the social interactions among humans in work processes, such as those found in the operation of an aircraft carrier flight deck (Rochlin, LaPorte, & Roberts, 1987). Such double-checks only exist as a result of social interaction among multiple individuals. Authors such as Rochlin (1998), Dreyfus and Dreyfus (1998), and Von Hippel (1998) argued that as technology threatens to replace many such human processes, decision failure will increase because the loss of friction will allow many errors to continue that were previously prevented during the course of normal social interaction among the humans involved in the process. For example, friction would not exist if computer automation were to take over the launching and landing procedures aboard aircraft carriers (Rochlin et al., 1987).

Frictionless knowledge (Rochlin, 1998) would initially be more efficient, but it would also allow for a drastic increase in decision errors. Dreyfus and Dreyfus (1998) argued that their own model of novice, advanced beginner, competence, proficiency, and expertise provides the experiential elements required to reach the potential of true human intelligence. Frictionless knowledge would be knowledge that develops a "set of rules and principles that produce expert-quality performance in an entire domain of skill" (Rochlin, 1998, p. 284). In this view, frictionless knowledge could be easily transferred to or among countless individuals, and it would not be sticky as there would be no cost in transferring the knowledge. However, Dreyfus and Dreyfus (1998) argued for the necessity of the experience and thus the buildup of friction required for true expertise.

Scenarios, Stickiness, and Friction. Scenario planning is posited as a tool for reducing the cost of information transfer and increasing the friction among knowledgeable organizational decision makers. By reducing the cost of information transfer, in theory, decisions can be made more effectively and efficiently. By increasing the friction among decision makers, small errors may be caught and perspectives can be added that might have otherwise been overlooked.

Scenarios and scenario planning seem to address information stickiness by providing a forum for multiple individuals to develop similar expertise about the potentials of the organization. The strategic conversation (van der Heijden, 1997, 2005b; Wright & Goodwin, 1999) is one example of how developing a shared mental model, and thus a shared language, can reduce the stickiness of information within the organization. The process of creating a shared mental model facilitates the process of information transfer. By requiring frequent and intense interaction, scenario planning reduces the cost of information transfer, making information less sticky (Wright & Goodwin, 1999).

Scenarios might further help decision makers take full advantage of the necessary friction required for expertise in organizational decision making. The process of scenario building requires intense interaction for extended periods of time among managers and executives involved in the decision-making process. Through this interaction and friction, important forces in the environment are often detected that would not have been if a single decision maker were attempting to construct scenarios individually.

In scenario planning, van der Heijden (1997, 2005b) makes use of "remarkable people" (Wack, 1985b) to provide even more friction. *Remarkable people* are "those experts who are not in regular contact with the client organization, such that an original contribution can be expected" (Wack, 1984, p. 67). Remarkable people often provide insight, prevent groupthink, help with information gathering and processing, increase the friction and interaction among planning team members, and expand the rationality of the group.

Policies and Decision Premises. In this context, a policy is defined as "a formal statement giving the relationship between information inputs and resulting decision flows" (Forrester, 1994, p. 58). *Policies, decision premises*, and *decision rules* are all terms that describe this same phenomenon. "Informal policy results from habit, conformity, social pressures, ingrained concepts of goals, awareness of power centers within the organization, and personal interest" (Forrester, 1994, p. 58). Decision policies, premises, or rules can be thought of as the guiding norms within the context that help individuals make decisions when they are uncertain about the information at hand or the "best practices" that offer guidance. It is argued here that such policies, premises, or rules are developed according to the mental model in use as mental models house our biases, values, and beliefs about how the world works. Thus, to change or expand the decision rules, one must change the mental model.

Scenarios and Decision Premises. Decision premises and policies are linked to mental models. Because premises and policies "result from habit, conformity, social pressures, ingrained concepts of goals, awareness of power centers within the organization, and personal interest" (Forrester, 1994, p. 58), they can be changed through the alteration of mental models. The key idea with regard to decision premises is that through the expansion of mental models, guiding decision policies are revised to accommodate a more adequate view of the world and the system within which the individual is operating.

Scenarios may also provide a venue for testing new decision policies by manipulating forces and potential responses to them in an experimental environment. Decision makers can play out the possibilities of given decision policies and examine their long-term effects. Furthermore, by creating shared mental models and a strategic conversation within the organization, policies undergo constant scrutiny, modification, and adjustment to assure that they provide decision makers with an informed perspective when confronted with an uncertain situation.

MENTAL MODEL THEORY (COGNITIVE PSYCHOLOGY)

Mental model theory is important in scenario planning because of its ability to help understand individual learning and perceptions in organizations (Morecroft, 1990, 1992; Senge, 1990; Wack, 1984; Weick, 1979, 1990).

Mental models encompass people's assumptions, values, experiences, beliefs, and ideas. Reperceiving the organization and its environment is thought to occur through learning that forces participants to reexamine their assumptions and alter their mental models (Wack, 1984, 1985a). While it may sound simple, shifting mental models is a delicate process. Mental models are not like computer hard drives that, once full or faulty, can simply be removed or replaced.

Definition

Doyle and Ford (1999) defined a *mental model* as "a relatively enduring and accessible, but limited, internal conceptual representation of an external system (historical, existing or projected) whose structure is analogous to the perceived structure of that system" (p. 414).

Description

Originally introduced by Forrester (1961), mental models are the lenses through which we see the world. They incorporate our experiences, learning, biases, values, and beliefs about how the world works. These models embody how individuals see the world, how individuals know and think about the world, and how individuals act in the world. Furthermore, as a result of action and learning, mental models are altered, leading to different ways of seeing the world, knowing and thinking about the world, and, again, acting in the world. Mental models are constantly being adjusted, refined, and re-created in dynamic and ever-changing environments. Mental models both affect experience (active) and are affected by experience (passive). Having briefly established the active and passive roles of mental models in the construction and interpretation of reality, we can now turn to a detailed attempt at defining them.

Clarifying Mental Models. Different streams of decision-making literature refer to mental models, representations and cognitive maps. Each of these terms warrants clarification and description.

Mental Models. Allee (1997) stated that mental models are "important cornerstones for building knowledge and defining some of the cognitive processes that support change and learning" (p. 11). Senge (1990) defined *mental models* as "deeply ingrained assumptions, generalizations, or even pictures or images that influence how we understand the world and how we take action. Very often, we are not consciously aware of our mental models or the effects they have on our behavior" (p. 8).

Doyle and Ford (1998) explored the concept of mental models in detail: "Mental models are thus the stock in trade of research and practice in system dynamics: they are the 'product' that modelers take from students and clients, disassemble, and reconfigure, add to, subtract from, and return with value added" (p. 4). After providing a comprehensive literature review of the terms from both the systems dynamics and cognitive psychological perspectives, and some discussion in *Systems Dynamics Review*, Doyle and Ford eventually offered the following revised definition of mental models: "A mental model of a dynamic system is a relatively enduring and accessible, but limited, internal conceptual representation of an external system (historical, existing or projected) whose structure is analogous to the perceived structure of that system" (p. 414). Weick (1979, 1985, 1990) has argued consistently that mental models guide, shape, and provide the basis on which individuals interpret and make sense of organizational life.

Representations. Cognitive psychology literature focuses on mental representations. *Representations* refer to the way humans build "stand-ins" for reality in their minds. "One of the functions of representations is to stand in for things outside the system; once a system has representations, it can operate on them and not need the world" (Bechtel, 1998, p. 297). The concept of representation can best be introduced by considering that the mind and brain are involved in "coordinating the behavior of an organism in its environment" (Bechtel, 1998, p. 297). To coordinate such behavior, an organism must create some working understanding of its environment, and it does so by constructing a mental representation, or model of that environment (Johnson-Laird, 1983).

Freyd (1987) suggested that mental representations are also dynamic: "perceivers are sensitive to implicit dynamic information even when they are not able to observe real-time changes" (p. 427). The significance of Freyd's research is its suggestion that the human mind is itself anticipatory in its perception and construction of events. That is, the human mind naturally anticipates possible future sequences of actions based on immediate perceptions.

Cognitive Maps. Cognitive maps apply metaphor to the notion of mental models. Weick (1990) recounted a favorite story about a Hungarian military unit on maneuvers in the Swiss Alps:

Their young lieutenant sent a reconnaissance unit out into the icy wilderness just as it began to snow. It snowed for two days, and the unit did not return. The lieutenant feared that he had dispatched his people to their deaths, but the third day the unit came back. Where had they been? How had they made their way? Yes, they said, we considered ourselves lost and waited for the end, but then one of us found a map in his pocket. That calmed us down. We pitched camp, lasted out the snowstorm, and then with the map we found our bearings. And here we are. The lieutenant took a good look at the map, and discovered, to his astonishment, that it was a map of the Pyrenees. (This story was related by the Nobel Laureate Albert Szent-Gyorgi and was turned into a poem by Holub, 1977.) (p. 4)

Thus, the "cognitive map" refers to the way the mind creates a map or model of a territory, or situation that it uses as a reference point. Weick (1990) further explained that any map, no matter that it may be an incorrect one, provides some reference point and increases the likelihood that an individual or group will be able to navigate unfamiliar terrain. Weick's point seems to be that it is better to operate with a set of assumptions that may be incomplete than to forego operating completely.

Global Business Network, a consulting firm with specialization in scenario planning and strategic thinking, suggests a story of map use to illustrate its point—a point that differs a bit from that of Weick (1990):

This map [Figure 2.2] was made in 1701 by a Dutch mapmaker named Herman Moll, working in London. He based his map on the explorations of the Spanish, who came up the western side of the Americas, and originally encountered the southern point on the map, the tip of today what we call the Baja Peninsula. And actually the first maps were right. Everything north of that was drawn as terra incognitas, one great land mass. But then a few years later, around 1635, the Spanish sailed to the northern points along this map and encountered what we call the Straits of Juan de Fuca and the Puget Sound. Being good Cartesians, they connected the northern point with the southern point and created the Island of California.

Now, this would only be a historical curiosity were it not for the problem of the missionaries, because the missionaries actually used this map. They would land near what is today Monterey and go inland to bring the word

FIGURE 2.2   A Map of North America

of God to the American Indians. Now, if you're on the western shores and you want to go inland, what do you have to do? Well, of course, you have to take your boats with you. So these poor missionaries disassembled their boats, packed them on mules, hauled them across California and 12,000 feet up the Sierra Nevada, and then down the other side—only to find a beach, that went on and on, and on, and on. Until, of course, they finally recognized that they were in the middle of the deserts of Nevada, and there was no Island of California. So they wrote to the map-makers in Spain and said, "Hey, listen, there's no Island of California; your map is wrong!" And the mapmakers would write back and say, "No, no, no! You're in the wrong place; the map is right!"

Well, finally, in 1685, the Spanish changed their maps. Sixteen years later, when Moll was challenged by the Spanish about his map, he claimed,

"I have actually talked to sailors who sailed all the way around the Island of California. It's an island." Finally, in 1721, he changed his maps too.

So, what's the point? The point is, if you get your facts wrong, you get your map wrong. If you get your map wrong, you do the wrong thing. But worst of all once you believe a map, it is very, very hard to change. We all have deeply ingrained maps—all of us—and particularly successful corporate executives. Because, of course, they are successful precisely because they have had good maps of the world as they have understood it. They would not have risen to positions of power if they did not understand their business, the business environment, the evolution of their industry, and also function effectively using this map. However, these executives have a problem: the map that got them to the top is unlikely to be the map that they need for the future. And worst of all, challenging those deeply ingrained perceptions takes an enormous amount of skill, intelligence, information, and judgment. (www.gbn.org/scenarios/maprap, accessed April 14, 2003)

These two stories illustrate conflicting notions about the purposes and pitfalls of cognitive maps. We are therefore left with something of a paradox: any map is better than no map; however, an inaccurate map often leads to an undesired location. Scenarios work to continuously adjust the maps, based on new understandings of the terrain. New understandings of the terrain come from rigorous research and constant "strategic" conversations with other "explorers" of the terrain.

LEADERSHIP THEORY

Leadership is included here as a key ingredient of scenario planning because leadership is a critical component of any organization change and development effort. As with any other change project, if the leadership of the organization is not involved and supportive, the project is likely to fail. Because leadership is such an extensive topic itself, a lengthy review will be avoided here. Instead, some recent research, led by colleagues Rochell McWhorter and Susan Lynham, is summarized as an emerging foundation for developing links between leadership capabilities/capacities and scenario planning.

Definition

The *Oxford English Dictionary* (2006) defines leadership as "[a]n act or instance of guidance or direction" (p. 549).

Description

Leadership is obviously critical in organizations. The body of work examining and analyzing leadership is far too vast to examine in depth here. Suffice it to say that leadership is clearly a complex phenomenon concerned with how decision makers move organizations forward and inspire people around them. Leaders drive virtually all aspects of organizational life, including policy, human resource practices, structure, and compensation, among many, many others.

Emerging Research Linking Scenario Planning and Leadership

Research thus far on leadership as a critical component of scenario planning has focused on interviews with scenario planning experts (Lynham, 1998, 2000a, 2000b, 2002a, 2002b; McWhorter, Lynham, & Porter, 2008). Studies have explored the link between leadership development and scenario planning by asking experts to describe their interpretation of this relationship. Some exciting developments have included descriptions of scenario planning used as a leadership development activity. Companies have been experimenting by asking emerging leaders to manage various aspects of the scenario planning effort as a development activity. Interviews have suggested that leaders in some organizations are realizing that planning will be an increasingly critical skill set for the future, and they expect their future potential leaders to be familiar with scenario planning techniques (McWhorter et al., 2008).

Kleiner and Roth's (2000) *Oil Change: Perspectives on Corporate Transformation* and Lynham's (2000a) *The Development of a Theory of Responsible Leadership for Performance* provided strong additional conceptual starting points. Several emerging research studies are promising in that they suggest a clear link between leadership and scenario planning; however, such research is in the early stages of documenting this link technique (McWhorter et al., 2008). Additional studies will clarify the strength and importance of the relationship between leadership development and scenario planning, but for now, the suggestion is that leadership must be involved with and supportive of any scenario project in order for it to succeed. Perhaps in the near future, scenario projects can be designed specifically as leadership development activities. More research must be done to understand how leadership is linked to scenario planning and how the two systems interact.

ORGANIZATION PERFORMANCE AND CHANGE

Performance is one of the most talked-about aspects of organizational improvement efforts. Swanson's (1999) discussion of performance improvement foundations provided a broad yet well-defined perspective of performance along with the means to assess it, describe it, and explain it in more detail. Although the performance perspective has received criticism on the grounds that it neglects the human elements in organizations and improvement efforts, "the best [performance improvement] theory and practice will in the end validate the need for and contribution of human expertise to [performance improvement]" (Swanson, 1999, p. 4). The collective influence of dialogue, conversation quality and engagement, learning, decision making, mental models, and leadership on organization performance and change was shown in Figure 2.1. These elements combine to create performance-based scenario planning.

Definition

Performance has been defined as "the valued productive output of a system in the form of goods or services" (Swanson, 1999, p. 5).

Description

Performance occurs in four core domains: organization, process, group, and individual. Performance has also been placed at the center of a lengthy debate over the intended outcome of organizational interventions. The perspective advocated here is that performance is *necessary*, although not necessarily *sufficient*, for organizational effectiveness. Clearly, responsible scholars and practitioners must address both of these perspectives and concerns, and the position argued in this model is that the scenario planning system inherently requires that both learning and performance are necessary outcomes. Research in this area also suggests it is a promising area to continue exploring (Phelps, Chan, & Kapsalis, 2001; Visser & Chermack, 2009).

Levels of Performance

Regarding the link between performance and strategy, Rummler and Brache (1995) stated, "The most powerful strategy implementation tools we have found are those that help us effectively design and manage performance at the organization, process and job/performer levels" (p. 84). Thus, a clear strategy for evaluating the outcomes of the scenario planning processes is to evaluate changes in performance at these three levels.

The Organization Level. Rummler and Brache (1995) defined performance at the organization level in terms of three core variables: organization goals, organization design, and organization management. Organization goals frequently include a focus on productivity, cycle time, cost, and profit improvement efforts. Performance-focused analysts "design an organization that enables the goals to be met" (Rummler & Brache, 1995, p. 37); thus, a focus on the input-output relationships within the organization allow a design that accommodates and supports the organization's goals. Goals, performance, resources, and interfaces between functions are all areas requiring frequent assessment to "help identify what needs to get done (goals), the relationships necessary to get it done (design), and the practices that remove the impediments to getting it done (management)" (Rummler & Brache, 1995, p. 43). The organization level of performance provides the foundation for understanding, analyzing, and managing performance at the process and individual levels.

The Process Level. Commonly viewed as how work is accomplished, *processes* can be more specifically defined as value chains in which each step adds value to the previous step. Based on a view that effective process produces effective organizations, Rummler and Brache (1995) asserted that process goals, design, and management are the key variables to address for improving process performance. Process goals are considered subgoals of organization goals, and they should be designed to efficiently convert process inputs to process outputs. Managing, analyzing, and adjusting processes goals, performance, resources, and interfaces ensure the maintenance of high levels of process performance (Rummler & Brache, 1995). Targeted as the level with the greatest opportunity to contribute to performance improvement, the process level is largely ignored and often misunderstood.

The Job/Performer Level. Jobs must be designed to support process steps, enabling the achievement of process goals and, in turn, organization goals. Job goals must be aligned with process goals, and jobs must be designed and structured such that the performer can achieve those job goals (Rummler & Brache, 1995). Job management is considered a function of (1) performance specifications, (2) task support, (3) consequences, (4) feedback, (5) skills and knowledge, and (6) individual capacity. These components of job management, if effectively addressed, help job performers achieve process goals, leading to the fulfillment of organization goals.

Scenario Planning and the Levels of Performance Improvement

The link between scenario planning and performance improvement theory seems obvious, yet scenario planning is increasingly applied without a performance need and without a theoretical basis, making evaluation a difficult exercise. Thus, the importance of the performance need in the performance improvement context cannot be overstated. Van der Heijden et al. (2002) identified a "lack of purposefulness" (p. 3) as a major reason that scenario projects fail. It is in the performance need, determined by a thorough analysis, that such purposefulness can be discovered and acted upon (Holton, 1999; Swanson, 1994).

Scenario Planning at the Organization Level

Scenario planning must produce results at the organization level. While evaluation efforts have been minimal, one study in particular attempted to analyze the link between engagement in scenario planning and firm performance. Phelps, Chan, and Kapsalis (2001) evaluated scenario planning projects in the water and IT industries. In the water industry, firm performance measures included return on capital employed, water quality, variance in water pressure over time, and supply interruptions. In the IT industry, firm performance measures included annual growth rates of client companies, return on capital employed, and net profits. The authors concluded that scenario planning had a considerable positive effect on firm performance in the water industry, although the service score showed a considerable decrease. The IT industry also showed a positive association between scenario planning and performance, although it was less powerful and was based on a questionably small sample size. Further studies such as these are needed to establish the link between scenario planning and performance in terms of economic benefit. Studies focused on the relationship between scenario planning and the achievement of organization goals are particularly advocated as one step in a comprehensive program of scenario evaluation.

Several case studies—for example, Royal Dutch Shell (Wack, 1985a, 1985b), British Airways (Moyer, 1996), and Nokia (van der Heijden et al.,

2002)—examine the abilities of organizations to revive and renew themselves, and the fact that these companies are still flourishing despite some extremely challenging situations is one indicator that scenario planning might help an organization and its leaders cope with uncertainty. A company's ability to survive may be the most basic indicator of performance at the organization level. Other indicators may be specific to industry or company, but effective scenario planning will select these specific indicators, measure them, and address them.

Scenario Planning at the Process Level

Only one study was found that explicitly examined the effects of scenario planning on process capabilities or functions. A case study by Burt and van der Heijden (in Ringland, 2002) had as one of its primary aims the reconfiguration of supply chain processes. While it is clear that scenario thinking might be used to develop alternative processes and explore more efficient means of delivering products and services, scenarios have rarely been applied in this context. However, some scenario projects such as the IT company International Computers Ltd. (Ringland, 2002) have incorporated systems diagrams to map information markets in process formats; or, as in the case of Daimler-Benz Aerospace (Tessum, 1997), systems diagrams were used to map early warning systems as processes of contingency planning. Van der Heijden et al. (2002) suggested that organizational change is effectively brought about through process change, although "process gain requires persistence and consistency over an extended period" (p. 84).

Some preliminary conceptual arguments for using scenarios in the process context include the use of scenarios as "cognitive objects" (P. E. Johnson, personal communication, April 2003) in which scenarios are vehicles for process management and knowledge transfer. These are key areas for further investigation that might use scenarios to explore alternative processes for improved efficiency and storage spaces for descriptions of knowledge work. Research studies that document the effects of scenarios applied to processes would provide much value by potentially providing an additional application area for scenarios. As Rummler and Brache (1995) stated, "[T]he process level has been the least understood level of performance" (p. 44); as such, the process level provides the most potential for improving performance.

Scenario Planning at the Job/Performer Level

Perhaps more than any other level, anecdotal evidence has supported the claim of individual performance improvement. Whether through learning via intense trend analysis (Wack, 1985b), shared mental models (van der Heijden, 1997), or increased availability of information for more precise, long-view-oriented decision making (Schwartz, 1991), virtually all reports of scenario application address the performance of the individual. However, none reports an empirical study, with measures of individual performance improvement. Van der Heijden et al. (2002) stated that scenarios help individuals reperceive reality from multiple perspectives, provide a forum for people to think creatively, and are effectively used as communications tools. These uses of scenarios are all aimed at improving performance, although there is little beyond participant claims of improvement in these areas.

INTEGRATING THE THEORETICAL FOUNDATIONS FOR A THEORY OF SCENARIO PLANNING

Scenario planning is believed to contribute to organization performance through the collective effect of each of the theories described in this chapter. To some, this explanation may seem obvious, but such a system of concepts explaining how scenario planning contributes to the organization and its goals is not found in the literature. The goal of this chapter has been to justify the theory of scenario planning and to capture what scenario planning is and how it works (Torraco, 1997). In the proposed theory, conversation quality and engagement, learning, decision making, mental models, and leadership are positioned as drivers of organization performance and change. What is unique about scenario planning is that it integrates these critical drivers of organization performance and change (Visser & Chermack, 2009).

The components of the theory of scenario planning are useful in understanding what scenario planning is and how it works in numerous ways. First, the theory provides a thinking tool for conceptualizing how scenario projects might be facilitated. It presents several "targets"—or items that scenario planning is designed to change. The results of these changes are intended to alter how participants view the internal and external environments. Participants can therefore reperceive their environment and the options contained within it. Second, the components of the theory provide convenient measurement points for assessing and evaluating the outcomes of scenario planning. Finally, this theory provides a way of categorizing new knowledge that is generated about scenario planning. To be sure, theories in organization sciences require adjustment, refinement, and development as new insights are gained.

CONCLUSION

This chapter has reviewed the major theory domains that inform the practice of scenario planning: (1) dialogue, conversation quality, and engagement; (2) organizational learning; (3) mental models; (4) decision making; (5) leadership, and (6) organization performance and change. These theoretical foundations have been explored in detail, with an aim of explaining how each one is relevant in scenario planning practices and models. The theoretical foundations were integrated into a theory of scenario planning that attempts to present a conceptual explanation of what scenario planning is and how it works. This chapter is critical in understanding scenario planning practices as theories, and theoretical foundations provide a set of "hooks" on which to hang knowledge as one navigates through the implementation of any scenario planning project. In addition, the theories presented in this chapter help to identify the elements that must be considered in any scenario planning project intended to contribute to enhanced organizational performance.

3

The Performance-Based Scenario System

This chapter situates scenario planning in the organizational context. It explains how scenario planning fits into the organizational system as a subsystem with its own inputs, processes, outputs, and feedback loops.

To accomplish this goal, the state of the economic, business, and societal environment and its influence on organizational activity is described. Not only does the environment make the case for scenario planning, but it also sets up the reality of systems within systems and ever-changing conditions. This chapter also explains organizations as systems, describes scenario planning as a system within the organization, and introduces the phases of scenario planning that form the content for Part Two of this book.

THE EXTERNAL ENVIRONMENTAL CONTEXT

The nature of the environment was established in Chapter 1. To reiterate, things change too rapidly for forecasts or other predictive planning models to be useful. There are no signs that the rate of change will slow. Coupled with the rate of change is its depth. Economic hiccups are deeper and disasters more devastating than ever. Decision makers are just trying to make sense of a context that changes significantly and frequently. Many have tried other tools and been frustrated by the lack of ability to understand and account for uncertainty. Today's business context plainly leaves people in the midst of turbulence.

SYSTEMS WITHIN SYSTEMS

Much has been written about systems theory applied in business organizations, so there is no need for a lengthy explanation here. But what does require some explanation is viewing strategy itself as a system within the larger organization system.

Within its environmental context, each organization relies on a performance system. For public companies, the most common measure of this performance system is stock market performance. This overall performance measure over time is thought to include other indicators of performance, such as product innovation, competitor successes and failures, and market share, among others. Any of these indicators can also serve as overall performance indicators. The performance system for any organization is the set of components that decision makers have organized to sell products, goods, and services.

Within this performance system is the planning system. Decision makers and organizational leaders engage in planning as a means of influencing organizational performance, and as such, the planning system is a system within the performance system. Planning has always been intended as a means of satisfying the innate human need to think about the future, but in an organizational context, it is also intended as a means for people to consider the results of their potential activities. Most commonly, decision makers engage in planning in hopes of maximizing optimal growth, production, or delivery of services, which are then sold to optimize profit. All of this is happening amid the chaos of the external environmental context (Figure 3.1).

Figure 3.1 positions the performance system within the organizational and contextual environment, and the planning system within the performance system. Of course, this is a simplified view, but the key point to stress is that planning is a system *within* the organization system. However, planning is most often viewed as a *process*—a series of steps to be carried out to "do" the plan without regard for its inputs and outputs.

PLANNING AS A PROCESS

Most planning models are process models indicating the required planning steps, but a systems approach may provoke new insights related to planning. Such a reconceptualization creates new ways of thinking about planning performance.

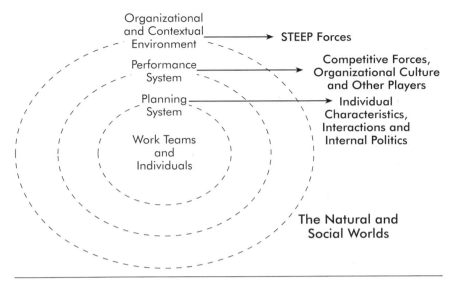

Organizational
and Contextual ─────────► STEEP Forces
Environment

Performance ──────────► Competitive Forces,
System   Organizational Culture
                        and Other Players

Planning ──────────► Individual
System   Characteristics,
                     Interactions and
Work Teams   Internal Politics
and
Individuals

The Natural and
Social Worlds

FIGURE **3.1**   The Context of Scenario Planning

The availability of countless guides to organizational planning and strategy serves as testament to the fact that there are as many different sets of steps for planning as there are consultants to help organizations through them. Much of the research concerning various planning processes is conflicting or ambiguous (Hitt, Hoskisson & Ireland, 1990; Micklethwait & Woolridge, 1996). Unfortunately, planning is mostly thought of as a stand-alone process or event in organizations with little concern for the nature of the organizational engagement in strategy or its ultimate outcomes (Micklethwait & Woolridge, 1996). Thus, a problem is that most approaches to planning are divorced from the inputs to, and outputs from, the strategy system.

The basic design school model of strategy is based on a process approach to planning and summarizes the early approaches to strategy in a delineated, step-by-step model (Mintzberg, 1994). Notably, the basic design school model is still the basis of strategy in most organizations today. The design school model uses the strengths, weaknesses, opportunities, and threats (SWOT) analysis as its foundation.

This basic design school model has been used to integrate a variety of common approaches to planning in organizations. The foundation of planning for many organizations, this model is inherently valuable because of its ability to synthesize a great deal of planning literature, research, and experience in a single model. However, the design school model includes an implicit assumption that the environment will stay relatively stable and predictable. It promotes a process approach to planning, giving people the steps to "do" planning, but it does not place any emphasis on the inputs and outputs relevant to the strategy system. There is no clear link to the rest of the organization. In contrast, a clear connection to organizational inputs and outputs defines the performance-based scenario system presented in this book.

PLANNING AS A SYSTEM

Planning is a system. Thus, as a system within the organization—a system within a system—it might be better approached from a more integrative perspective than current practices promote. While this distinction may seem trite, its implications have a considerable influence on the nature of planning and strategy in organizations. In addition, viewing planning as a system allows strategists a greater amount of flexibility in their efforts to obtain glimpses of the future.

The word system is used purposefully in this context. Planning has its own set of inputs, processes, and outputs and can therefore be labeled as a system itself. Conceptually, this system can be divided into two key components, the first concerning the exploration of options and the second composed of making decisions and moving forward. However, this separation is conceptual only: these components are iteratively linked, and scenario planning as a particular approach to strategy in the end is an ongoing approach to strategy that is never complete. Viewing strategy as a system means that time is spent analyzing the inputs and outputs; and, therefore, each instance of strategy is a customized, tailor-made effort.

THE SCENARIO SYSTEM: SCENARIO BUILDING AND SCENARIO DEPLOYMENT

The rationale for approaching planning as a system leads to a description of scenario planning as a system within the organization. The scenario system is divided into two parts:

- Scenario building
- Scenario deployment

These parts represent the two major components of engaging in scenario planning in organizations. This division is important, as building scenarios is not enough. Equally important is what is done with the scenarios once they are developed.

Scenario Building

Scenario building is the content covered in existing scenario planning books. The focus deals explicitly with the conduct of data gathering, analyzing, synthesizing, and eventually the construction of scenarios. In other words, existing writing on scenario planning covers how to create scenarios. Few authors demonstrate what to do with scenarios after they have been developed. Each of the approaches to scenarios covered in Chapter 2 are different ways of creating scenarios—scenario building. Numerous sources detail procedures on how to build scenarios, but this is where most books on the topic end.

Scenario Deployment

The second part of the scenario system—scenario deployment—centers on how to use the scenarios in ways that work toward outcomes. This book offers several strategies that have been used effectively, in addition to detailed descriptions and processes for using the scenarios to explore current organization issues, resources, strategies, and mental models. The key to making scenarios work is in using the scenarios to change the way decisions are made, shifting the thinking of managers, reframing decision-making processes, and examining numerous organizational issues in the context of each scenario.

Figure 3.2 illustrates the distinction between scenario building and scenario deployment Scenario building is represented by the first cone, opening up toward the middle of the model. The scenario building process is likewise designed to "open up" the thinking inside the organization, to expand the frame and include a wider range of possibilities, and to "see" things differently (Lynham, Provo, & Ruona, 1998; Provo, Lynham, Ruona, & Miller, 1998; Swanson, Lynham, Ruona, & Provo, 1998). The second cone, tapering down toward the right of the figure, represents scenario deployment. Scenario deployment is the process by which decisions must be made in light of a deeper understanding of possibilities inherent in the environment, an expanded set of decision premises, and a wider range of options

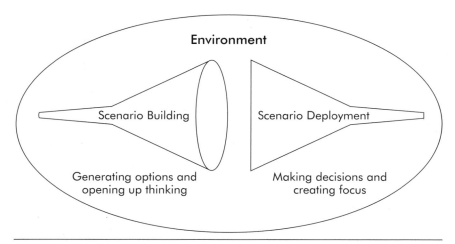

FIGURE **3.2**   Conceptual Model of the Scenario System

Source: Based on Swanson, Lynham, Ruona, & Provo, 1990.

that have been considered. The second cone is not intended to suggest that decision makers should move toward a single desired future state; rather, the most robust path, given an array of potential futures, should be sought.

The first component—option generation—can be characterized by divergent and challenging thinking. Conversely, decision formulation is concerned with convergent thinking and the fact that, ultimately, options must be reduced through decision making. The assumption in this model is that increasing the options that are considered in planning allows decision makers a better view of the potential future; thus, they are more prepared to make decisions under uncertain conditions.

THE PERFORMANCE-BASED SCENARIO SYSTEM

In this book, the performance-based scenario system is described in five phases:

1. Project preparation
2. Scenario exploration
3. Scenario development
4. Scenario implementation
5. Project assessment

These five phases capture the main ideas required to conduct a scenario project and have been used extensively in practice. The first three scenario system phases describe the process of *scenario building*. The last two phases describe what to do with the scenarios once they are developed—*scenario deployment*. The project preparation phase includes contracting with the client, identifying the purpose of the scenario project, clarifying and developing it, and creating an agenda and timeline for the project. The scenario exploration phase moves into detailed research of the purpose and issue identified in Phase 1. Internal and external environmental analyses are conducted in this phase. Phase 3, scenario development, covers the workshops used in the creation of multiple scenarios, writing scenario details, and the selection of four challenging and fundamentally different scenarios (using four scenarios helps to avoid some common thinking traps, which are explained in detail in a later chapter). The scenario implementation phase involves the facilitation of conversations to consider the implications of the scenarios that have been developed. Risk management and contingency planning are elements evident in the implications phase. Strategic insights discovered in the scenario implementation phase also require reflection, and events that signal the potential unfolding of a given scenario are identified. The final phase, project assessment, involves evaluating the scenario project. Scenario projects are difficult to assess, and their assessment has generally been neglected in the scenario planning literature. This book offers a practical approach to scenario planning project assessment.

Figure 3.3 presents a visual overview of the whole scenario system. The system includes inputs, outputs, and the phases of scenario planning. Part Two of this book focuses on the details of the phases of the scenario system, with specific tools and workshops for accomplishing the key purpose of each phase.

THE SCENARIO-BUILDING COMPONENT

Once the major inputs to the scenario system are considered, the scenario-building activity begins. Scenario building includes the first three phases—project preparation, scenario exploration, and scenario construction (see Figure 3.4).

These three phases build on ideas and use specific techniques to develop a set of four scenarios. The four scenarios are used to challenge the thinking in the organization and provide a common understanding of the dynamic

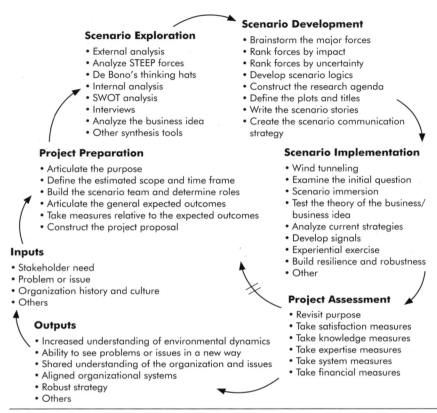

Scenario Exploration

- External analysis
- Analyze STEEP forces
- De Bono's thinking hats
- Internal analysis
- SWOT analysis
- Interviews
- Analyze the business idea
- Other synthesis tools

Scenario Development

- Brainstorm the major forces
- Rank forces by impact
- Rank forces by uncertainty
- Develop scenario logics
- Construct the research agenda
- Define the plots and titles
- Write the scenario stories
- Create the scenario communication strategy

Project Preparation

- Articulate the purpose
- Define the estimated scope and time frame
- Build the scenario team and determine roles
- Articulate the general expected outcomes
- Take measures relative to the expected outcomes
- Construct the project proposal

Scenario Implementation

- Wind tunneling
- Examine the initial question
- Scenario immersion
- Test the theory of the business/ business idea
- Analyze current strategies
- Develop signals
- Experiential exercise
- Build resilience and robustness
- Other

Inputs

- Stakeholder need
- Problem or issue
- Organization history and culture
- Others

Outputs

- Increased understanding of environmental dynamics
- Ability to see problems or issues in a new way
- Shared understanding of the organization and issues
- Aligned organizational systems
- Robust strategy
- Others

Project Assessment

- Revisit purpose
- Take satisfaction measures
- Take knowledge measures
- Take expertise measures
- Take system measures
- Take financial measures

FIGURE 3.3   The Performance-Based Scenario System

forces at play in the environment. At Shell, Pierre Wack often clarified that the scenario-building activity is actually a method of separating issues into things he called predetermined elements and critical uncertainties—in other words, separating the consequences of events that have already occurred and been perceived from the things that are truly uncertain.

THE SCENARIO DEPLOYMENT COMPONENT

When scenarios have been developed, they are used to explore organizational strategies, capacity, key decisions, and other important items. This is often called "wind tunneling," but scenarios can be used in a variety of ways to maximize their collective impact. The Scenario Implementation

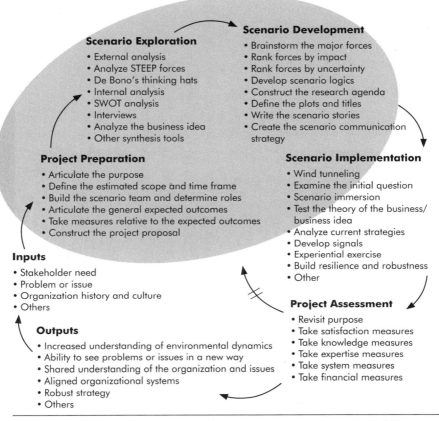

Scenario Exploration

- External analysis
- Analyze STEEP forces
- De Bono's thinking hats
- Internal analysis
- SWOT analysis
- Interviews
- Analyze the business idea
- Other synthesis tools

Scenario Development

- Brainstorm the major forces
- Rank forces by impact
- Rank forces by uncertainty
- Develop scenario logics
- Construct the research agenda
- Define the plots and titles
- Write the scenario stories
- Create the scenario communication strategy

Project Preparation

- Articulate the purpose
- Define the estimated scope and time frame
- Build the scenario team and determine roles
- Articulate the general expected outcomes
- Take measures relative to the expected outcomes
- Construct the project proposal

Scenario Implementation

- Wind tunneling
- Examine the initial question
- Scenario immersion
- Test the theory of the business/business idea
- Analyze current strategies
- Develop signals
- Experiential exercise
- Build resilience and robustness
- Other

Inputs

- Stakeholder need
- Problem or issue
- Organization history and culture
- Others

Project Assessment

- Revisit purpose
- Take satisfaction measures
- Take knowledge measures
- Take expertise measures
- Take system measures
- Take financial measures

Outputs

- Increased understanding of environmental dynamics
- Ability to see problems or issues in a new way
- Shared understanding of the organization and issues
- Aligned organizational systems
- Robust strategy
- Others

FIGURE 3.4   The Performance-Based Scenario System—Scenario Building Component

and Project Assessment phases are aimed at how scenarios can be used to provoke changes in organizations and help decision makers make sense of strategic insights (see Figure 3.5).

CONCLUSION

This chapter on the scenario system has discussed the nature of the external context facing organizations. This environment is highly turbulent, volatile, uncertain, complex, and ambiguous. Because of this context, traditional approaches to planning are not adequate because they assume the environment is relatively stable and predictable.

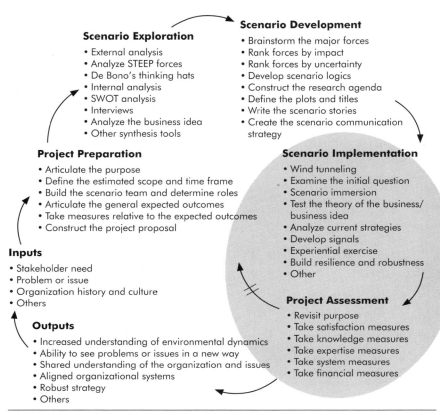

Scenario Exploration

- External analysis
- Analyze STEEP forces
- De Bono's thinking hats
- Internal analysis
- SWOT analysis
- Interviews
- Analyze the business idea
- Other synthesis tools

Scenario Development

- Brainstorm the major forces
- Rank forces by impact
- Rank forces by uncertainty
- Develop scenario logics
- Construct the research agenda
- Define the plots and titles
- Write the scenario stories
- Create the scenario communication strategy

Project Preparation

- Articulate the purpose
- Define the estimated scope and time frame
- Build the scenario team and determine roles
- Articulate the general expected outcomes
- Take measures relative to the expected outcomes
- Construct the project proposal

Scenario Implementation

- Wind tunneling
- Examine the initial question
- Scenario immersion
- Test the theory of the business/business idea
- Analyze current strategies
- Develop signals
- Experiential exercise
- Build resilience and robustness
- Other

Inputs

- Stakeholder need
- Problem or issue
- Organization history and culture
- Others

Project Assessment

- Revisit purpose
- Take satisfaction measures
- Take knowledge measures
- Take expertise measures
- Take system measures
- Take financial measures

Outputs

- Increased understanding of environmental dynamics
- Ability to see problems or issues in a new way
- Shared understanding of the organization and issues
- Aligned organizational systems
- Robust strategy
- Others

FIGURE 3.5   The Performance-Based Scenario System—Scenario Deployment Component

In this chapter, planning has been positioned as a system within the larger organizational system. In this repositioning, the scenario system has its own set of inputs, processes, outputs, and feedback loops. Furthermore, the scenario system has been presented with its five phases:

1. Project preparation
2. Scenario exploration
3. Scenario development
4. Scenario implementation
5. Project assessment

4

Scenario Case Study

This chapter introduces a scenario case study based on events in a real scenario project. Later chapters provide clear examples of the outputs for each phase of the scenario system. When all of the examples are put together, we will have a complete scenario case study.

Scenario projects are a purposeful approach to solving difficult, ambiguous, and complex dilemmas. These projects require a high degree of motivation and commitment to continuously learn in a context that does not reveal simple "right" answers. The skills required for facilitating scenario projects are developed over time. While some organizations provide training workshops and seminars focused on scenario planning skills, there is no substitute for engaging in these complex problems firsthand.

One approach is to seek an experienced scenario planning professional with whom to apprentice. The mentor-apprentice relationship is perhaps the most powerful way to learn the tools, skills, processes, and nuances that make for effective scenarios. Studying the details of the scenario system through this book combined with serious intellectual engagement with the Technology Corporation case and expert tutelage in actual scenario projects forms an ideal approach to building scenario project leadership expertise.

The organization that serves as the core scenario case throughout this book is an actual research and development technology firm located in the northeastern United States. The company name used here will be "Technology Corporation" to disguise the organization. The organization currently employs 185 people. Organizational leaders had never used a formalized approach to their planning for the future. Their typical process was ad hoc and unstructured. On the surface, there appears to be no cohesive approach to developing strategy or thinking about the future at

Technology Corporation. As with so many fast-growing technology firms, executives tend to describe planning as an essential part of daily activities while having no formal strategy process designed to focus on the external environment.

COMPANY BACKGROUND

Technology Corporation was founded in 1971 and altered its focus to technology product research, design, and development in 1984, shortly after the U.S. government launched the Small Business Innovation Development Act. The act was designed to promote innovation through research and development (R&D) that was seen as lacking in small business due to limited funding sources. Small businesses are encouraged to seek funding through the Small Business Innovation Research (SBIR) and Small Business Technology Transfer (STTR) programs managed by the U.S. Small Business Administration (SBA). These agencies develop technologies used by eleven federal departments (e.g., Department of Defense, Department of Energy, and National Science Foundation). Technology Corporation developed expertise in writing proposals for SBIR and STTR funding. For thirty-eight years, its primary revenue was generated by the SBIR/STTR funding, with limited success in the commercialization of new technology products. Its primary output was intellectual property intended for development into innovative technology products. The business model of the organization never fully realized the intended outcomes of the SBIR/STTR funding. Instead, the company used the writing of proposals and success in winning SBIR and STTR funding as its primary business model. The results were the development of numerous technology products that were never brought to market because they did not move beyond the testing phase.

In 2002, a new owner purchased the company. The new owner had a strong vision that included a more diverse set of funding sources and the ability to deliver new products to market. While the new owner acknowledged the success of the organization's ability to secure and process numerous SBIR/STTR awards through Phase I (start-up) and Phase II (R&D), she felt the future of the organization would lie with the commercialization (Phase III) of the technology and diversification into new markets through intercompany development, partnerships with larger corporations, or venture capital agreements. The owner and members of the leadership team are experienced technology, innovation, and design managers, having worked most of their careers in large international technology, computing, and data distribution organizations. Their business acumen in the technology industry combined with the intellectual power of the scientists, designers, and R&D staff, affords the organization the ability to expand and explore its potential in new technologies that did not exist prior to the acquisition.

STRUCTURE

Figure 4.1 presents a simplified version of Technology Corporation's organizational chart to focus on the major functional areas.

ORGANIZATION PERFORMANCE RECORDS

The purchase of Technology Corporation was welcomed by employees, as was the focus on pushing products through to commercialization. However, little had changed in the first two years of the new leadership. Technology Corporation was still having success with SBIR and STTR funding. As long as its success was bringing in dollars, there was little motivation to change. Company performance was consistently high, as long as the proposals for government funding continued to be successful. However, the ongoing reliance on a single source of funding can be a worry to any organization. An upcoming presidential election had implications for dollars available in the SBIR and STTR programs, and some were speculating that these funding streams could be shut down completely.

Perhaps a more relevant aspect of organization performance centers on the number of proposals funded and the number of design projects in progress at a given time. Consider Figures 4.2, 4.3, and 4.4 and their implications.

Casual conversations with three senior-level decision makers suggested themes about the organization culture. Most employees were described as hardworking, creative, and intelligent people. However, leaders describe the culture as independent. That is, collaboration is not a priority; and once proposals are funded and projects are initiated, people work on their individual parts with little interaction and connection to the other product components (e.g., design, development, engineering, and marketing). Decision makers expressed a desire for more collaboration and cross-functional

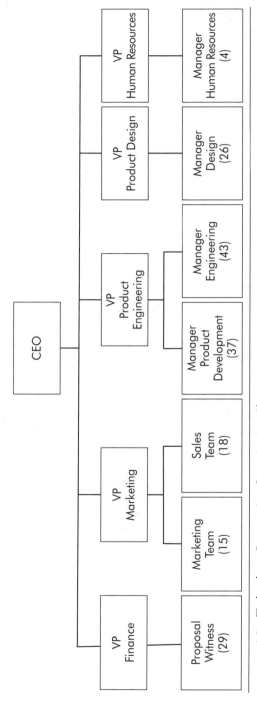

FIGURE 4.1 Technology Corporation Organization Chart

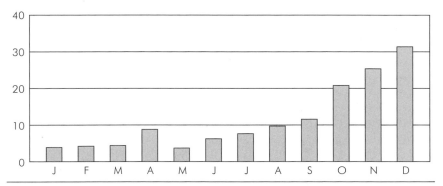

FIGURE **4.2**   Technology Corporation's Small Business Innovation Research/
Small Business Technology Transfer Proposals Submitted
2007–2008

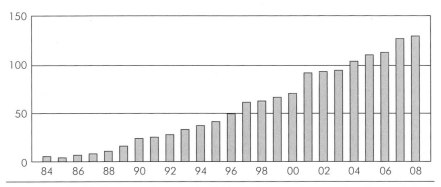

FIGURE **4.3**   Technology Corporation's Small Business Innovation Research/
Small Business Technology Transfer Proposals Funded 1984–2008

interaction. They believe this would lead to additional creative insights and would leverage more collective intellectual capital inside the organization.

Decision makers also commented that the organization is a classic case in which the creative designers often clash with the logical engineers. These thinking processes are not always compatible, but both are necessary for Technology Corporation to develop into the organization that the new owner has in mind. In the past, the most rewarded group has been the proposal writers because they are seen as the revenue generators. Decision makers recognize that reward systems may need to change to support

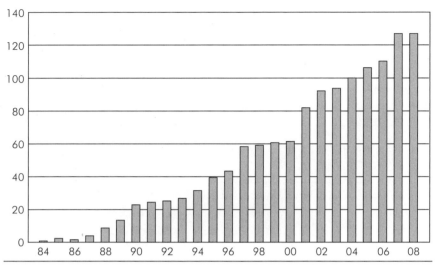

FIGURE 4.4   Technology Corporation's Active Projects 1984–2008

collaboration and also to wean the organization from its dependence on a single source of revenue. The radical variance in salaries has also been a factor in that it has dictated the perceived value of each functional area.

A FEW RELEVANT INDUSTRIAL DYNAMICS

One of Technology Corporation's major current initiatives is a new mobile communications device. Currently, iPhone and BlackBerry dominate the market, and Samsung, LG, and Palm are also players. Displacing these popular brands is a tall order. Device interface and network capabilities (e.g., 4G, 5G, and beyond) are obvious topics of interest for decision makers.

Another major current initiative is the technology for an organ transport system (to replace the low-tech Igloo cooler). The device would monitor temperature, pressure, and other factors influencing the length of time an organ can remain viable for transport. Prototype designs have been shown to support organ life twelve hours beyond the Igloo cooler.

These are just two examples of product development underway at Technology Corporation. Considering the charts depicted in the figures, we see that many other developments are in the pipeline, each carrying a different level of priority, resources, and commitment. Again, without a formal approach to strategy, no time is being dedicated to exploring the external environment relevant to any of these items. Past conversations about strategy have been financially based annual events.

SCENARIO PROJECT INITIATION

Imagine you are approached by a member of the executive team to discuss the possibility of a scenario project at Technology Corporation. You were recommended by a previous scenario project participant. The major issue discussed was the lack of a structured approach to planning. Given the dynamics described in this case, decision makers have expressed a desire to use a systematic approach to strategy to understand the external environment. Simultaneously, they view a collaborative approach to strategy as an opportunity to get the functional areas more integrated. Another critical question increasingly troubling decision makers is how to prioritize projects to optimize the fit between resource investment and likelihood the product can be taken to market and sold. The organization has experienced high growth in terms of the number of projects it is working on at any given time. Decision makers realize this growth is not likely to continue; but if it does, they will become increasingly scattered across even more projects and industries.

CONCLUSION

Clearly, several strategic issues exist in Technology Corporation. The case incorporates some classic, common elements (e.g., lack of cross-functional communication, a history of financial budgeting described as strategy, and internal conflict). Striking elements presented here are the continued growth and success with proposals and funding. It is easy to see why decision makers may be concerned. Yet, transitioning to other funding sources before reducing successful SBIR/STTR funding will be a tricky negotiation. Fostering a more collaborative culture, overhauling reward systems, and managing a variety of projects in a variety of industries are complex activities that have important implications. While this case may seem simple at first glance, complex issues will unfold in the following chapters as scenario planning tools are applied.

PHASES OF THE PERFORMANCE-BASED SCENARIO SYSTEM

EFFORTS AT PLANNING without defining objectives or expected outcomes are likely to fail. Furthermore, approaches to planning that focus on development and leave off implementation will lose momentum once the plan is complete. Scenario planning has proven itself as an upgrade to traditional strategic planning, but scenario planning experts have not established a set of best practices, and every firm that offers scenario planning goes about it differently. Most approaches to scenario planning adhere to vague, ill-defined outcomes, focus on scenario development, pay minimal attention to how to use the scenarios, and completely neglect the idea of project assessment.

Part Two provides a comprehensive approach to scenario planning. These chapters show you how to work with your colleagues or other organizations to develop a proposal with defined purposes and expectations and to create a set of scenarios that are compelling, novel, and useful. These chapters show you how to use those scenarios in specific ways that increase the likelihood of generating strategic insights and how to assess whether the project has added value.

Part Two consists of Chapters 5 through 9, and these chapters correspond to the phases of the Scenario System:

- Phase 1—Project Preparation
- Phase 2—Scenario Exploration
- Phase 3—Scenario Development
- Phase 4—Scenario Implementation
- Phase 5—Project Assessment

Chapter 5, "Project Preparation," is focused on how to develop the purpose of the project, define the key issue or question that is the focus of the project, and build support. This phase also includes building the scenario team, the time line and scope of the project, and conversations about expected outcomes.

Chapter 6, "Scenario Exploration," describes how to gather data relevant to the purpose, issue, and question of the project. Various activities including SWOT analysis, forecasts, trend analysis, internal interviews, and others are described to help understand the dynamics of the internal and external environments.

Chapter 7, "Scenario Development," clearly shows how to use a variety of workshops and exercises to build a strategic conversation inside the organization and create scenarios. Methods for gauging the effectiveness of the scenarios are also provided with detailed application guidelines.

Chapter 8, "Scenario Implementation," shows how to put the scenarios to use. This chapter describes additional workshops designed to get the most of scenarios and increase the likelihood that they will shift the thinking inside the organization.

Chapter 9, "Project Assessment," outlines the necessary components of a comprehensive scenario project assessment. These activities include measuring the outcomes relative to the expected outcomes defined early on, looking at a cost/benefit analysis of the project, and checking for knowledge and expertise increases among participants.

The activities described in Part Two come together to form the complete scenario system, designed to be used in any organization. Using the phases described here will help you create a scenario project with impact.

5

Phase 1— Project Preparation: Understanding Purpose and Building Support

This chapter presents the first phase of the scenario system—project preparation. The goal of this chapter is to describe and explain the important elements that should be defined in the project preparation phase of a scenario system and that culminate in a project proposal (Figure 5.1).

Project preparation requires careful attention to decision makers, leaders, and sponsors of the project. Listening to people express what they are frustrated with and excited about helps to develop an initial understanding of the situation. Follow-up questions to these key people can reveal additional important information, including constraints, biases, misperceptions, and glimpses of expected outcomes.

Scenario projects are initiated with a meeting (or series of meetings) to discuss the organizational issue, problem, or need for scenarios. This initial meeting (or meetings) provides valuable insight for understanding the inputs to the scenario effort. Project inputs are clarified as more information is shared among all participants through the activities of the early phases in the scenario system.

Whether the project is being led by internal or external professionals, there should be a formal proposal to the organizational decision makers and sponsors laying out the key elements of the project. The importance of establishing a clear purpose is critical. It will become the basis for everything else that follows, including, eventually, assessment of the project. The more clarity in the purpose at the onset, the more direct and elegant the flow of the project and assessment can become.

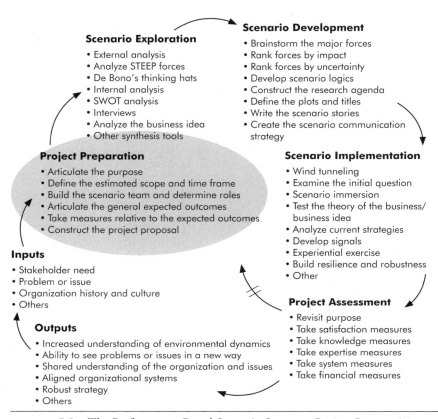

Scenario Exploration
- External analysis
- Analyze STEEP forces
- De Bono's thinking hats
- Internal analysis
- SWOT analysis
- Interviews
- Analyze the business idea
- Other synthesis tools

Scenario Development
- Brainstorm the major forces
- Rank forces by impact
- Rank forces by uncertainty
- Develop scenario logics
- Construct the research agenda
- Define the plots and titles
- Write the scenario stories
- Create the scenario communication strategy

Project Preparation
- Articulate the purpose
- Define the estimated scope and time frame
- Build the scenario team and determine roles
- Articulate the general expected outcomes
- Take measures relative to the expected outcomes
- Construct the project proposal

Scenario Implementation
- Wind tunneling
- Examine the initial question
- Scenario immersion
- Test the theory of the business/business idea
- Analyze current strategies
- Develop signals
- Experiential exercise
- Build resilience and robustness
- Other

Inputs
- Stakeholder need
- Problem or issue
- Organization history and culture
- Others

Project Assessment
- Revisit purpose
- Take satisfaction measures
- Take knowledge measures
- Take expertise measures
- Take system measures
- Take financial measures

Outputs
- Increased understanding of environmental dynamics
- Ability to see problems or issues in a new way
- Shared understanding of the organization and issues
- Aligned organizational systems
- Robust strategy
- Others

FIGURE **5.1**   The Performance-Based Scenario System—Project Preparation Phase

CONSTRUCTING A SCENARIO PROJECT PROPOSAL

The process of constructing a project proposal involves building agreement among the project leader and organizational decision makers on five critical items. These five items should be documented in the scenario project proposal:

- The purpose and question of the scenario project
- The estimated scope and time line of the scenario project
- The scenario team and defined roles for each team member
- The general expected outcomes of the scenario project
- Measures to assess the achievement/success of the expected outcomes

ARTICULATING THE PURPOSE OF THE SCENARIO PROJECT

Most organizational interventions begin with the identification of a problem. Effective interventions are based on plans for tackling these problems and gaining approval to work toward solutions. Problems are usually related to continuously trying to optimize fit with the environment, or they can be classified into one of a few general categories. No matter what the problem is, the first phase in the scenario system is focused on listening to key people talk about the situations they are facing. The project leader also becomes oriented to the problem and begins gathering general perceptions of the problem and the project that is designed to address it. Remember, the term problem in this context means to put forth for conversation, and the purpose of the project drives subsequent activities (Burt & van der Heijden, 2003).

Increasingly, decision makers are overwhelmed by volatility, complexity, and uncertainty. Many are frustrated with current planning processes, stating that the methods they are using don't work. Many express a desire to make sense of a complex set of forces and variables in the external environment that seem to have no structure or pattern of behavior that might suggest how things will play out in the future. A key overarching purpose of scenario planning is to develop a variety of alternatives so that decision makers will be more prepared for anything that might come to pass.

Scenario Planning Categories of Purpose

Four distinct purposes for engaging in scenario planning logically flow from the interactions between content and process on one continuum, and between thinking and action on another (van der Heijden, 2004). Content and process form the horizontal axis, while thinking and action form the vertical axis, creating four cells. These four cells delineating distinct purposes of scenario planning are as follows:

- Making sense
- Optimal strategy
- Anticipation
- Adaptive learning

A scenario planning project can focus on one or more of these purposes.

Making Sense

The content-thinking combination—or making sense—is aimed at understanding the external environment. Scenario projects framed from this purpose result in contextual scenarios, or what Wack called "learning scenarios." Making-sense scenarios do not often provide major strategic insights for practicing managers because they do not provide a framework for decision making. These projects are useful for defining uncertain elements or exploring the external environment in general. Success in making-sense projects depends on defining appropriate questions for analysis. However, the intent of this purpose is to gain a new understanding of things in the environment that are unclear and need definition, exploration, and analysis.

Optimal Strategy

Developing the content and action—or the purpose of optimal strategy—is aimed at using scenarios specifically to test a strategy already in place. Projects based on this purpose often feature an organization "trying out" scenarios as a one-time effort. Few success stories are documented using the optimal strategy purpose in that stand-alone scenario efforts do not often lead to strategic learning or insights. Reasons for the lack of success include difficulties in shifting away from predictive thinking, inability to truly entertain multiple possible futures, variations on proven scenario planning processes, and a lack of time and commitment to the project.

Anticipation

Thinking-process projects—those with the purpose of anticipation—are new projects initiated within in a continual, ongoing scenario planning cycle. Think of these scenario projects as continuous quality improvement for planning in organizations. Combining thinking and process into anticipation, these projects are focused on developing and continuing what van der Heijden (2004) calls "the strategic conversation" in organizations. Such an ongoing conversation builds shared mental models of the external environment and of the organization itself. Organizations that are successful with this purpose are able to prevent groupthink by continuously generating new ideas in the scenario planning project, and they also prevent fragmentation by building an organizational community and generating collective understanding.

Adaptive Learning

The action-process combination—adaptive learning—is the scenario purpose in which an organization is continually using scenarios to understand the environment, holding internal strategic conversations, and taking action to leverage strategic opportunities. Adaptive organizational learning is the ultimate aim of scenario work because it signals an organization that learns and changes from its own experience to navigate the turbulent business environment. Furthermore, these organizations are simultaneously developing a better understanding and awareness of uncertain elements in the environment and improving the quality of the internal strategic conversation.

Learning-Decision Scenarios

Beyond these four purposes of scenario projects, scenario planning literature and many of the documented processes clearly state that scenarios are also effectively used to consider a specific decision, project, or issue. For example, leaders at Royal Dutch/Shell often faced key specific decisions that required the kind of analysis presented in scenario planning, such as the possibility of constructing a new oil-drilling rig in a new location. Scenarios were built around the possibilities of how such an investment might turn out.

In the early years at Royal Dutch/Shell, Wack repeatedly had a response of "So what?" from managers after they would participate in his scenario presentations. The first-generation scenarios were always learning scenarios; their purpose was not to impel action but to gain understanding and insight (Wack, 1985a). Wack therefore called the first-generation scenarios "learning scenarios." Initial scenarios rarely have an impact on managers' mental models because they often do not provide a basis on which managers could exercise their judgment.

The World Economic Forum has developed and published scenarios for a variety of regions throughout the world. These scenarios are clearly learning scenarios, and they explore several different economic contexts, setting the stage to tell the stories that speculate on their implications. A variety of reports and scenario projects are free to download directly from the World Economic Forum at www.weforum.org/en/initiatives/Scenarios/index.htm.

Eventually, a high degree of utility was realized in a second round of scenario development. Second-generation scenarios became the "decision scenarios." Wack's insights developed when he realized that to affect the managers' core thinking, he needed to target the scenarios to the deepest concerns of the decision maker; and to accomplish that, he needed to tailor-fit the scenarios to challenge the mental models of the managers who would use them. Moreover, the scenarios also had to be targeted at a key issue or decision the managers were facing.

"Decision scenarios explore for facts out there, but they aim at perceptions inside the head of critical decision makers. Their purpose is to gather and transform information of potential strategic significance into fresh perceptions that then lead to strategic insights that were previously beyond the mind's reach—those that would not even have been considered" (Wack, 1985a, p. 88).

The two-tiered approach to scenario planning was effective at Shell. To summarize, the first round of scenarios were context-setting scenarios—learning scenarios—that explored the external environment. The second round of scenarios were tailor-fit to the mental models of the managers—decision scenarios. This tiered approach is reflected in Wack's (1985a) use of a cherry tree as a metaphor (see Figure 5.2):

> Scenarios are like cherry trees: cherries grow neither on the trunk, nor on the large boughs; they grow on the small branches of the tree. Nonetheless, a tree needs a trunk and large branches in order to grow small branches. The global, macro-scenarios are the trunk; the large branches are the country scenarios developed by Shell operating companies, in which factors individual to their own countries—predetermined and uncertain—are taken into account and added. But the real fruits of the scenarios are picked at the small branches, the focused scenarios which are custom tailored around a strategic issue or a specific market or investment project. (p. 83)

To apply scenarios in this tiered way, decision makers would have to entertain several rounds of scenario construction. This is why most single instances of scenario planning fail. For example, first the global/macro scenarios should be constructed. These simply set the context for the appropriate industry. These are likely to be scenarios that capture external factors only. Once complete, and depending on the size of the organization, decision makers can move into more specific scenarios focused on a region (in the case of a truly global organization with numerous regional offices) or a specific strategic issue. When scenario planning is adopted as a way of

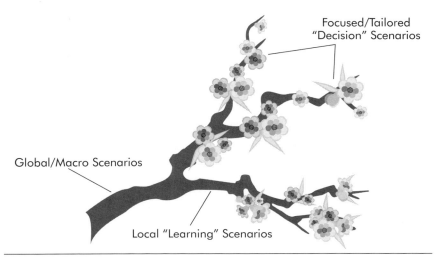

Focused/Tailored
"Decision" Scenarios

Global/Macro Scenarios

Local "Learning" Scenarios

FIGURE **5.2**   Scenarios Are Like Cherry Trees

thinking in organizations, the ways in which scenarios can be used expands drastically.

> To do specific analyses of parts of the business, one develops "focused scenarios" custom-tailored around a strategic issue, or a specific market or investment project. But you cannot start with such focused scenarios because you will almost certainly miss key things, or cast the focused scenarios in the wrong way. You must wide-angle first, to get the big picture, and them zoom in on your business specifics. (Wack, 1985a, p. 92)

Some scenario planning experts favor a highly specific approach from the start. For example, Louis van der Merwe tells stories about scenario projects he has observed in which the facilitator spent two full days defining the initial strategic question. Asking the right question is important; and the more specific the purpose, the easier it is to assess upon project completion. However, the context, situation, decision maker conversations, and other information will determine the level of focus required. There are no hard rules here, but the context will usually indicate when enough detail is reached. Gaining people's understanding and readiness to move forward is both hard to miss and a key indicator to proceed.

ASKING THE QUESTION

The question that is posed directs the purpose of the scenario project. The first priority is to develop a clear question that will set the tone of the project. Time should be spent refining the question. The goal of the project is to examine the range of possible environments in which strategic choices can play out, and all of these have significant implications for how the initial question can be answered. It is important to remember that when dealing with complex, strategic puzzles, there is no perfect answer. Therefore, asking the question is not meant to find a single correct answer. Rather, it is to explore a variety of answers and the implications that each carries with it. Scenario thinking "isn't a magic 8-ball, a process where all you need to ask is 'should we do x?' (and getting 'ask again later' as a result is neither useful nor surprising)" (Cascio, 2009, p. 1). The original question of purpose should be revisited as the project progresses. Examining the question repeatedly suggests a willingness to continuously check progress and make sure the project is on track, which in turn may lead to a better question. The rest of this book is aimed at how to go about providing a variety of answers to the initial question, considering their implications, and assessing the range of answers that can be developed.

A few sample questions to consider are as follows:

- How can we retain our current value proposition in a high-change environment?
- Should we introduce a completely new product or service?
- How can we more effectively integrate our strengths to enhance the value we provide to our customers and increase our efficiency?
- What are the major technological advances on the horizon that we have not thought about?

Once the purpose of the project has been clarified, it can be documented in the project proposal. The next step is to move on to estimating the scope of the project and a general time frame.

TECHNOLOGY CORPORATION'S PURPOSE AND QUESTION

The case study of Technology Corporation started with an initial meeting and conversation with corporate leaders, including the CEO, the vice president of finance, the vice president of human resources, and the vice president of product design. It was decided that the purpose for using scenarios was part anticipation and part organizational learning. The priority of the project was to anticipate major potential changes in Small Business Innovation Research (SBIR) funding policy, as well as major developments in the technology industry. In part, the project was also aimed at making sense of the external environment, and organization leaders were clear that they wanted to spend time exploring the things they didn't know they didn't know. While it would be the first scenario project inside Technology Corporation, two of the leaders had prior exposure to scenario planning. Both expressed interest in the learning orientation that scenario planning demands, adding that learning something unexpected about their industry would be of high value. Leaders settled on the following question to frame the scenario project:

> How can we balance the number of projects we initiate, with a firmer commitment to producing marketable products and generating revenue, and wean ourselves from relying on a single source of funding?

DEFINING THE ESTIMATED SCOPE AND TIME FRAME

The next task is to develop a sense of the scope of the project. This is largely dependent on the defined purpose of the project. Key items to consider are the amount of time and resources the organization is willing to invest in the project, deadlines that may be relevant, and how far into the future the scenarios will reach.

Before attempting to estimate details about the time frame, it is useful to know what is generally involved in scenario projects. Although each project is different, most can be expected to involve interviews and initial data gathering, two to three full-day workshops (spaced out over a few weeks) to build the scenarios, and two to three full-day workshops (spaced out over a few weeks) to consider the implications of the scenarios. The space between workshops is important for allowing participants to reflect on and absorb ideas and information. Given these general guidelines, projects can be expected to require five to nine weeks of commitment at a minimum. Small projects with a clear focus may be able to move faster, and, of course, large projects involving multiple organizational units over varying locations can take longer. The purpose of this part of the scenario project proposal is simply to estimate how long the project will take, clarifying any deadlines or other critical dates that may pose barriers to the project.

The time line can be represented graphically, in a list, or in a particular software program. The point is to have a general estimation of the project. Will it be five weeks or nine? Are there other critical deadlines that may draw attention and participation away from the project that must be considered?

The time line should also include general agreement on the estimated number of workshops that will be aimed at scenario development and the number that will be used for scenario consideration. In other words, the proposal should include a framework for the approximate time investment on the part of the decision makers and key stakeholders in the organization.

How Far into the Future?

This part of the scenario proposal must also consider how far into the future the scenarios will reach. Will they explore five years or twenty-five? This span is commonly referred to as the time horizon in scenario literature. "If it takes three years to set up the widget factory, a five year target for the future exercise would be useful to think through initial operating environment, while a 12 year exercise will help to think about what things will be like over time" (Cascio, 2009, p. 1). Cascio (2009) also recommends using political cycles for considering how far the scenarios should explore. For example, in the United States, scenarios that extend at least eight years into the future are assured a change in the presidency, which will have pros and cons associated with the party in power. Another strategy is to consider key forces that one is already familiar with and play them out beyond what is known (e.g., what does the 5G wireless network look like?) (Cascio, 2009).

A recent project I facilitated involved cell-phone technology. Given the pace of current technological development, the scenarios we created reached just five years into the future. The organization was looking at a few specific decisions driven by competition and emerging, cutting-edge technology. As a team, we looked at forces in the more immediate future to inform the specific decisions in question. Certainly, it would have been a useful exercise to look further into the future beyond, say, the 5G cell-phone network. However, we chose a time frame that fit the purpose of the project as the decision makers had defined it.

The time horizon should also be included in the project proposal, but it may be adjusted as the project progresses. Incoming information, reshaped perceptions, and new understandings of the internal and external environments can reshape how far the scenarios should explore.

TECHNOLOGY CORPORATION'S SCOPE AND TIME FRAME

Leaders in Technology Corporation were excited about using scenarios to explore the question they had defined and were ready to commit substantial time to the project. Leaders agreed to three half- to full-day workshops focused on developing scenarios, and three half- to full-day workshops focused on using scenarios, with additional time as needed by team members to prepare for the workshops and conduct further research. We expected the project to be completed in approximately three months (see Figure 5.3).

Leaders further agreed that scenarios reaching fifteen years into the future would be useful in provoking strategic insights about the organization, its market, and how it might evolve.

BUILDING THE SCENARIO TEAM AND DETERMINING ROLES

Getting the right people involved in the scenario project is absolutely critical. To be effective, projects must involve the people who will use the scenarios, as well as a representative from each level of the company. During the project preparation phase, important stakeholder groups should be identified, individuals with a high degree of organization knowledge should be recruited, internal leaders at all levels of the organization should be identified, and the scenario team can be assembled. The scenario team manages the project. Some suggested roles are described next.

PROJECT LEADER

The project leader is obviously responsible for directing the scenario project. This person is often an external consultant with expertise in the scenario planning system, and he or she should have significant experience in a variety of business processes and change interventions. It is a good practice to partner an internal expert to colead the project if an external consultant is the main facilitator. Such a partnership allows the internal leader (and

Initial Meeting and Project Initiation	Interviews with 7–10 people (all senior managers and a cross section)	3 Workshops for Scenario Development	Scenario Presentation	3 Workshops for Scenario Implementation	Follow-up Evaluative Interviews
Survey Research Data Collection (Pretest)				Survey Research Data Collection (Posttest)	
2 hours	1 hour per interview	4 hours each = 12 hours	2 hours	4 hours each = 12 hours	1 hour per interview
September	September/October	October	End October	November	Late November/ December

FIGURE 5.3 Technology Corporation's Time Line and Scope

therefore the organization) to gain scenario planning expertise, and it can help navigate the project inside the organization.

TEAM MEMBERS

Team members will participate in all of the workshops, generally be responsible for developing the detailed scenario story lines, and will accomplish much of their work through subteams. For example, a subteam is often assigned to work on each scenario, provide further details, and write the scenario narrative. The team should include someone from each level of the organization, so that the team is ultimately cross-level and cross-functional.

COORDINATOR

One individual should be responsible for convening the group, managing schedules, reserving spaces and locations for scenario work, creating internal mechanisms for the scenario team to communicate, and performing other administrative functions.

REMARKABLE PEOPLE

Because scenario planning is a system designed to stretch the thinking inside the organization, it should involve people with diverse backgrounds and expertise. Perhaps Pierre Wack's greatest contribution to modern scenario planning is the inclusion of what he called "remarkable people." By this, he simply meant people with a completely different outlook or mental model than those inside the organization working on the issue and who were known for their ability to think unconventionally. Global Business Network has continued this tradition by frequently using musicians, artists, bench scientists, and other people from a wide range of backgrounds to provide alternate perspectives in scenario projects.

In one of my own early projects, I did not consider the importance of building a solid scenario planning team. I neglected spending time defining roles and responsibilities, and with a team loosely formed within the organization, the project suffered because no one was responsible for basic functions of the project. For example, workshops and meetings were ill attended because no one was coordinating the project activities. With few participants attending the workshops, one can imagine that there was little learning, ownership, buy-in, and implementation of the project outcomes. In the end, the scenarios were never communicated throughout the organization because they did not involve enough of the managers' thinking. In this case, my own failure to see the importance of establishing clear roles and responsibilities led to an ineffective project. However, it was a valuable learning experience that I will not forget. Once the scenario team members and roles have been identified, important conversations about outcomes can begin.

TECHNOLOGY CORPORATION'S SCENARIO TEAM AND ROLES

Technology Corporation's scenario team and roles were defined after some conversation and clarification. Names have been omitted, but the roles were as follows:

- *Project leader*
- *Team members.* The team was composed of the CEO, the vice president of finance, the vice president of human resources, the vice president of product design, three managers, and two line workers.
- *Coordinators.* Two coordinators were involved in this project, the CEO's Executive assistant and another manager.
- *Remarkable people.* Three remarkable people participated in the project, at various times. One was invited by the CEO, and two were recruited by the project leader.
- *Others.* Other participants from Technology Corporation helped at specific times, but they were not attached to the project as intimately as team members. It is common for additional members to move in and out of the project, with a base of consistent team members.

ARTICULATING THE GENERAL EXPECTED OUTCOMES

It is important to know at the outset if a financial analysis, a recommendation regarding a specific decision, ongoing organizational learning, or something else is sought as a result of the project. Time spent on clarifying the initial purpose of the project provides a general idea of what is expected, but additional conversations should consider any specific expectations. The bulk of the scenario literature has ignored any process for assessing scenario planning efforts. In contrast, this book assumes that scenario planning can and should be assessed. Specific strategies for assessing scenario projects are covered in Phase 5—Project Assessment, but it is wise to decide how the project will be assessed from the beginning.

Precisely how to measure the effects of scenario projects can be tricky. Assessing the costs associated with a major industry shift that did not happen because it was anticipated through the scenario planning system is a challenging activity. However, estimates can be made. Estimates of savings due to anticipating major business discontinuities, or profits gained through strategic insights, or both, can and should be part of the scenario project.

Chapter 10 provides further details and examples for estimating the financial benefits of a scenario planning project, but in the project preparation phase, it is useful to consider a basic financial assessment model. Swanson's (2004) cost/benefit model is a simple tool for thinking about the financial benefits of any scenario planning project:

Performance Value − Cost = Benefit

In the context of scenario planning, the costs of a project are relatively easy to estimate. The performance value is the tricky part. It can be helpful to simply ask decision makers, "What is the value that you place on a single novel strategic insight?" (van der Merwe, 2005), and the ensuing conversation will further clarify expected outcomes and intended goals of the project. An additional useful question to pose is "If this project exceeded your expectations, what would be true?" It is not a requirement that scenario planning projects carry a financial assessment component, but if they do, they are more likely to garner support from executives and project stakeholders. It is also important for those interested in furthering the discipline of scenario planning to think about the value of the contributions that are made through the scenario planning system. The more evidence that is built in to show the benefits of scenario planning, the more confidently its benefits can be promoted.

Outside of financial data, many other tools can be used to assess individual learning, mental models, decision making, and other important outcomes of scenario planning. These tools tend to be more academic in nature and may not be appropriate in some situations. However, when used, they can make a very compelling case. These tools can provide valuable information about learning, perceptions, decision making, and other critical outcomes of scenario planning. Projects using these tools may look like research projects—but why wouldn't they? The purpose of these projects is to discover new knowledge about some organizational element as it may relate to the scenario project. For the purposes of project preparation, it is useful to know if decision makers are interested in assessing particular items.

The literature suggests that scenario planning can benefit organizations in several ways. Outcomes commonly associated with scenario planning include the following:

- Individual and organizational learning
- Improved decision making
- Stronger communication systems
- Shared mental models of the internal and external environments
- Heightened organizational performance
- Greater organizational agility
- Stronger ability to fit with the environment
- Deeper anticipatory capacity
- Increased strategic insights

These are all domains that have related measures that can be assessed at the start and again at the end of a scenario planning project. Measures that are important to stakeholders and that are related to the purpose of the project should be agreed on as part of the purpose and documented in the project proposal.

TECHNOLOGY CORPORATION'S GENERAL EXPECTED OUTCOMES

Leaders in Technology Corporation expressed interest in knowing whether employees viewed the organization as a place that emphasized learning, whether decision making could become a more team-oriented activity, and whether better communication could be facilitated through the scenario project. Leaders also placed a high value on the potential to know what things to pay attention to. In other words, if certain events were indicators that other events were about to happen, there was great value in indentifying these "indicators." Finally, although leaders and executives in Technology Corporation did not expect a tangible return on investment, they were interested in considering how the project could add financial value.

TAKING MEASURES RELATIVE TO THE EXPECTED OUTCOMES

Once the expected outcomes of the scenario planning project have been decided, any measures relevant to those expected outcomes can be taken. Think of this as any measure that can be taken at the start of the project and then compared to a second measure of the same item at the conclusion of the project—a simple pretest/posttest assessment strategy. The general plan for what will be measured, where, how, and for what purpose should be included in the scenario project proposal.

RELATED MEASURES AT TECHNOLOGY CORPORATION

The measures taken at Technology Corporation mapped directly to the expected outcomes that were identified. We chose instruments that had a history of validity and utility to measure the expected outcomes. The selection was a collaborative process based on conversations that clarified what project sponsors were hoping to achieve and other desirable changes that might logically flow from a scenario planning project.

Learning Orientation	→ Watkins and Marsick's Dimensions of Learning Organization Questionnaire (DLOQ)
Team Decision Making	→ Scott and Bruce's General Decision-Making Style Survey (GDMS)
Communication	→ Van der Merwe's Conversation Quality and Engagement Checklist
Indicators	→ A list of indicators or "signposts"
Value-Added	→ Swanson's Cost/Benefit Analysis

CONCLUSION

The components presented in this chapter represent the critical first steps of any scenario project. Defining these components at the start of the project will create anchors for other parts of the project later on. The scenario project proposal, the major output of the project preparation phase, is designed to clarify assumptions, expectations, and get the project moving. Done well, the project's purpose, scenario team, time frame, estimated measures, outcomes, and benefits have been articulated and provide a starting point. In the event that disagreements ensue about the content of the improvement proposal, expectations can be clarified and changed before moving ahead. The scenario project proposal provides a general outline for the project and serves as a contract for moving forward with the scenario planning effort. What follows is a sample that illustrates the components discussed in this chapter.

SAMPLE SCENARIO PROJECT PROPOSAL

DATE: Month / Day / Year
TO: Organization Contact / CEO / Relevant Decision Maker [title]
FROM: T. Chermack
RE: Scenario Project Proposal

The purpose of this document is to establish the general, agreed-on objectives for a scenario project in Technology Corporation. This document describes the purpose of the project, the estimated scope and time frame, the composition of the scenario team, the general expected outcomes, and the measurements to be taken prior to the start of the project. Also included is a general financial benefit estimate.

Purpose

The purpose of a scenario project at Technology Corporation is to help make sense of a rapidly changing technology industry and environment, and to help Technology Corporation anticipate possible major shifts in the industry. More specifically, Technology Corporation is struggling with the ineffectiveness of outdated planning models and intends to develop a learning-focused approach to strategy. Rather than hike profit expectations, Technology Corporation desires to shift its culture toward one that supports continuous learning and development, improved communication across silos, and shared, collaborative decision making. Specific issues include questions about the amount of resources invested in each R&D project. Based on learning scenarios generated for the technology/R&D industry, Technology Corporation also intends to understand how to better distribute its resources across more viable projects expected to eventually lead to marketable technology products.

Estimated Scope and Time Frame

The project will begin with an initial organizing meeting starting on [mm/dd/yy]. Technology Corporation estimates that six subsequent full-day workshops will be used over approximately eight weeks to develop scenarios and use them in examining potential futures. Technology Corporation also agrees to allow [internal or external consultant name] access to interview participants from multiple levels of the organization, access to internal organizational records, and other items relevant to the project. The scenarios will have a horizon year of [fifteen years out], which extends the scenarios into the creative future of the technology industry.

Scenario Team and Roles

The scenario team will include Pierre Wack as the project leader. Deepak Chopra, Katherine Eisenhardt, Sansai Hosokawa, Candace Pert, Joe Dispenza, Bikram Choudhury, and Sen no Rikyu will be team members. Pema Chodron will be the on-site project coordinator, and will serve as the general administrative contact for the project. Pierre Wack will recruit additional people with diverse backgrounds as he sees fit throughout the project workshops and meetings to introduce alternative thinking.

General Expected Outcomes

Technology Corporation expects several outcomes from the scenario project. These are assessments of (1) perceptions of organizational learning characteristics, (2) team decision

making, (3) communication and conversation skills, (4) clear indicators or "signa
about to unfold, and (5) a cost/benefit analysis. Additional outcomes that are standz
planning are strategic insights about products and services in the technology industry, iour unique
and detailed scenarios of the industry, and time devoted to dialogue about strategic issues.

Measurements

Given the expected outcomes of this project, measurements will include financial benefit
estimates of the scenario projects and assessments of participant learning, decision making, and
conversation quality. The following measurements will be taken from project participants before
the project begins and at the end of the scenario project so as to determine changes:

1. Dimensions of Learning Organization Characteristics
2. General Decision-Making Style Survey
3. Conversation Quality and Engagement Checklist
4. Indicators or "signals"
5. Cost/Benefit Analysis

The cost/benefit estimate is provided here. We defined the performance value as the value of the
scenario project with the assumption that it will provoke a strategic insight. We then estimate
the value of such an insight in the case that it provides a competitive edge or prepares us to react
faster. From this value, we subtract the costs of the project to derive the benefit:

Performance value	$250,000	(details of estimate below)
− Cost	$100,000	(total breakdown of costs below)
Benefit	$150,000	

Performance Value Estimate

The performance value estimate follows. Assumption: The organization is able to generate a
significant, innovative idea as a result of the scenario project that leads to a new technology
product/service. Let's assume the product is a technology communication device. In 2009, RIM
reported shipping fifty million BlackBerry smart phones, generating $11 billion in revenue.
Technology Corporation is much smaller, but based on a similarly priced device, assume that
Technology Corporation is able to develop, patent, market, and sell five million devices,
generating (conservatively) $8 million. Start-up, R&D, marketing, patenting, prototyping, and
other development costs can be estimated at approximately $5 million, which leaves $3 million.
Again, being highly conservative, we reduce the performance value to $250,000 based on other
potential development costs.

Cost Estimate

Costs related to facilitating the scenario project are as follows:

Consulting Fees	= $40,000	(6 days of facilitation at $5,000 per day = $30,000 + $10,000 for other meetings and time spent on the project)
Materials	= $5,000	(includes printing, transcription, software, participant materials, preparation of all reports and scenario packages, and all other project materials)

Travel	=	$5,000	(6 air tickets from Denver, CO, to [location] at $300 each = $1,800 + 15 nights' lodging [location] at $150/night = $2,250 + $950 miscellaneous or extra travel)
Meals	=	$6,300	(6 workshop days × 3 meals per day × 7 participants [assume $50 per person, per meal] = $6,300)
Time away from regular work	=	$47,000	(This figure assumes approximately 27 participants at any given time and estimates that each participant may cost approximately $2,000 in time away from his or her normally assigned functions)
Total Project Cost Estimate	=	$100,000	

6

Phase 2—
Scenario Exploration:
Breathing In

The scenario exploration phase of the scenario system focuses on analyzing the external and internal environments of the organization. During these analyses, the initial issue or purpose of the project from the project preparation phase must be kept in mind as information is gathered. This chapter describes a variety of methods and tools that can be used to assess the external and internal situation, context, and problem (see Figure 6.1).

Scenario exploration is divided into two general parts, external analysis and internal analysis. These two parts establish the boundaries of the project in preparation for the next phase, scenario development. Several tools for gathering information about the external environment and two workshops for the internal analysis are detailed. The workshops are intended to stimulate strategic thinking, familiarize participants with key issues, and prepare participants for constructing scenarios as described in Chapter 7.

EXTERNAL ANALYSIS

Information gathering is the foundation of the analysis of the external environment. The scenario exploration phase involves data gathering both on a general level and about the specific issue under consideration. The goal of information gathering is to learn and to expand the project team's familiarity with the industry and relevant economic and social factors. A secondary goal is to gather information relevant to the specific issue or decision articulated in the project proposal. "Being a scenario planner, therefore, means

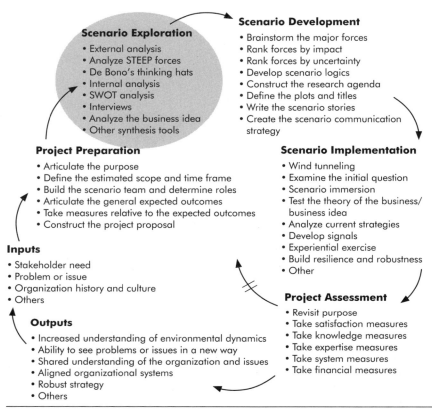

Scenario Exploration

- External analysis
- Analyze STEEP forces
- De Bono's thinking hats
- Internal analysis
- SWOT analysis
- Interviews
- Analyze the business idea
- Other synthesis tools

Scenario Development

- Brainstorm the major forces
- Rank forces by impact
- Rank forces by uncertainty
- Develop scenario logics
- Construct the research agenda
- Define the plots and titles
- Write the scenario stories
- Create the scenario communication strategy

Project Preparation

- Articulate the purpose
- Define the estimated scope and time frame
- Build the scenario team and determine roles
- Articulate the general expected outcomes
- Take measures relative to the expected outcomes
- Construct the project proposal

Scenario Implementation

- Wind tunneling
- Examine the initial question
- Scenario immersion
- Test the theory of the business/ business idea
- Analyze current strategies
- Develop signals
- Experiential exercise
- Build resilience and robustness
- Other

Inputs

- Stakeholder need
- Problem or issue
- Organization history and culture
- Others

Project Assessment

- Revisit purpose
- Take satisfaction measures
- Take knowledge measures
- Take expertise measures
- Take system measures
- Take financial measures

Outputs

- Increased understanding of environmental dynamics
- Ability to see problems or issues in a new way
- Shared understanding of the organization and issues
- Aligned organizational systems
- Robust strategy
- Others

FIGURE 6.1   The Performance-Based Scenario System—Scenario Exploration Phase

becoming aware of one's filter and continually readjusting it to let in more data about the world, but without becoming overwhelmed" (Schwartz, 1991, p. 61). Everyone has biases, and they show up in scenario planning. A key skill is the ability to be aware of biases and head off confinement in thinking. Thus, another purpose of the scenario exploration is to expand the assumptions, beliefs, and possibilities evident in the industry or environment being studied, thereby expanding one's filter.

There are many ways to approach the data-gathering stage. Three tools for helping to structure information about the external environment include STEEP forces, De Bono's (1990) thinking hats, and a SWOT analysis (focusing on the opportunities and the threats).

While each of these approaches is reviewed in further detail, the best solution is to develop a method that works for a particular situation. In other words, there are many tools and processes for exploring the external environment, and good scenario planners use tools that fit the organization and the purpose for engaging in a scenario project. The ultimate goal of this phase is to develop a rich understanding of the context in which the organization is operating. Data gathering, analysis, and synthesis are a complicated function to perform in today's complex organizations, and there are no hard and fast rules. "Don't worry about your files; worry about your perceptions" (Schwartz, 1991, p. 62). Stated another way, in this phase, you have to develop awareness of and expand your perceptions of the external environment.

The start of a scenario project requires getting up to speed with the general industry. It is helpful to visit and revisit several aspects of a given industry looking for trends, key factors, and other forces that have an obvious influence on the industry. At this point in a scenario project, it is important to create time for rigorous investigation of the industry and reflection on the dynamic and relevant forces at play. Pierre Wack referred to this as "breathing in," and he was known to go to great lengths to put himself into new unrelated physical environments to think about his projects. For example, he spent significant amounts of time in Japan, India, and the Saudi desert thinking about scenario projects he was working on. The primary purpose is to learn as much as possible about the industry—its composition and complexity—and to see it all from a new perspective.

SOCIAL, TECHNOLOGICAL, ECONOMIC, ENVIRONMENTAL, AND POLITICAL (STEEP) FORCES

A tool for structuring thinking and key categories to make sure you do not overlook any is the well-known STEEP analysis. The STEEP analysis is a logical and effective way to begin. In reality, these are simply general categories to include in any exploration of the external environment (Burt & van der Heijden, 2002). This section offers examples of each force that might be considered in the general and global context.

Social Forces

Population trends are clear social forces. Usually, population is also classified as a predetermined element—something that can be estimated with a high degree of certainty. This means that at any given point in time, we have access to data that will indicate population numbers. Estimates with high accuracy can be made of what the population growth will look like over any specified number of years. Cultural diversity is another social force that will be a significant driver over the next half century. Literacy, population migration, and emerging societies can also be considered social forces.

Technological Forces

It is difficult to conceive of all the possible technological drivers of our time. Advances such as multimedia, the Internet, various mobile technologies, alternate fuel sources, and music format are just a few. Technology may be the greatest single category of change drivers that we will cope with over the next millennium. Web 2.0 technologies such as Second Life, Facebook, Twitter, and others are popular though their true contributions to organizational efficiency are yet to be determined. Key questions about technology continue to relate to how technology's role in increasing efficiency and supporting collaboration over great distances can be leveraged, and whether they can increase firm performance or are simply social distractions.

Economic Forces

As I write this, the global economy is without doubt, the headlining issue. Fluctuating markets are the high-priority questions on everyone's minds. The economies of China and India are likely to continue to influence other economies around the globe. The growth of these countries in terms of the economic development will affect the social forces not only in each of these countries, but throughout the rest of the world as well. Other economic forces include fluctuating currency exchange rates, changing interest rates, taxes, fees, and costs of doing business, to name a few.

Environmental Forces

Limited oil reserves are driving nations to consider alternate fuel sources. Global climate change, storm activity in various parts of the world, and the limits of physical and geographic space in some countries are all examples of environmental forces that will have an impact on business and society in the future.

Political Forces

In today's global economy, political forces have the potential to shape industries like never before. Governmental transitions in countries like China and India have led to outsourcing trends that have altered and will continue to alter the global economy. Policies and plans of national leaders also shape global perceptions. There is no denying the power of political forces in our world.

These categories should be kept in mind when reading newspapers and magazines, watching the news, surfing the Web, and doing any other activities. The best advice in exploring these forces is to read widely and frequently. Really Simple Syndication (RSS) feeds can help to stay connected to a user-defined set of news feeds from an endless variety of sources and are a very effective way to efficiently scan headlines from around the world.

FORECASTS

Scenarios generally ask what happens if forecasts are wrong, and a STEEP analysis will undoubtedly turn up forecasts. During this phase, it is useful to understand what the forecasts are saying; and in the next phase, the project turns toward asking what if they are wrong. These forces and forecasts should be treated with skepticism, but they clearly contain information about the industry. Forecasts are "someone else's understanding and judgment crystallized in a figure which then becomes a substitute for thinking for the person who uses it" (Wack, 1985b, p. 89). The forces and forecasts contained in a STEEP analysis may provide useful information. However, the goal of scenario planning is to think deeply about the future, to learn about it, and to develop one's own understanding and judgment about how to navigate uncertainty.

DE BONO'S THINKING HATS

Thinking hats (De Bono, 1990) are a technique for thinking about complex issues. The approach is based on an assumption that when people think about complex issues, they are overcrowded with emotions, logic, data, hopefulness, and creativity. These factors are simply too much to make sense of at once. People need help breaking apart their thinking by dealing with each of these particular factors independently before combining them. The thinking hats represent six critical views for thinking about any complex issue. Each is represented by a different color:

- The White Hat—Neutral and objective, this hat is concerned with data and an analytical view. Most of us are stuck here.
- The Red Hat—This hat represents the emotional view.

- The Black Hat—The "devil's advocate" hat, this is the cautious view.
- The Yellow Hat—This hat represents the completely positive, optimistic view.
- The Green Hat—The creative hat, this hat is for new ideas and perspectives.
- The Blue Hat—The blue hat is an organizing, synthesizing hat, representing overviews, summaries and conclusions.

The six thinking hats can be used in a variety of ways, and not only for external thinking. These hats can be used at any time during the scenario project, but they are sometimes most helpful when soliciting and capturing initial reactions and comments about the initial issue. Two different strategies for using the hats are (1) single use and (2) sequential use (De Bono, 1990).

In the course of a conversation, it may be useful to inject a different kind of thinking, in which case any of the hats can be called upon. The different hats can be used to explore a subject and introduce alternate perspectives.

Sequential use of the hats is also a flexible approach and can be done in a variety of ways. A facilitator can choose one hat and ask the group to think from that perspective. Then another hat is chosen, and so on. Another approach is to assign a hat to each individual and ask that individual to think about the issue from that perspective.

Two critical factors are important in using the thinking hats: discipline and timing. When individuals are asked to think according to a specific hat, they must stay with the hat's perspective and represent that viewpoint for the sake of the group and the intent of the hats. If people are allowed to abandon their assigned hat, the danger is that they revert to their original, comfortable perspective, and the project gets more of the same. The other issue is timing. Because thinking in different ways can be uncomfortable for some people, using a short amount of defined time for thinking in these alternate perspectives is effective because people will concentrate and focus on what they are being asked to do.

In Technology Corporation, we used the thinking hats with great effect. From the start, buy-in was high, thanks to an engaged CEO. This set the tone for experimenting with different modes of thinking, and participants began to enjoy playing the various roles. The activity certainly got them consciously out of their default thinking patterns.

Again, the thinking hats can be used in a variety of ways. They can be used in a group workshop to stimulate diverse thinking on the initial scenario project purpose, to frame obvious issues in the external environment, and as a consulting tool to see the project in different ways, among many others. They can also be aimed at the external or internal environments.

SWOT ANALYSIS

SWOT (strengths, weaknesses, opportunities, and threats) analysis is probably the most common tool used in strategic thinking and planning. Although the O and T especially are externally focused, SWOT analysis is described in detail in the next main section on internal analysis.

SUMMARY

News media can often be more of a representation of what people are thinking than a reflection of the facts, so perusing numerous samples from varying "filters" is important when conducting an external analysis. For example, "[r]outinely pick up a dozen magazines from a newsstand and scan them. Include magazines you would not otherwise read" (Schwartz, 1991, p. 81).

While each scenario project will have particular investigative requirements, the following are subjects worth paying continual attention to (Schwartz, 1991):

- Science and technology
- Perception-shaping events
- Music
- Fringes

Online sources are also valuable in expanding your personal filter. Recommended newsfeeds include *Strategy+Business*, *Fast Company*, BBC News, the *New York Times*, *Wired*, the *New York Times* Editorials, the *Wall Street Journal*, the World Economic Forum, Earth Trends, and the United Nations Development Programme.

INTERNAL ANALYSIS

The internal analysis is focused on understanding forces within the organization. The most important tool for accomplishing this is interviews with key stakeholders of the organization. Additional tools include questionnaires, observations, and existing organizational data. Other tools for internal analysis include the SWOT analysis, the theory of the business (Drucker, 1994), van der Heijden's (1997, 2005a) business idea, Rummler and Brache's (1991) levels of performance, and Swanson's (1994, 2007) performance diagnosis matrix. Expert scenario planners use any tools that can help them understand an organization's internal dynamics efficiently and effectively.

SWOT ANALYSIS

Readers may be surprised to see the recommended use of a SWOT analysis here because some people consider it an outdated strategic tool. A SWOT analysis is still a useful way to stimulate strategic thinking and get people into the mind-set to think about their organization. Odds are, most have used this approach before, and so it is a comfortable way to begin engaging. Using a tool that decision makers are familiar with is a helpful bridge into scenario planning.

Research warns that the biggest problem with SWOT analyses is that the outcomes are never used in any meaningful way (Chermack & Kasshanna, 2007). In a scenario project, the insights from a SWOT analysis are highly useful in understanding the organization and its internal politics, and they can increase the relevance of scenarios when inserted into the scenario stories developed later on. For example, if information from interviews with managers is used in the second round of scenario construction, it is likely that the scenarios will be more relevant and provide a better framework for decision making. The key to a successful SWOT analysis is to use the information, even if it is as simple as feeding the results back to the participating group. Another common oversight with using SWOT is that the strengths and weaknesses relate to the internal environment, and the opportunities and threats relate to the external environment. The SWOT analysis is misused when the internal/external distinction is not made.

SWOT analysis is useful as long as it is not the sole means of internal environmental analysis. It contributes useful information and can be used in two distinct ways: (1) as a tool to structure data once collected and (2) as a tool to provoke further insights and areas in which to conduct further research. Figure 6.2 depicts the structure of a typical SWOT analysis.

At its essence, a SWOT analysis is a brainstorming exercise. Using a SWOT analysis at this stage of the planning system is beneficial in that it explores the perceptions of strengths, weaknesses, opportunities, and

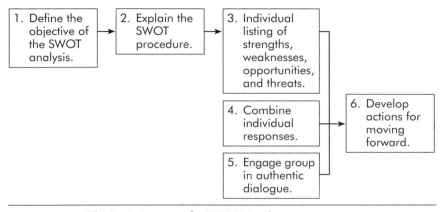

FIGURE 6.2   The Basic Process of a SWOT Analysis

threats. However, it is important to keep in mind that the analysis usually contains only the perceptions of managers and executives inside the organization. A useful SWOT analysis follows up with considerable investigation and confirmation.

It is also important to recognize that an item that falls under the strengths category can often be argued as a weakness as well. Thus, the danger of a SWOT analysis is in its forced dichotomies. Something is forced to be either a strength or a weakness when in reality it could be both, depending on the contextual circumstances. This dilemma provides an appropriate opportunity to use De Bono's thinking hats to consider alternate perspectives.

SWOT Analysis Workshop

A SWOT analysis can be conducted in about a half day, with some preparation, depending on the number of people involved, and should be structured according to the model in Figure 6.2. Begin by communicating the objective to participants, explaining the process, and answering any questions. Next, simply ask individuals to list their perceptions of the organization's strengths, weaknesses, opportunities, and threats. These perceptions can be combined on a wall chart, computer-projected document, or other format. Dialogue is the natural outcome, as there will be varying perspectives, ideas, and disagreement on the category to which a given force may belong. Keep in mind two critical points at this stage: (1) participants are verbalizing their perceptions, and (2) the outcomes of the conversation must be fed back to the participants. The strategic conversation has begun.

Corporate leaders in Technology Corporation decided to begin with a SWOT analysis because most of them were familiar with the process. It would be a comfortable way to get started. A conversation with leaders suggested a few important factors for the SWOT analysis, including specific objectives and actions. Figure 6.3 shows the basic process of a SWOT analysis for Technology Corporation.

Combined and Distilled SWOT Data. Figure 6.4 shows the combined and synthesized SWOT analysis for Technology Corporation. With redundancies eliminated, and after clarification and dialogue, the strengths, weaknesses, opportunities, and threats are relatively simplified. The real utility was in the conversation about items that are perceived to be strengths, which can often be argued as weaknesses. The sharing of perspective is how participants learn and begin working toward a shared mental model.

Several individuals had noticeable insights that came simply from taking the time to talk about strategic issues. It was clear that little to no time had been previously dedicated to having conversations about important issues, and having them now was like a breath of fresh air. Once these conversations began, participants enjoyed the ability to reflect, and thinking out loud became contagious.

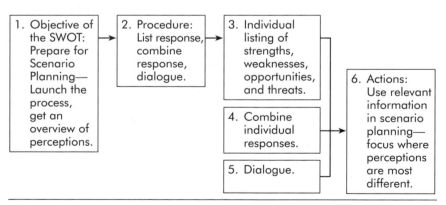

FIGURE **6.3** Technology Corporation's Basic Process for SWOT Analysis

Strengths	Weaknesses
Intellectual capital	Reliant on funding strategy
Agile	Small—limited capacity
Hardworking	Tendency for ego-driven projects
Innovative	Lack of teamwork/communication
Proposal writing expertise	Marketing strategy needs
Ability to focus	improvement
Leaders at each level	Internal functional silos
Opportunities	**Threats**
Leveraging skills to move projects to Phases II and III	Political removal/changes in SBIR funding
Fewer projects and more focus	Inability to collaborate more effectively
Collaborative effort	
Leveraging brainpower—communication	Economic impact on funding sources
Opportunities in manufacturing our own products (phase III–dependent)	Competition—emerging companies doing what we do . . . better?

FIGURE **6.4**   Technology Corporation's SWOT Analysis

INTERVIEWS

Interviewing individuals or groups of people in an organization is a time-consuming and detailed process that requires commitment and skill. Interviews can be considered as much an art as a science, and the only way to develop interviewing skills is through experience.

In scenario planning, the foundation of internal analysis is the content of interviews. They are a highly critical piece of the scenario planning system as the interviews will reveal opinions, facts, experiences, beliefs, organizational symbols, history, and more. Most important, interviews reveal what managers and executives are concerned about. Evoking, addressing, and highlighting these concerns is a requirement for scenarios to be effective.

Interviews can be (1) structured, (2) unstructured, or (3) a combination of structured and unstructured. Structured interviews follow a predetermined list of questions and can be scripted so that each interviewee is asked exactly the same questions. This approach limits responses to the content covered by the questions. Unstructured interviews usually follow a much more casual track and take the shape of a conversation. In this type of interviewing, the content can extend to cover a much wider range of subjects and questions, and each interviewee can be asked a completely different set of questions. Combination-type interviews contain structured questions and also allow for follow-up and spontaneous questions.

Group and telephone interviews and focus groups are other types of interviews, but they are not necessarily recommended for use in scenario planning. People are less likely to share their true opinions if interviewed in a group setting. Workshops tend to take care of group conversation and interaction, and they can even function as team-building exercises. Telephone interviews do not allow for the face-to-face interaction that is important in scenario planning. Body language, mannerisms and other nonverbal communication are valuable, as is the establishment of rapport and a relationship with project participants. In addition, it is unlikely that an individual would share his or her true concerns with a stranger over the phone.

Interviews in scenario planning projects should follow the combination-type approach. That is, specific questions should be asked of each participant, but room for other issues and conversation should be allowed. The "seven questions" have gained popularity in scenario planning because they can surface the strategic agenda of decision makers. While there are a few varying interpretations of these seven questions, they generally fall into the following categories:

1. Clairvoyant
2. Good Scenario
3. Bad Scenario
4. Inheritances from the Past
5. Important Decisions Ahead and Priorities
6. Constraints in the System and Changes That Need to Be Made
7. Epitaph

Specific sample questions that pertain to each of these seven categories are as follows:

1. If you could speak with an [industry] oracle from [year], what three things would you like to know about the [organization]?

2. If the [organization, industry] were to collapse by [year] (a "bad" scenario), what might have caused the collapse and why?

3. If the [organization, industry] were thriving, growing, and moving in a genuinely positive direction (a "good" scenario) by the year [year], what would be true of it?

4. (a) What has surprised you (pleasantly or unpleasantly, specifically or generally) about the [organization, industry] in recent years? (b) What have been the memorable "turns" and why?

5. (a) What are the major challenges to be faced by [organization, industry, etc.] professionals in the next five years? (b) What are the obstacles to be overcome that keep you awake at night?

6. (a) What would hinder the field from moving past these obstacles? (b) What forces could constrain the [e.g., organization and industry]?

7. Imagine that your program is in danger of being completely cut. What is your argument for keeping it?

Two common additional questions:

1. What would be some signs that the [organization, industry] is moving in a positive direction?

2. Any other uncertainties in the environment that might impact the future [organization, industry]?

The purpose of the interview stage is to become familiar with the mental models (values, beliefs, assumptions, experiences, hopes, and dreams) of a cross section of the organization. The seven questions are the standard tool for accomplishing this, but in order for these questions to be effective, the establishment of a good relationship with each interviewee is critical. Interviewees should be allowed to add anything else they feel is relevant to the project, and they may want to know more about the scenario planning project as well.

OTHER DATA COLLECTION METHODS

Three other data collection methods can be useful in understanding the internal dynamics of an organization: questionnaires, observations, and existing data. Though these are not often featured or highlighted in published scenario cases or in existing scenario planning texts, they deserve mention because there may be times when their use is appropriate.

Questionnaires

Questionnaires allow the collection of data from a large number of people, across locations, in a relatively efficient manner. They are useful in getting a snapshot of current perceptions in the organization. For example, culture questionnaires might be used before starting the scenario construction workshops if culture comes up in several interviews as a barrier to engagement in the scenario project. Change-readiness questionnaires can be useful if there has been a lot of recent consulting activity in the organization, mergers, leadership changes, or reorganizations. Custom questionnaires can also be developed to access targeted information, but they can take some time.

Observations

Observations are useful in understanding abstract behaviors such as thinking, planning, and estimating (Swanson, 2007). Some think these behaviors are unaccountable, but observing people perform their work functions on the job can yield a great deal of qualitative and quantitative data. Observation requires a high level of skill, patience, and the ability to be unobtrusive and avoid changing how the individual being observed performs his or her work. However, if these assets are used expertly, great insights can be generated about the nature of knowledge-based work and how masters of specific content knowledge perform.

Existing Data

Existing data should be used to the extent possible. Use of this data collection method usually happens informally as one becomes oriented to the organization and its personalities, issues, industry, and culture. Particularly relevant in scenario planning are previous uses of scenario planning and the outcomes, other planning tools that have been used, and other recent change initiatives. Financial and performance data, employee survey data, and customer data are all other useful data pools to examine. It is useful to know previous successes and failures with planning, and to know what was gained through such processes and where they may have collapsed. It is also useful to review reports from other external consultants who may have been working with the organization to get a general feel for other recent change activity.

THEORY OF THE BUSINESS/BUSINESS IDEA

In 1994, Drucker published "The Theory of the Business," which was an attempt at understanding the primary growth loop of any organization. Drucker wrote:

> These are the assumptions that shape any organization's behavior, dictate its decisions about what to do and what not to do, and define what the organization considers meaningful results. These assumptions are about markets. They are about identifying customers and competitors, their values and behavior. These are about technology and its dynamics, about a company's strengths and weaknesses. These assumptions are about what a company gets paid for. They are what I call a company's theory of the business. (p. 96)

Four critical aspects form the theory of the business:

- The assumptions about the environment, mission, and core competencies must fit reality.
- The assumptions in these three areas must fit each other.
- The theory of the business must be known and understood throughout the organization.
- The theory of the business must be tested constantly.

From a diagnostic perspective, it is helpful to know the status of each of these specifications. Scenario planning will address all of these points, but it is important to know at the start if, for example, the business idea is known, understood, and articulated throughout the organization.

Related to the theory of the business is the business idea developed by van der Heijden (1997, 2005b). The business idea is based on system theory and system dynamics concepts. The business idea is simply a visual display of the primary growth loop—it is the business model. The business idea shows how the organization has understood a social need, created a novel idea about how to address that need, developed expertise in addressing that need, and created a viable business based on the perceived value of that need.

THEORY OF THE BUSINESS WORKSHOP

It is very useful to conduct a workshop based on understanding the theory of the business/business idea. This workshop can be completed in a few hours and can alone initiate strategic insights, but it also will generate thinking directly relevant to the work that takes place in the scenario construction phase (see Chapter 7). Gather the relevant participants in a setting conducive to creative thinking (e.g., a meeting room with large whiteboards or newsprint on the walls so that participants can think and draw out loud). Ask each participant to use a single sheet of paper and briefly describe

- whether the assumptions about the environment, mission, and core competencies fit reality;
- whether the assumptions in these three areas fit each other;
- the extent to which the theory of the business is known and understood throughout the organization; and
- the extent to which the theory of the business is tested.

Next, ask each participant to draw or write out the business idea on another sheet of paper. When all participants have completed the exercise, ask them to individually report their responses to the four specifications of the theory of the business, and then ask them to share their business ideas. The variety in responses to both of these activities indicates how unified or scattered the thinking is about the core purpose of the organization and how well it is understood. A useful goal is to create one unifying business idea. Participants can present their models and work together to build a business idea and set of assumptions that capture the essence of what the organization is trying to accomplish. This is a simple exercise in eliciting individual mental models and working toward a shared one. As the strategic conversation was started in the SWOT analysis workshop, it continues here as participants share ideas, perspectives, and insights.

In my own experiences, if I ask twelve participants to draw or write out the business idea, they will draw or write out twelve different things. I have found a tremendous amount of utility in then asking participants to create a single business idea out of what they have individually generated. This simple activity has frequently produced "aha" moments in participants I have worked with, and the resulting theory of the business is a critical item later on in the scenario project.

Technology Corporation's Theory of the Business/Business Idea

Technology Corporation's scenario team met for a half day with a general purpose of understanding and sharing perceptions of the organization's business model. Before presenting the organization's theory of the business and business idea, some background information on perceived core competencies, vision, and other internal thinking will be useful to set the context.

> *Core competencies:* Developing innovative products in the chemical, contracting, manufacturing industries, developing human capital (expertise and innovation), and listening to customer needs
>
> *Activities:* Technology Corporation researches and develops intellectual property to license and sell technologies related to innovations in energy, chemicals, and technology.
>
> *Vision:* Technology Corporation develops ideas and products that meet the energy, chemical, and technological challenges of the future.
>
> *Model:* Three concentric circles for the business model illustrating short-term, midterm, and long-term strategies (Figure 6.5):
>
> 1. Short-term: Current funding sources including Small Business Innovation Research.

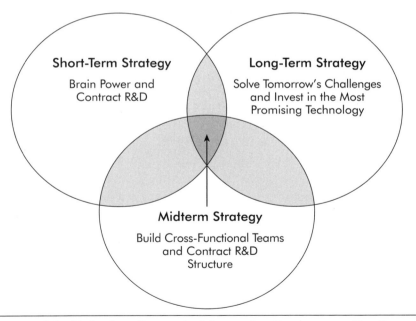

FIGURE **6.5** Technology Corporation's Innovation-Development of Intellectual Property

2. Midterm: Lessen dependence of SBIR.
   Contract R&D. Delays in time horizons.
   This midterm strategy is an opportunity to lay the foundation for future success (develop cross-functional teams, build the infrastructure for R&D, and listen to customers to build trust). Midterm activities build Technology Corporation's reputation.
   Cross-functional teams allow everyone to be involved in the project at all times. If an issue comes up, decisions can be made quickly. Teams are involved early to understand the big picture and help reduce time to market.
3. Long-term: Innovation—development of intellectual property
   Key questions for Technology Corporation:
   - When does Technology Corporation stop pouring resources into technologies that have achieved their purpose? In other words, what will Technology Corporation stop doing?
   - Will Technology Corporation consider partnering with other companies to develop technologies?
   - Will Technology Corporation offer incentives to cross-functional teams to innovate?
   - Will Technology Corporation look to outside resources to fill gaps in core competencies needed to execute the innovation?

Technology Corporation's Theory of the Business

1. **Do the assumptions about the environment, mission, and core competencies fit reality?**
   Yes. Decision makers in Technology Corporation realize it is risky to be committed to a single funding source, but the purpose of the organization meets a significant need in society. The key will be in moving beyond simply idea-based projects and into design and manufacturing processes to see their products built to suit specific actual needs. The mismatch is in any assumption that the current stream of SBIR funding will be consistent. Most members of the organization agree that this is the only assumption that may not fit reality.
2. **Do the assumptions in these three areas fit each other?**
   Yes. Again, the only potential problem here is if change strategies fail and decision makers fall back into relying on the same sources they have relied on over the past several years.

3. **Is the theory of the business known and understood throughout the organization?**

   It is unclear how well the theory of the business has been communicated and understood. An additional purpose of the scenario project is to communicate the current theory of the business and create a shared understanding of how and why it needs to change.

4. **Has the theory of the business been tested?**

   No. One other key purpose of the scenario project will be to document the current theory of the business, show where it is weak, develop an alternative, and test it in each scenario.

Technology Corporation Business Idea

The business idea in Figure 6.6 is a simple model that captures the essence of Technology Corporation's current overall strategy. The organization has key expertise in writing proposals that garner funding. Funded proposals account for the majority of Technology Corporation's operating budget, and currently, few if any products are produced. Under the current model, the corporation uses funding to work on good ideas and enhance its intellectual property. The result of this is increasing brainpower—Technology Corporation continues to provide intellectual challenges for its scientists and developers, but these ideas are never brought to fruition or taken to market.

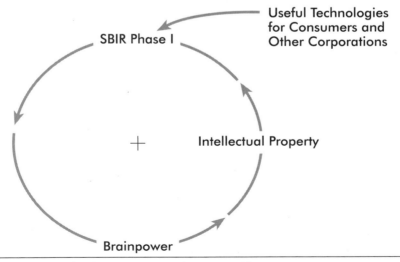

FIGURE **6.6** Technology Corporation's Business Idea

The workshop for creating the business idea involved thirteen people from Technology Corporation. Each participant drew a similar model, but significant insights were not achieved until each one was able to see what his or her colleagues were drawing. Combining and simplifying these models was extremely useful, and all thirteen participants agreed that significant changes would need to be made. First, the reliance on a single funding source was clarified to a couple of individuals who were not totally aware of it, and the implications discussed. Second, all thirteen people saw that significant cultural changes would result from changing the business model to include additional funding sources, and moving into Phases II and III of existing funding protocols.

SYNTHESIS TOOLS

Two additional analysis/synthesis tools can be used to summarize the information that is collected in the scenario exploration phase. These are Rummler and Brache's nine performance variables and Swanson's performance diagnosis matrix. Not all scenario planning projects will use a depth of analysis that makes these tools relevant, but where appropriate, these tools have the capability to structure and summarize a great deal of information in a relatively simple format.

RUMMLER AND BRACHE'S NINE PERFORMANCE VARIABLES

The individual, process, and organizational levels are the critical divisions of the organization (Rummler & Brache, 1995). The greatest opportunity for performance improvement is in understanding and leveraging the process level. The key strategic perspective is based on fit among the levels of the organization (Rummler & Brache, 1995). The nine performance variables are shown in Figure 6.7.

Job/performer goals must support process goals, which must in turn support organization goals. If the organization goals change (as a result of a planning process), then logically, the process goals and job/performer goals should change. Likewise, job design must support process design, which must support organization design (Rummler & Brache, 1995). The utility of the nine performance variables are in achieving fit or alignment among these nine key variables. For example, simply describing the cells of the matrix will yield useful insights. Asking questions about alignment is the

The Three Performance Needs

	Goals	Design	Management
Organization Level	Organization Goals	Organization Design	Organization Management
Process Level	Process Goals	Process Design	Process Management
Job/Performer Level	Job Goals	Job Design	Job Management

The Three Levels of Performance

FIGURE 6.7   Rummler and Brache's (1995) Nine Performance Variables

logical next step and can reveal where there may be significant breakdowns in alignment of goals, design, and management. The team/group level has become a common addition to the nine performance variables.

SWANSON'S PERFORMANCE DIAGNOSIS MATRIX

Swanson's performance diagnosis matrix (2007; see Figure 6.8) is another high-utility synthesis tool. The matrix provides a means of synthesizing the vast amount of information that has been collected about the internal function of the organization. More specifically, the matrix includes a number of critical variables to consider in the context of performance problems. While some of these might not be immediately relevant to the scenario exercise, the overall utility of the matrix is in its use as a snapshot of organizational performance. The critical variables in Swanson's matrix are mission/goal, system design, capacity, motivation, and expertise. These variables can be assessed at the levels of the organization proposed by Rummler and Brache (job/performer, process, and organization). Swanson's matrix is also frequently updated to include team/group levels just like the performance improvement matrix by Rummler and Brache.

A properly used matrix will reveal many issues inside any organization. It is not realistic to assume all of these issues can be solved. The critical issues must be worked on, particularly those related to the strategic agenda of the organization, if scenario planning is to be used.

These two synthesis tools were developed as tools for general organizational analysis. Their use in scenario planning is not required and, in some cases, may not even be recommended. However, their utility is in

Performance Levels

Performance Variables	Organizational Level	Process Level	Individual Level
Mission/Goal	Does the organizational mission/goal fit the reality of the economic, political, and cultural forces?	Do the process goals enable the organization to meet organizational and individual missions/goals?	Are the professional and personal missions/goals of individuals congruent with the organization's?
Systems Design	Does the organizational system provide structure and policies supporting the desired performance?	Are processes designed in such a way as to work as a system?	Does the individual design support performance?
Capacity	Does the organization have the leadership, capital, and infrastructure to achieve its missions/goals?	Does the process have the capacity to perform (quantity, quality, and timelines)?	Does the individual have the mental, physical, and emotional capacity to perform?
Motivation	Do the policies, culture, and reward systems support the desired performance?	Does the process provide the information and human factors required to maintain it?	Does the individual want to perform no matter what?
Expertise	Does the organization establish and maintain selection and training policies and resources?	Does the process of developing expertise meet the changing demands of changing processes?	Does the individual have the knowledge, skills, and experience to perform?

FIGURE 6.8   Swanson's (2007) Performance Diagnosis Matrix

synthesizing information about the internal state of the organization. These synthesis tools are particularly helpful in cases with a history of ongoing scenario planning or other change initiatives. In these instances, problems may be hiding in places not often investigated in the commonly used scenario planning tools. Moreover, these tools are intended to assess overall organizational viability, which fits well with scenario projects aimed at organizational learning, or the continuous quality improvement of anticipatory and strategic thinking inside the organization.

Technology Corporation's Performance Diagnosis Matrix

Figure 6.9 shows a snapshot of Swanson's (2007) performance diagnosis matrix applied to Technology Corporation. The matrix shows where there are issues and indicates leverage points for starting to work on them.

FIGURE **6.9**   Technology Corporation's Performance Diagnosis Matrix

Performance Variables	Performance Levels			
	Organizational Level	*Process Level*	*Team Level*	*Individual Level*
Mission/ goal	Does the organization mission/ goal fit the reality of the economic, political, and cultural forces?	Do the process goals enable the organization-, team-, and individual-level goals to be met?	Do the team goals enable the organization-, process-, and individual-level goals to be met?	Are individual goals (job descriptions) supporting team, process, and organizational goals?
	No, problems here—changing environment, need to reevaluate goals.	**Not sure—if organization goals change, these will change, too.**	**If organization goals change, these will change, too,**	**If organization goals change, these will change, too,**
Systems design	Does the organization system provide structure and policies supporting the desired performance?	Are the processes designed in a logical, efficient, and systematic way?	Are the teams assembled in a logical, efficient way that also takes advantage of individual strengths?	Does the job design enable the individual to perform in the team as required by the process?
	Yes—but could be altered to reward team performance more completely.	**Yes—but they may need to change.**	**No—collaboration is a problem. Possible leverage here to get people working together more.**	**Yes**
Capacity	Does the organization have the leadership, capital, and infrastructure to achieve its mission/goals?	Does the process have the capacity to meet the quantity, quality, and time line requirements?	Do teams demonstrate the capacity to meet the quantity, quality, and time line requirements?	Do individuals have the mental, physical, and emotional capacity to perform as required by the team and the process?
	Yes	**Yes**	**No—more collaboration and teamwork is needed.**	**Yes—absolutely**

(continued)

FIGURE 6.9   Technology Corporation's Performance Diagnosis Matrix *(continued)*

Performance Variables	Performance Levels			
	Organizational Level	*Process Level*	*Team Level*	*Individual Level*
Motivation	Do the policies, culture, and reward systems support the desired performance?	Does the process provide the required information? Is the process motivating for the workforce?	Is the reward system structured to enable maximum performance from each team member?	Are individuals motivated to perform as required by team and process goals?
	Generally, yes, but not in the case of team performance	**Yes**	**Yes, but needs adjustment to reward collaboration**	**Possibly internally, but they are not formally rewarded for doing so.**
Expertise	Do the selection and training policies and resources enable the desired performance?	Is the expertise required by the process continuously determined and developed?	Are teams developing collective expertise, or are teams continually reconfigured to share expertise?	Do individuals have the knowledge, skills, and expertise required by the team and process?
	Yes	**Yes**	**Opportunity here—teams are not performing well, but individuals are.**	**Yes**

CONCLUSION

This chapter has described the scenario exploration phase, covering general tools in assessing the external and internal environments. The purpose of this phase is to learn about the industry and external environment, as well as the internal dynamics of the organization. Simultaneously, participant viewpoints, ideas, and perspectives can be gathered. Two workshops were recommended (on SWOT analysis and theory of the business/business idea) to stimulate strategic thinking and prepare participants for the scenario construction that is to follow.

The core outcomes of this phase are summaries of the state of the internal and external environments. Items that should be included are the following:

- A listing of STEEP forces, with major issues in each category
- A report of the SWOT analysis
- An executive summary of the internal interviews
- A summary of information gained through use of other data collection methods
- A summary report of the theory of the business/business idea workshop

Optional but useful synthesis tools include these:

- A completed table summarizing Rummler and Brache's nine performance variables
- A completed version of Swanson's performance diagnosis matrix

This chapter includes examples of these elements as applied in the scenario case. These reports do not need to be lengthy. In fact, they should be short, providing the core, relevant information for the project. The goal is to present an understanding of the basic internal and external dynamics, recognizing that the next phase, scenario construction, delves more deeply into the external environment.

7

Phase 3—Scenario Development: Digging Deeper

The scenario development phase consists of workshops used to build scenarios. Most scenario planning books cover the materials presented in this chapter. These activities are the signature of scenario planning. The prior phase on scenario exploration included several tools for assessing the external and internal environments. This follow-up phase digs deeper into both of these environments. The key outcome of scenario development is two to four scenarios that are relevant, plausible, and challenging. During the creation of scenarios, participants challenge each other's viewpoints and set the foundation for a shared mental model of the organization and its environment.

KEY TERMS AND APPROACHES

Before getting into the details of scenario development, it is important to review some key scenario terms and cover some philosophical approaches to scenario development.

PREDETERMINED ELEMENTS

Predetermined elements are predictable elements that do not depend on a particular chain of events (Schwartz, 1991). Predictable elements are divided into four categories: slow-changing phenomena, constrained situations, in the pipeline, and inevitable conclusions. The most obvious example of a predetermined element is demographics. Populations are predictable. Populations are also an example of elements in the pipeline. Much has been written about the baby boom generation, because the aging of that generation can be predicted with precision. Likewise, we will know how many teenagers there will be in 2010–2020 because they have already been born. The U.S. dependence on foreign oil is a constrained situation, meaning that it is likely that the dependence will continue until alternate fuel sources are developed. However, given the technological and infrastructural implications of the United States (or almost any other nation), switching to a non-petroleum-based fuel is unlikely in the near term. "In the pipeline" refers to things that have happened, but the consequences have yet to unfold. For example, Apple's dominance of online media is unexpected to some, and how far that company will take it is not yet certain, but its presence is undeniable. The U.S. deficit is an example of an inevitable conclusion, meaning that the debt has a direct influence on other obvious decisions such as raising taxes (Schwartz, 1991). If an element seems certain, no matter what scenario comes to pass, then it is probably a predetermined element.

CRITICAL UNCERTAINTIES

"Critical uncertainties are intimately related to pre-determined elements. You find them by questioning your assumptions about pre-determined elements" (Schwartz, 1991, p. 115). Thus, what might happen to change the U.S. dependence on foreign oil? While the U.S. deficit is often a predetermined element, what are the forces that could change the U.S. debt. Ultimately, decision makers will identify the critical uncertainties in a workshop designed for a group to identify forces with the highest potential impact on the organization and that are the most uncertain. What is uncertain, however, is intimately related to what is predetermined. So, playing with these forces in different configurations is where insight can be found.

Great care is needed in sorting out the predetermined elements (Burt, 2006). This is because "a poorly observed fact is more treacherous than a faulty train of reasoning" (Wack, 1985a, p. 18). Many of the errors in judgment observed at Shell were cases in which predetermined elements and critical uncertainties became mixed up. Thus, a hallmark of scenario planning is in separating what is predictable (predetermined) from what is truly open to change (uncertain).

Understanding these forces is the basis of the scenario development phase and will shape the structure of the entire scenario planning project. Initial scenario construction occurs through a series of workshops in which participants dialogue about important issues affecting the organization. The task is to separate out the forces that have both the highest relative potential impact on the organization and the highest relative uncertainty. This is a subjective task, accomplished by intense dialogue and debate. Exchanging ideas allows participants to understand each other's perspectives, open up their mental models, and create the basis for a shared mental model of the organization and the situations it may face.

INDUCTIVE VERSUS DEDUCTIVE SCENARIO CONSTRUCTION

Induction is usually described as moving from specific ideas or factors to general laws, whereas deduction begins with general overarching concepts and clarifies toward the specific. Arguments based on personal experiences are best expressed inductively, while arguments based on laws or widely accepted principles are best expressed deductively. Either approach can be applied to scenario projects, and both have benefits and drawbacks. It is always wise to adopt the technique best suited to the culture of the organization. For example, engineers and academics will probably be more comfortable with the deductive method, while designers will love the freedom of the inductive method (Wright, Cairns, & Goodwin, 2009).

The simplest approach to scenario planning is through inductive scenario construction. This method has two different strategies: (1) a simple brainstorming approach and (2) using the "official future."

The first method is to brainstorm a variety of different scenarios. Effectively using this method requires that users be highly "tuned in" to their industry and organization. Few rules apply in this method, and the only goal is to develop different stories that are based on major events or innovations that have dramatic implications. For example, how can cell-phone companies think beyond Apple's iPhone, instead of simply copying it? What could be the next surprising evolution in mobile information technology?

The second method within the inductive approach is to consider the official future, which is usually a forecast, and then ask, "Where might our forecast be wrong?" The official future is a surprise-free, status quo, growth-as-usual scenario. It carries its own set of driving forces, and if they can be understood, varying them will introduce some thought-provoking alternatives. The elements of the official future are usually found in the interviews. Therefore, the interviews are the critical method of information gathering in the inductive approach to scenario development.

The unstructured nature of the inductive scenario approach lends itself to small organizations or situations in which participants have considerable prior experience with scenarios. Early scenario work was inductive, and the use of the official future was a "bridge" into the world of scenario thinking for managers who were initially resistant. The inductive approach may not be suitable for cultures unfamiliar with scenario planning or those lacking patience and comfort with debate (Ogilvy & Schwartz, 1998). Because the inductive approach is informal and unstructured, it does not necessarily require the clearly defined question, scenario project proposal, or external and internal analyses that have been presented thus far. The inductive approach is best suited to experienced users of scenarios and organizations in which scenario thinking has become "a way of planning." The inductive method is most useful in situations in which specific people are dedicated to thinking about strategy as their core function for the organization.

Inductive scenario construction is also the result of resident geniuses, or great men and women who parlayed their thinking skills and established track records of helping companies avoid major discontinuities. Thinking in alternative futures is a natural human ability, but most have lost those skills. We need to be reminded, and the first step is a structured way to think about the future. This book provides that structure, which begins with the deductive approach. Working through the scenario system presented in this book is a reminder of how we naturally approach dilemmas—we think in alternatives.

The deductive approach to scenario planning is structured; thus, it is common. The deductive approach typically features the workshops, ranking exercises, and a 2 × 2 matrix that have become a hallmark of scenario planning. The workshops in the deductive approach create time and space for participants to think and talk about strategic issues. Bringing a cross section of organizational decision makers together to work on strategic issues is believed to draw on the collective thinking within the organization to tackle difficult problems and dilemmas. The fact is, few organizations create ways for colleagues to jointly reflect on strategic issues. Using the deductive approach, by its nature requiring involvement, contributes to community building in the organization. The deductive approach is a modern version of sharing stories and having conversations about difficult issues around a campfire.

EIGHT COMPONENTS OF SCENARIO DEVELOPMENT

Having established these important terms and approaches to scenario development, we can now turn to the details of the scenario development phase. There are eight important and well-known pieces of scenario development:

1. Brainstorming the issues the organization is facing
2. Ranking those issues according to their relative impact on the organization
3. Ranking those issues according to their relative uncertainty
4. Developing the scenario logics by selecting issues "high" on both rankings to build a scenario matrix
5. Constructing the research agenda
6. Defining the scenario plots and titles
7. Writing the detailed scenario stories
8. Creating the scenario communication strategy

These pieces are the focus of this chapter, with the goal of understanding the forces that drive the organizational system and its environment. The first four of these pieces are best done as workshops. These workshops are described, one for each of the pieces of the scenario development phase (Figure 7.1). The first three workshops are all aimed at identifying and separating the predetermined elements and critical uncertainties. The fourth workshop describes how to hone the critical uncertainties to build scenarios. Tips are provided for deriving the scenarios and writing the scenario stories. Finally, methods for presenting the scenarios to the organization are covered.

OVERVIEW OF THE SCENARIO CONSTRUCTION WORKSHOPS

Once the initial issue is defined, the purpose of the project has been set, and a general understanding of internal and external dynamics is developed, a series of workshops must be designed to build scenarios. The number and length of these workshops will vary according to the number of people involved, the size of the organization, and the complexity of the issue. This

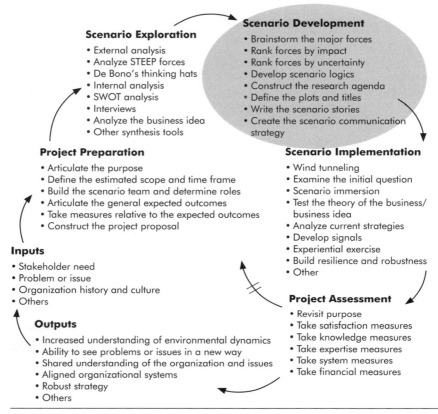

Scenario Exploration

- External analysis
- Analyze STEEP forces
- De Bono's thinking hats
- Internal analysis
- SWOT analysis
- Interviews
- Analyze the business idea
- Other synthesis tools

Scenario Development

- Brainstorm the major forces
- Rank forces by impact
- Rank forces by uncertainty
- Develop scenario logics
- Construct the research agenda
- Define the plots and titles
- Write the scenario stories
- Create the scenario communication strategy

Project Preparation

- Articulate the purpose
- Define the estimated scope and time frame
- Build the scenario team and determine roles
- Articulate the general expected outcomes
- Take measures relative to the expected outcomes
- Construct the project proposal

Scenario Implementation

- Wind tunneling
- Examine the initial question
- Scenario immersion
- Test the theory of the business/ business idea
- Analyze current strategies
- Develop signals
- Experiential exercise
- Build resilience and robustness
- Other

Inputs

- Stakeholder need
- Problem or issue
- Organization history and culture
- Others

Outputs

- Increased understanding of environmental dynamics
- Ability to see problems or issues in a new way
- Shared understanding of the organization and issues
- Aligned organizational systems
- Robust strategy
- Others

Project Assessment

- Revisit purpose
- Take satisfaction measures
- Take knowledge measures
- Take expertise measures
- Take system measures
- Take financial measures

FIGURE 7.1   The Performance-Based Scenario System—Scenario Development Phase

chapter presents a series of workshops for constructing scenarios. In some cases these can be combined, particularly if the project is small. The first task is brainstorming the issues and concerns of the group, and beginning a general group dialogue.

Dialogue is a key component of the scenario-building process. Dialogue is the mechanism for uncovering individual mental models and working toward a shared group mental model of the issue, the organization, and its external environment. Workshops following the brainstorming activity are more specific and are aimed at separating major forces into predetermined elements and critical uncertainties. The workshops are a way to leverage the collective capital inside the organization, build a collective mental model of the issue, and cull out what is truly uncertain. However, these workshops are not a substitute for deep research and reflective, critical thinking on the driving forces of a given industry. The project leader and the scenario planning team must continue to identify areas that require further research as the project proceeds.

BRAINSTORMING THE MAJOR FORCES—WORKSHOP 1

The brainstorming workshop is simple in concept. The purpose is to capture what participants perceive are the major forces the organization is facing that relate to the problem or issue defined. This workshop usually takes a half-day to a full day. It is important to get input from all participants and allow enough time to capture everything that is said. An effective way to structure this workshop is in a meeting room with empty wall space, whiteboards, or newsprint taped to the walls. Give each participant a pad of sticky notes (or hexagons), and ask them to write a single issue on each note and stick it to the wall (see Figure 7.2). Because this is a true brainstorming session, everything is included, and order does not matter, nor does the location in which sticky notes are placed. When dominating personalities are present, it can be helpful to establish ground rules, such as no talking during a portion of the activity until the placement of sticky notes is complete. Once participants have exhausted their ideas, it is useful to have an open dialogue. Specific brainstorming methods can be used, such as the nominal group technique (Delbecq & Van de Ven, 1971), to ensure participation from each member, and to rein in dominant personalities.

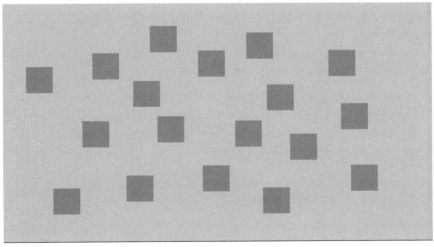

FIGURE **7.2** Brainstorming Key Forces

An important point of the brainstorming exercise is to strive for granularity. That is, each force should be written such that they are all relatively equally big or small forces. It is also important that the forces are written ambiguously so that normative judgment can be added later on. For example, use "technology skills," not "technology is here to stay."

Brainstorming is usually a lot of fun. The goal is to get the ideas flowing freely and include everything—no matter how far-fetched things may initially seem. The workshops for Technology Corporation were a lot of fun because the participants were engaged. This could be attributed to leaders who were committed to the project and created an atmosphere in which people felt comfortable contributing their ideas. While a few individuals felt intimidated by the hierarchy, for the most part, participants were set at ease, and the exercises became engaging, fun exchanges among colleagues. A simplified version of Technology Corporation's initial brainstorm session is in Figure 7.3.

Brainstormed items should be grouped when there is overlap. Duplications should be combined so that a cleaner, more efficient scattering of major forces is built. Once completed, these are the forces perceived to be driving the environmental system in which the organization is operating.

The categories used in the scan of the external environment should be kept in mind while brainstorming and distilling these issues. The major factors affecting any business are usually found in examining the social, technological, environmental, economic, and political environments. These are usually macro issues. For example, many current scenario projects would include the volatility of the U.S. economy and its time line to recovery as major issues in the external environment.

Before moving on to the ranking workshops, sometimes it is helpful to look at the list of brainstormed forces and simply ask:

- Which of these are predetermined? (Which are outcomes of things that have already taken place or are currently underway?)
- Which of these are truly uncertain? (Which forces carry truly uncertain outcomes?)

RANKING THE FORCES BY RELATIVE IMPACT ON THE ORGANIZATION—WORKSHOP 2

The next step in understanding the major forces is ranking the issues according to their potential impact on the organization's strategic agenda.

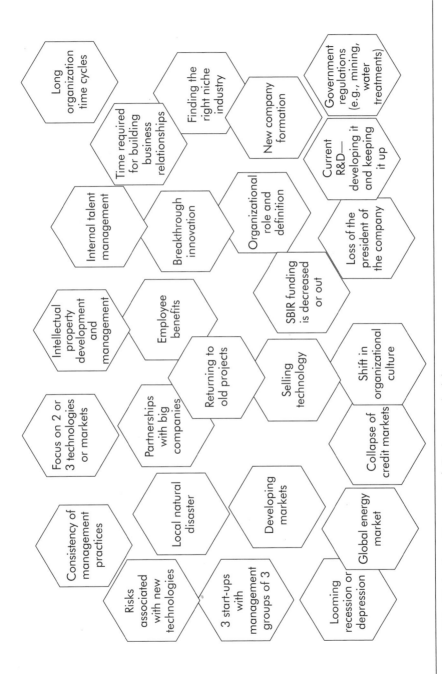

FIGURE 7.3 Technology Corporation's Brainstorm Activity

This ranking occurs horizontally across the working space—preferably a long empty wall in an open meeting room with newsprint taped to it—simply ranging from "Low" to "High" (Figure 7.4). The goal is to separate the truly critical factors from the other. This is not to say that the other factors are not important. Rather, the high-impact items are those that have the power to fundamentally reshape the business. If these factors are perceived differently, they can provoke significant strategic insights. Figure 7.5 shows the brainstorming activity from Technology Corporation with forces simplified, and then ranked horizontally according to impact.

This ranking exercise can take several hours to a full day, depending on the number of participants involved. Viewpoints will differ, and conversations that develop around understanding the varying viewpoints are how mental models continue to be shared. This face-to-face dialogue is critical to scenario planning. The knowledge friction (meaning the resolution of multiple viewpoints into a more complete understanding) is what allows many participants to experience a significant shift in insight (Rochlin, 1998). This has been referred to as an "aha" moment, and it happens when participants are able see the situation with new eyes.

FIGURE 7.4 Ranking Forces by Relative Impact on the Strategic Agenda

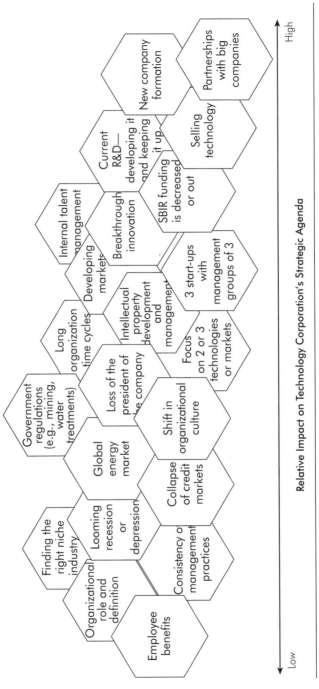

Low ← → High

Relative Impact on Technology Corporation's Strategic Agenda

FIGURE 7.5 Technology Corporation's Brainstormed Forces, Simplified and Ranked by Relative Impact on the Strategic Agenda

RANKING THE FORCES BY RELATIVE UNCERTAINTY—WORKSHOP 3

The next exercise is focused on ranking the issues by uncertainty. This ranking is done vertically, again according to "Low" and "High" uncertainty (see Figure 7.6).

Again, significant disagreement will arise. Conversation, debate, and dialogue are intended to support the extension of participant perceptions. By listening to a variety of perspectives and describing their own, participants build their own mental scaffolding. Once the scaffolding is in place, the group can work toward a shared mental model. Figure 7.7 shows the uncertainty/impact matrix for Technology Corporation.

BUILDING THE SCENARIO LOGICS—WORKSHOP 4

The next workshop is aimed at creating the scenario logics. The scenario logics are the general frameworks—or the plots of the scenarios. These are also known as proto-scenarios (van der Merwe, 2008). Once the participants have ranked the issues by impact on the strategic agenda and by uncertainty, the ranking space is divided roughly into quadrants (see Figure 7.8). Figure 7.9

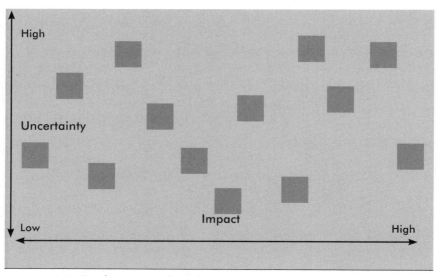

FIGURE 7.6 Ranking Forces by Relative Uncertainty

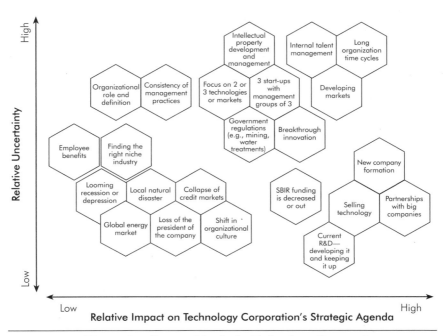

FIGURE **7.7** Uncertainty/Impact Matrix for Technology Corporation

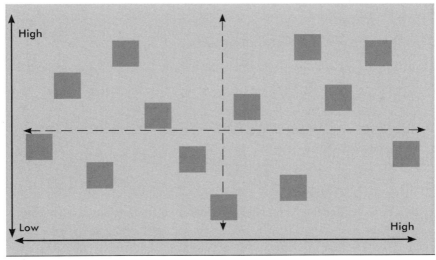

FIGURE **7.8** Quadrants of the Ranking Space

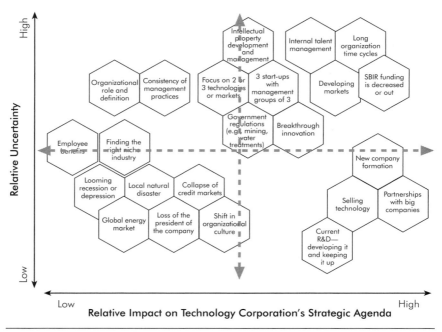

FIGURE 7.9   Technology Corporation's Quadrants

shows the ranking space divided into quadrants for the Technology Corporation case.

The Quadrants of the Ranking Space

By dividing the ranking space, the issues can be grouped into general areas as follows:

- High impact–Low uncertainty
- Low impact–Low uncertainty
- Low impact–High uncertainty
- High impact–High uncertainty

Issues that are ranked high impact–low uncertainty are major issues but are also relatively stable. Major industry shifts that are already underway, such as new government regulations, would characterize this category. Issues that are low impact–low uncertainty are issues that can be readily dealt with. These issues generally do not require a significant investment of analysis to better understand. Items in these two categories are also, by definition, predetermined elements. It is worthwhile going over each of these again to make sure they really belong in this category. Things that are misread and grouped as predetermined elements, but are actually quite uncertain, can lead to significant errors in judgment (Wack, 1985a, 1985b).

Issues ranked low impact–high uncertainty require further research because of the high uncertainty ranking. High uncertainty rankings simply mean that the eventual outcomes of these issues are unknown. Even though the group has agreed that their impact is low, it is worth conducting some extra research because of the potential volatility of these issues.

Finally, issues ranked high impact–high uncertainty are called the critical uncertainties (Figure 7.10). These are the issues that have the potential to fundamentally shift the assumptions under the strategic agenda and issues whose outcomes are highly uncertain. These critical uncertainties are used to construct the scenario logics.

The 2 × 2 Scenario Matrix

Scenario logics are built by choosing two critical uncertainties and plotting them in a 2 × 2 matrix (see Figure 7.11). Remember that the critical uncertainties are the items ranked high on their potential impact and high on uncertainty. The two critical uncertainties chosen for the scenario matrix must

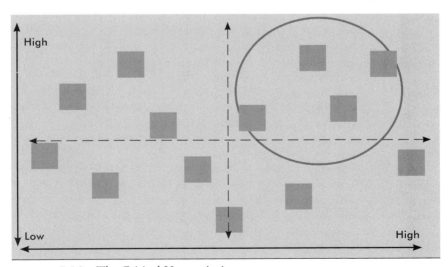

FIGURE 7.10   The Critical Uncertainties

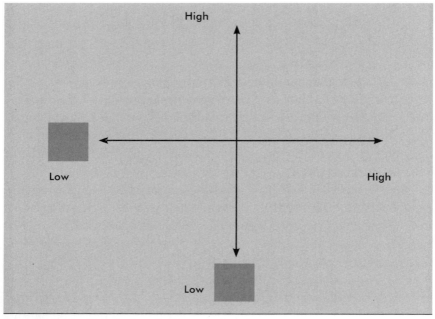

FIGURE 7.11   Developing the Scenario Matrix

be independent variables. Facilitators should steer the group toward "useful" variables, not "right" variables. By combining two critical uncertainties, the themes of the four scenarios become apparent. Normative judgment is now applied to each critical uncertainty, generally adding a high and low value to each.

A variety of methods can be used to choose the two critical uncertainties, such as value voting, poker chips, and the nominal group technique (Delbecq & Van de Ven, 1971). All are variations on the same process. For example, in value voting, each participant is given twenty one-dollar bills (real or not) and asked to allot their dollars among the critical uncertainties. As each participant "spends" his or her money, the critical uncertainties are prioritized, and the top two can be chosen for use in the 2 × 2 matrix. It is worth the time to experiment with a few different 2 × 2 matrices to get a sense of the different scenario logics that can surface from this part of the workshop. The goal of this workshop is to develop four scenario logics.

In Technology Corporation, the scenario team worked through the initial brainstorming exercise, the two ranking exercises, and prioritized the critical uncertainties. After several hours of debate and dialogue, the team settled on two critical uncertainties: funding sources and talent management. These items were placed on the *X* and *Y* axes of the matrix in Figure 7.12.

These scenario logics must be plausible, challenging, and relevant. Strategies for assessing scenarios are presented in detail in Chapter 9. At this point in the project, the scenario logics must meet three criteria as a face validity check. The scenarios must be plausible in that they can potentially draw from data and facts, and present an acceptable view of the future. They must be challenging in that they can assemble events and facts in a way that challenges the current mental models. They must be relevant in that they relate to the key issues that have been expressed during the project and draw on real concerns of managers in the organization.

If some of the scenarios resulting from the 2 × 2 matrix do not meet these criteria, two more critical uncertainties can be mapped on another matrix until four useful scenarios come together (see Figure 7.13). The issue with using another set of two critical uncertainties becomes keeping

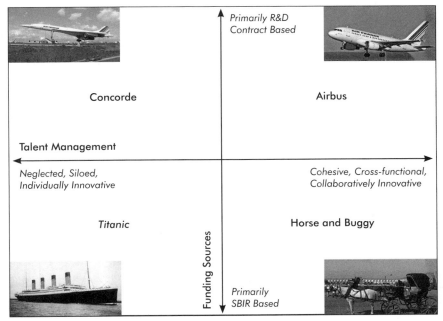

FIGURE **7.12**   Technology Corporation's Scenario Matrix

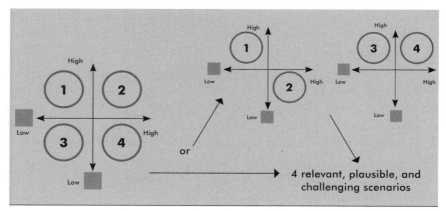

FIGURE **7.13**   Developing the Scenario Matrix Using Additional Critical Uncertainties

a coherent "set" of scenarios with a common theme. However, it is a mistake to sacrifice the validity of the scenarios (based on their being plausible, challenging, and relevant) to maintain the common theme. The priority is developing scenarios that are plausible, can challenge current thinking, and are relevant to managers' deepest concerns.

The Number of Scenarios to Use—Why Four?

There is debate about the number of scenarios that should be developed. One approach is never more than four, and some have suggested the optimal number is one status quo scenario, plus two genuine alternatives (Wack, 1984). The status quo scenario is used to get decision makers to take the bait. Then two genuine alternatives can be presented that deliver compelling stories of fundamentally different futures.

When two scenarios are used, there is a tendency among novice scenarists to have a "good" scenario and a "bad" scenario. When using three scenarios, the tendency is to fall into "best case," "worst case," and "status quo" thinking. Five scenarios are too many for decision makers to entertain. For years, Royal Dutch/Shell has used two scenarios. The key is to make sure the scenarios are distinctive and memorable.

In my experience, I have often found that four scenarios seem to be the optimal number and can help in avoiding some common thinking traps. This number is also a natural outcome of the 2 × 2 matrix approach. There is no clear rule here, and many successful documented projects have used two or three scenarios. No matter how many scenarios are used, attention must be paid to make sure these common mistakes are avoided. The best way to do this is to make sure that the scenarios do more than simply present different quantifications of obvious variables. They have to present a story line, laying out the "characters" and data to support their actions in the scenarios in a surprising or interesting way.

Using the "Official Future"

It can be useful to include a surprise-free status quo scenario, called the "official future" or the "consensus forecast." This scenario is an extension of the past into the future, and it holds little that is challenging or useful for decision making. The official future is a common feature of first attempts at scenario planning when executives are unable to leave behind their training to seek "the answer" and a reliance on forecasts and predictive approaches to strategy. The official future is a safe option and can be included when managers are presumed to have a difficult time adjusting to scenario thinking. This way, managers can see their forecasted scenario in the set of scenarios, and entertaining the other options is not quite as uncomfortable. The official future can be a bridge into the future and into the discipline of scenario thinking for those unfamiliar with it (Wack, 1984).

Technology Corporation Scenario Logics

The Technology Corporation scenarios are based on the deductive approach and feature four scenarios. Technology Corporation is based on a real scenario project (with some changes to conceal the identity of the organization). The scenario team reviewed all of the critical uncertainties, focusing on two that were particularly relevant. As noted, the team settled on using "talent management" and "funding sources" as their critical uncertainties for building the scenario matrix (see Figure 7.12, earlier).

An interesting unexpected outcome for Technology Corporation was the emerging awareness of extent to which the organization relied on its CEO. With no clear succession plans, the scenario team had discussed what would happen if the CEO suddenly became ill. Technology Corporation's CEO was in his second career after retirement and was getting to an age at which health problems are somewhat common. The point is that the scenario project provoked conversations that the organization did not previously have the capacity to have. Although the issue of the aging CEO was not selected as one of the items for building the scenario matrix, it is an example of a "character" that could appear in any of the scenarios, adding an interesting twist to the story. Figure 7.14 presents each of the four scenarios, capturing its essence with a photo and short description.

CONCORDE

Neglect of talent with significant wins in contract R&D

We're getting there, but success depends on the work of a few . . .

AIRBUS

Sincere collaboration and cross-disciplinary cohesion with significant wins in contract R&D

We're getting there and everybody is going with us!

HORSE AND BUGGY

Sincere collaboration, but continued reliance on SBIR funding exclusively

An archaic approach to progress

TITANIC

Individual success, silos, and continued reliance on SBIR funding exclusively

We're slowly heading precisely where we don't want to go . . .

FIGURE 7.14 Technology Corporation's Scenario Matrix

THE SCENARIO RESEARCH AGENDA

Before outlining and writing the scenario stories, further research must be conducted for each scenario logic. A practical way to accomplish this is to assign a member from the team to gather more information on the driving forces in each scenario. Or, if the team is large, it is effective to have subgroups work on each scenario. The goal is to share the workload and stimulate further inquiry into each set of variables that come together in the scenario. In a few meetings, the scenario planning team can talk about the features of each scenario logic and determine where further research is required. Then, individuals or subgroups can tackle each scenario, gather research on the driving forces, and begin thinking about plots. Groups should develop detailed responses to the following questions for each scenario (Schwartz, 1991):

- What are the driving forces?
- What do you feel is uncertain?
- What is inevitable?

The scenario team can be reconvened to discuss answers to these questions. Conversations get going and ideas start flowing. When the ideas are flowing naturally, it is good to take a break and let individuals reflect. After an overnight break, team members often return with excitement and scenario plots almost completely conceptualized (Schwartz, 1991).

PLOTS

Each scenario must have a plot. The general plot is outlined and defined before the story line is written. It is helpful to use subgroups of the scenario planning team to brainstorm plots and exchange ideas. Three common plots include "winners and losers," "challenge and response," and "evolution" (Schwartz, 1991).

- The "winners and losers" plot is based on the familiar story of a protagonist against an antagonist. The story involves a struggle, and only one character can "win." Therefore, the other character must "lose."
- In the "challenge and response" plot, a situation is presented in which the actions of a group and related consequences become the basis for

the story—for example, the current economic crisis and how companies can manage through times of layoffs, low growth, and declining stock value. A flu pandemic is another example of a challenge and response plot.

- "Evolution" plots involve slowly changing phenomena. Technology is the most common example of this kind of plot. Technological innovations start small with early adopters, and at some point, they explode and become mainstream. Being ahead of or behind the explosion can carry dramatic implications.

Here are five other plots that can be main plots or subplots within the three just described:

- *Revolution*—an unpredictable, dramatic change (e.g., natural disasters and political revolutions)
- *Cycles*—Economies often move in cycles of growth and decline. Investors who believe in economic cycles would suggest that the current economic crisis provides tremendous opportunity for those who can see them. Cities can behave similarly. Real estate investors base their careers on being able to anticipate high-growth sections of cities.
- *Infinite possibility*—This story line is based on a perception that a given force will continue to grow and expand, infinitely. Some stories about technology fit this plot—that technology will continue to improve the quality of our lives by making things easier. However, there is usually a counterplot or a dark side to stories based on infinite possibility.
- *Lone ranger*—The lone ranger plot features a hero confronting a corrupt system. The "underdog" and "David and Goliath" stories are other names for this plot. Apple Inc. is an example of the lone ranger plot—a small business gaining victories against the IBM corporate conglomerate (Schwartz, 1991).
- *My generation*—Some plots can effectively feature major social shifts that show up in the form of significant generational differences. For example, the generation known as the "Millennials" has a comfort with technology the world has never seen. In many scenarios, the values of this generation can provide an interesting twist, using technology as the driving force.

A quick online search of standard movie plots suggests many others that could be considered for scenario plots. Here is a sampling:

- Friendships (friendship, followed by separation, followed by reconciliation)
- Epic (a group or individual travels from A to B having adventures along the way)
- Heist (something must be stolen from an inaccessible place—the "impossible")
- Coming of age (a critical time of life, with some tragedy reshaping personalities)
- Do the right thing (the main character facing an ethical dilemma)

Don't Forget the Work Already Done

Plots should involve key factors and trends from the interviews, brainstorming, and ranking exercises. If managers can see their thinking and concerns from previous exercises in the stories, they are more likely to entertain the idea of the scenario. Certainly, there were more than two critical uncertainties than the two chosen for Technology Corporation's scenario matrix. Other forces in the high impact–high uncertainty category should appear in the scenarios that can provide interesting twists. The challenge is developing plot lines that integrate dynamics, present them in an interesting way, and summarize the information effectively. Using standard movie plots, classic stories, and time-tested literary hooks are helpful ways of building a compelling set of scenarios.

You can begin by considering the newspaper headlines that might appear in each scenario (Flowers, 2003). Using newspaper headlines, the team can create a simple time line with three major events occurring every five years for each scenario. The template provided in Figure 7.15 is designed to help flesh out the major events in each scenario simply by using bullet points for each five-year block.

TITLES

The scenario titles are critical. Recent brain research suggests that people remember things more easily if there is an associated image so that the idea can somehow be related to a past experience (Dispenza, 2007).

5-Year Block	Event Event Event
5-Year Block	Event Event Event

FIGURE 7.15 Template for Scenario Plot Construction

Quick—what are the four scenario outlines for Technology Corporation? You probably remember the images of airplanes, the *Titanic*, and a horse and buggy—these are memory cues for the titles and content of each scenario. Another example is a set of scenarios using the titles of Beatles songs: "A Hard Day's Night," "Help," "Magical Mystery Tour," and "Imagine" (Ogilvy & Schwartz, 1998). One can easily see how these titles represent four different perspectives (even stories), having read nothing but the titles. One set of scenarios I worked on recently used board games to represent each scenario (Monopoly, Slip N' Slide, Scrabble, and Go Fish). Be creative and use intuition in generating titles that are recognizable and convey the essence of each scenario.

Naming scenarios also has to do with branding and providing names that conjure up the gestalt of the scenarios will make them memorable. The name provides a sort of mental Velcro for the members of the organization. The chosen names provide an easy way to talk about the different worlds that may confront the organization and its decision makers. It is therefore appropriate to have the images drawn from a family of images.

WRITING THE SCENARIO STORIES

Once the scenario logics have been constructed and the basic plots of four scenarios have been defined, each subgroup should ask an individual to write the detailed scenario story. Again, it is extremely important to use the key factors and trends identified in the previous workshops. Using these forces and trends gives the set of scenarios relevance and ensures that they address the things that are on the minds of managers.

Whereas brainstorming the general events of each scenario and plot development is best done in groups, writing the scenario details is best done as an individual activity. Some general strategies for scenario writing include the following:

- Assign each scenario to an individual.
- Assign each scenario to a pair of authors—one as the writer, and one as a veteran of the organization.
- Assign each scenario to an individual with access to an experienced scenario writer/editor.
- Assign all scenario writing to one individual (usually a talented writer) (Ogilvy & Schwartz, 1998).

All four are useful strategies, but the one chosen will depend on the situation, how many people are involved, and the knowledge capital within the group.

As the time line emerges, the major events that correspond to each scenario become clear, and further details can be filled in. Creative writing skills are an asset in this part of scenario planning, and many organizations seek writing expertise at this stage. I have found it useful to write two versions of the story for each scenario. The first is in the third person, laying out the facts of the scenario. This version helps to get the facts straight and reveals any holes or weaknesses in the plot. The second is a narrative, in the first person, and describes the scenario from its horizon year, looking back over what has happened throughout the scenario. Inevitably, the first-person narrative is more memorable, drawing on the reader's empathy more immediately.

Here are five more tips for writing scenarios:

- Give each story a beginning, middle, and end.
- Some elements should remain constant—not everything changes.
- Use characters in the scenarios. Inflation levels may be the villain, and policy options may be the hero. Build tension between the characters as the story unfolds. Present dilemmas, solve dilemmas, or provide twists.
- Include dramas and conflicts in the stories.

- Use present verb tenses—no "might haves" or "could haves" (Wilson & Ralston, 2006).

Decision makers must be involved in the scenario-writing process. Their involvement indicates the sense of ownership they will have for the scenarios. In other words, if decision makers don't participate in the scenario writing, they may be detached from the scenarios that are produced. Scenario planning is a participative process in which the decision makers create scenarios that challenge internal thinking. Thus, making the scenarios relevant is directly related to involving the people who will use them in their development.

TECHNOLOGY CORPORATION'S SCENARIOS

The following sections describe more fully the four scenarios introduced earlier (see Figure 7.14).

Concorde Scenario

World oil supplies remain sufficient, but prices fluctuate, making sustained investments in alternative solutions risky. During a new U.S. presidential administration, 50 percent of Small Business Innovative Research (SBIR) funding was redirected to national laboratories. Technology Corporation research had successfully won a few grants, all related to energy research.

Except for its Technology Corporation Water affiliate, Technology Corporation has experienced only sporadic and limited success with commercializing its own intellectual property. However, bolstered by several recent successful energy-related pilot plant rollouts through its other affiliate, Continental Technologies, Technology Corporation successfully recruits two world-renowned energy research scientists to join the organization.

World oil prices begin to stabilize at a relatively high level, sparking renewed pressure for alternative energy research. Technology Corporation's reputation in energy research has grown as its two world-renowned energy research scientists have enabled research partnerships with a national laboratory and a major research university. These partnerships are lucrative but create an emphasis on research to the detriment of development; as a result, Technology Corporation hires more energy-related scientists while engineering and other areas suffer due to a lack of funding and little interest by the prestigious scientists.

Technology Corporation's water patents expire, and although it retains a substantial market penetration, profit margins substantially decline due to competition from reverse-engineered products; it is soon sold. Because of the lucrative energy research partnerships, pressure to sustain that portion of the enterprise increases, and Technology Corporation's energy research emphasis dramatically increases, too. However, its engineering/development capacity has been severely hampered due to the lack of collaboration from the scientists.

Unable to turn Technology Corporation into the entrepreneurial enterprise originally envisioned, its owner decides to sell; a group of senior scientists buys. A funneling effect over the past twenty years has transformed Technology Corporation into a contracted, narrowly focused, world-class, energy research laboratory working with national laboratories, universities, and industry. However, the owning coalition of brilliant but egotistical scientists makes for a dysfunctional siloed organization, with each division operating as functionally separate enterprises. Eventually, the discord leads to a "brain drain" as scientists leave or are recruited to more stable environments. Ultimately, an entrepreneurial applied scientist and a like-minded engineer buy Technology Corporation with the intention of reintroducing, and capitalizing on, the "D" side of R&D.

Airbus Scenario

Technology Corporation continues working in its SBIR-focused model, but it increases R&D contract funding as the economy recovers from a recession. The contracts draw revenue from large and small companies. A focus on green technology emerges from a new presidential administration influencing a positive reception from market prospects and new clients. For example, a fundamental shift in the transportation field sparks new business contracts. Technology Corporation secures an R&D contract with a major U.S. automotive manufacturer to develop alternative transportation technology. Technology Corporation gains a strong reputation in the high-tech research and development industry. A large proprietary foundation takes interest in a partnership with Technology Corporation due to new high-profile contracts.

The president is reelected, and funding increases for energy innovation. The organizational vision and goals are aligned to take advantage of the opportunity. Technology Corporation is able to recruit top talent and maintain its innovative employees at a 98 percent retention rate. Technology Corporation's success has enabled the company to expand the Human Resources and Development (HRD) department to effectively manage their talent pool. The HRD department builds a comprehensive program to support a collaborative and innovative culture. The plan includes mentoring, offering incentives for innovation, and promoting cross-functional teamwork. Technology Corporation invests in new laboratory equipment and an electronic knowledge management system. The organization is able to reduce its fifteen-year turnaround for innovations to ten years from conception to market. Because of the looming 2016 election, Technology Corporation guards against threats of SBIR funding cuts by securing primarily R&D contracts.

Technology Corporation has shifted its business model to be primarily weighted on R&D contracts. The shift is successful although SBIR funding has been maintained. Technology Corporation steers away from the competition with revenue from new R&D contracts and bringing intellectual property to market. The company hires a mix of engineers, scientists, and business development employees and executives. The retention rate continues to hold stable.

The demand for clean coal and other green technologies improves, which stimulates new R&D contracts with automotive companies and firms in two new markets. The diversification in new markets pays off.

The proprietary foundation continues to fund Technology Corporation, which impacts the organization twofold: Technology Corporation gains recognition and success, and other R&D contracts spark from the publicity and reputation.

The HRD change is integrated into the culture, and the innovation turnaround is reduced to five years from conception to market. Top industry competitors were not prepared for the cut of SBIR funding and fold or merge.

Technology Corporation expands with a significant increase in new hires. The Technology Corporation culture embraces a collaborative and innovative philosophy and practice reflecting HRD success. There is continual demand for clean coal and other green technologies, sparking continual new and returning business. Technology Corporation Water becomes a market leader in water technologies. The company accomplishes a two-year innovation turnaround.

Horse-and-Buggy Scenario

It was a turbulent year, with a significant stock market falter in October followed closely by the demise of numerous financial institutions and the uncertainties of a newly elected Democratic administration. The current administration scrambles to address eight years of initiatives ranging from public school reform to the ongoing wars in Iraq and Afghanistan, all while negotiating a $700 billion bail-out package for the spiraling financial industry. Throughout national uncertainty, Technology Corporation remains focused on developing and promoting numerous technologies funded primarily through the SBIR program, which is renewed by the 111th Congress. Not only is the SBIR program renewed, but as part of the president's job stimulus package, the funding is increased 25 percent over the current rate in an effort to promote new technologies that will aid in the research and development of alternative transportation fuels.

The increase spurs a fresh level of interest among the current SBIR companies and attracts the attention of new entrants into the market. With over twenty-five years of experience working within the SBIR community, Technology Corporation is well positioned to take advantage of the opportunities as long as it can maintain the balance between the more risky contract R&D and manufacturing businesses it has developed. Because Technology Corporation's product is essentially intellectual property, the firm's success lies in the development of its human resources, knowledge management, and the alignment of its talent with the appropriate technological demand. By 2013, Technology Corporation has become known as the best R&D organization by developing a network of highly intellectual individuals who operate as a collaborative, cohesive team. It is able to recruit the best talent due to its reputation as the "Google" or "Apple" of high-tech research and development. Technology Corporation's research and development facilities are outfitted with the latest equipment, allowing research scientists and engineers to take a technology from conception to prototype with amazing accuracy, speed, and ability to replicate experiments and confirm hypotheses through a network of highly skilled individuals. One of the secrets behind the success lies within the company's talent management systems known as "E-Knows," which comprises not only in-house personnel but also contract agreements with other scientists around the country who have been "catalogued" using its extensive profiling systems. Prior to or during a project,

E-Knows can help determine resources that may be able to contribute a solution and be contacted immediately via secure communication. The success of E-Knows lies not only in the extensive knowledge database but also in a culture that knows what it does not know. The ability to manage knowledge while promoting creativity, innovation, entrepreneurialism, and flexibility have become the "Technology Corporation Way."

Over the next five years, the Technology Corporation Way is inculcated throughout the organization, and the firm's ability to execute to the highest of standards has become intuitive. The past eight years have been a roller coaster ride for the country as the economic slump followed by slow recovery and an overuse of bail-outs has resulted in numerous bankrupt companies with little to show for the promises of "reorganization" or control through regulation. The national debt has eclipsed $17 trillion, and the pressure to cut government spending is strong. The average American has lowered his or her debt by 30 percent over the past ten years, and savings are on the rise. The general perception among the public is that the government should listen to its own advice: "Quit spending what you don't have."

With most of the baby boomers in retirement, the strain on health care has become the "hot button" for certain generations, while the $6 gallon of gasoline has remained the "pulse check" for the working class. The Middle East continues to require attention and resources but is more stable than during the past two decades. Technology Corporation has numerous technologies ready for Phase III with potential clients interested in partnerships. It is managing over two thousand projects funded by SBIR and a few contract R&D projects. The staff of 175 scientists and engineers, with an average tenure of ten years, is proud of its accomplishments but also realizes that change is in the air. The success rates of receiving SBIR funding have continued to drop from 50 percent to 15 percent over the past year, and the chatter regarding new avenues for technologies seems to be less.

While the funding for any new SBIR projects was removed in late 2016 from the federal government's budget, the awarded contracts are still being funded. Anticipating this change, Technology Corporation was able to contact many of the SBIR companies and acquire their research awards, which resulted in enough R&D to not only support its 175 scientists and engineers but increased its resources through short-term contract agreements as well. The addition of these new resources grew their E-Knows database 150 percent.

The world of research and development has finally learned how to cross the "valley of death" by enhancing the ability to manage knowledge while promoting creativity, innovation, and entrepreneurialism through continuous improvement and collaboration.

Titanic *Scenario*

SBIR continues to be the bread and butter of the company. As a result of the recession, SBIR funding continues to decline, and contract R&D has a limited duration for specific projects. Although Technology Corporation prefers long-term, multiple-year contracts, companies are wary of commitment. Few incentives are offered for cross-functional teams' performance. Consequently, there is a lack of idea sharing and collaboration.

The current administration makes changes in public policy and decides to fund a particular type of research. However, Technology Corporation has been misaligned and spread thin with so many other projects; therefore, it is not prepared to act. Technology Corporation continues to invest in clean coal.

In an attempt to steer away from relying on venture capitalism and due to the inability to identify a select group of business partners, SBIR remains the major funding source. For fear that SBIR might not be reauthorized and that Technology Corporation might not be able to compete for the limited funding, some scientists leave the company. The remaining "brainpower" is content with the knowledge they have. Only one-third of the employees are willing to participate in job rotations and, consequently, do not learn about research strategies for other areas of the firm.

Furthermore, the remaining Technology Corporation employees are not prepared to fill the research void from the scientists who left due to the organizational silos and a limited focus on succession planning. As a result, Technology Corporation's R&D contracts continue to decrease.

News flash! The EPA standards on clean coal are not as stringent as in the last five years. There is increased interest in funding R&D related to clean coal technology. Technology Corporation has an opportunity to partner with another company. In the past, the "old" Technology Corporation did some partnering and licensed technology but got burned by it, so the firm is cautious. This partner has been successful in getting venture capital. Unfortunately, the partner has an existing lawsuit that has not been settled, so this challenge delays the contract. The venture capitalist pulls out. The competition capitalizes on clean coal technology.

Meanwhile, a firm in Turkey that specializes in a water treatment technology wants to relocate its production facilities to the northeastern United States. Technology Corporation has the equipment, and the company buys Technology Corporation Water. There are increased regulatory requirements, and the electrowinner—one of Technology Corporation's top projects—is a potential source of income, if it is marketed, but the technology is sold prematurely.

The economy is in slow recovery. SBIR is reinstated; however, there is a decrease in the amount of funding. One measure to alleviate fears about the limited funding is to freeze hiring for a while. There is an increased urgency to find funding sources, but the cross-functional teams, once created to help anticipate the needs of the market, are weak. Unfortunately, employee morale is low; the employees work alone and rarely collaborate. Technology Corporation's reputation is that it has feelers in too many areas to be effective.

Technology Corporation has developed two new technologies that help solve pressing environmental issues. However, due to the lack of business development expertise and market timing, Technology Corporation sells the technologies too soon. It loses most nonfederal contracts that helped fund the bottom line and increased its expertise.

A market-minded employee, who previously left Technology Corporation, misses living in the western United States. The former employee has a proven track record in partnering with large firms. The president of the company wants to rehire this employee, hoping to ignite some entrepreneurial spirit. There is talk of bonuses for teams that innovate. The president tries to sell the idea, but Technology Corporation's staff loudly protests the hire and threatens to leave. The president concedes.

Biotechnology R&Ds are being funded. Previous partners with Technology Corporation, which were hurt by the recession, are now obtaining venture capital related to biotechnology. They want Technology Corporation to contract with them since it has had a great reputation, but there is not time for Technology Corporation to hire needed expertise. Employees take a significant pay decrease in order to help Technology Corporation's cash flow. The president retires and another firm hires a majority of the remaining scientists and engineers of Technology Corporation.

CRITERIA FOR ASSESSING THE UTILITY OF THE SCENARIOS

As mentioned earlier, scenarios must be relevant, challenging, and plausible in order to be useful tools for managers (Kahane, 2004; Ringland, 2002; Schwartz, 1991; van der Heijden, 1997, 2005a; van der Merwe, 2007).

- *Relevant*—Scenarios must be relevant to the managers who use them. Three clear strategies for creating relevance are to include interview data in the scenarios, include a variety of forces from the brainstorming and ranking exercises, and involve mangers in the scenario writing process.
- *Challenging*—Scenarios must stretch the thinking inside the organization (Wack, 1985b). This means they must organize and present variables in surprising ways. Scenarios must challenge the assumptions inside the minds of managers. Challenging scenarios come from well-executed external and internal analyses, and a thorough understanding of the forces at play.
- *Plausible*—Plausible scenarios are scenarios that might actually happen. If scenarios are too challenging or not well researched, they are in danger of being dismissed on the basis of being implausible. On the other hand, one of the true crafts of scenario planning is to bring things that seem implausible into the realm of the plausible (N. Collyns, personal communication, November 20, 2009). The term *plausibility* sometimes carries a link to *probability*, which is the certain death of any scenario project. Using this criterion requires attention to ensuring that the term is interpreted more as "possible," rather than "probable."

These three criteria are a result of the scenario experiments over approximately thirty years at Shell and the scenario planning pioneers who spent time there. It is important to ask the scenario planning team to consider the extent to which each of the scenarios satisfies these criteria before moving ahead. If the situation is conducive, it can also be beneficial to pilot-test the scenarios with a group of managers. Satisfying these three criteria creates a kind of face validity for the scenarios and increases the likelihood they will be useful in provoking managers' insights.

The three criteria are highly interdependent. For example, the more plausible or realistic a scenario is, the more relevant it will usually be for managers. Likewise, the more challenging a scenario is, the more it runs the risk of losing plausibility. The key is to strike a balance among these criteria so that they can be used as a quick estimate of the scenario's potential utility.

Wack (1985a) wrote that scenarios require a component of rigorous research that is frequently missed. It is not enough to simply think creatively and produce a fun set of scenarios. Many scenario exercises fail to gather the necessary data to support the options and events they present. Significant detailed research is a key characteristic of effective scenarios.

A More Comprehensive Assessment

Six critical skills for the next decade of knowledge workers are described in Daniel Pink's (2006) book *A Whole New Mind*:

- Design
- Story
- Symphony
- Empathy
- Play
- Meaning

Referred to as "senses," these skills can be part of a unique approach to assessing scenarios.

Design

Developed countries are experiencing an age of material abundance. This means that consumers in developed countries are not limited in their choices. Now, more than ever, people can choose goods based on their preferences. People are attracted to things that are aesthetically pleasing.

The design of a set of scenarios is critical. Scenarios must incorporate themes such as songs by the Beatles (Ogilvy & Schwartz, 1998), catchy phrases that are easy to recall, and colorful images to make the set of scenarios visually pleasing. People need to want to read the scenarios, and the document itself is often the first contact some will have with the ideas that they carry.

Increasingly, how scenarios are distributed also matters. Technology (be it video, podcasting, narrated slides with photos, interactive websites, etc.) allows for great creativity in design and should be leveraged when finishing up a set of scenarios.

Story

People can remember information more easily if it is presented in the form of a story (Manning, 2002). From the studies at Xerox concerning the exchange of expertise through repair stories in small "knowledge management" teams to the shifting of organizational strategy at 3M from bulleted, logic-based lists of action items to stories (Shaw, Brown, & Bromiley, 1998), it is clear that some organizations are harnessing the natural tendency of the human brain to think in story format.

Most primitive, preindustrial cultures featured stories as a means for transferring history and critical knowledge. Native American tribes and South African Ubuntu tribes are but two examples. Storytelling is also a growing component of big business. From scriptwriters in Hollywood to descriptions of homes for sale in real estate ads and vineyard lore on wine bottles, story elements are now being used to do what they do best: influence and strike an emotional chord. Cutting-edge research at Columbia University Medical School called the "narrative medicine movement" suggests that the ability to understand patient stories plays an important role in diagnosis, treatment, and a whole-minded approach to healing (Charon, 2001). Thus, the contexts in which stories are effective seem almost endless.

Obviously, scenarios tell stories. Stories are the foundation of scenarios and scenario planning. Each scenario must contain an interesting plot that captures reader attention and contains tension that is ultimately resolved. The story criterion is the logical location of the three criteria discussed earlier: relevant, challenging, and plausible.

Symphony

Symphony is simply another word for systems thinking. To illustrate how symphonic thinking will be important for knowledge workers in the future, consider the need for people who can straddle cultures. For example, as more jobs are sent to India, there is an increasing demand for "people who can manage the relationships between the coders in the East and the clients in the West. These whole-minded professionals must be literate in two cultures, comfortable in the hard science of computing and the soft science of sales and marketing" (Pink, 2006, pp. 135–136).

Using the symphony criterion means checking that each scenario contains a "system" of interacting events, characters, and interactions. Each scenario must form a logical whole in which the various elements and their relationships can be seen. Using systems diagrams as part of the scenario construction process is one way to enhance the symphony criterion (Ward & Scheifer, 1998). Scenarios must also integrate numerous variables in their stories and present them in a novel way. Systems thinking is considered a cornerstone of scenario planning. The ability to see interrelated forces and integrate patterns that drive events can lead to compelling presentations in the scenario stories.

Empathy

Empathy is the ability to put yourself in someone else's shoes. As a result, high-value work will be unique, heartfelt, and based in communicating things that are difficult to describe with a removed sense of logic.

The ability to provoke empathy is one key to effective scenario planning. When scenario planning participants suspend disbelief and seriously consider the options presented in the scenarios, they begin to develop empathy for each other and for the complexity of the system in which they are operating. Facilitators must also be able to empathize with participants in order to make the scenarios compelling. The ability to empathize with managers and incorporate elements of concern from their initial interviews is one key to making the scenarios useful.

Play

Play is an increasingly fundamental part of important work in all kinds of organizations. A playful attitude is often an indicator of a creative personality (Csikszentmihalyi, 1996). The role of a playful attitude has been suggested as a business skill, leading to high emotional intelligence with many favorable side effects in the coming conceptual age.

The set of scenarios, and each scenario individually, must create a world in which managers can "play." One particularly effective strategy I have used is to create physical spaces or rooms that feature the qualities of each scenario. By putting decision makers into a physical space, the natural inclination to play can be enhanced. Drawing on experiential and constructionist learning theory, using physical spaces that reflect each story makes it easier for managers to suspend disbelief. Awakening the imagination can be a time-consuming process; and while the business world continues to move faster and faster, innovative ideas are often found by slowing down, stepping

away, changing the location, and allowing time to reflect (Csikszentmihalyi, 1998).

Meaning

People in developed countries are searching for more satisfying, meaningful
work and lives. Pink (2006) cited dissatisfaction with current global politics
(Koenig, 2001), research in current corporate environments in which spirituality is growing (Karlgaard, 2004), and the rising popularity of activities
like meditation as evidence that people seek meaningful, fulfilling occupa-
tions and lives.

Scenarios provide a forum for awakening creativity and innovative
thinking in the individuals who use them. Cases from companies that have
used scenarios (Ringland, 2002) suggest that scenarios, and the scenario
planning process itself, encourage organization members to take ownership
of ideas and processes. In some ways, creating a feeling of ownership signals
a sense of increased meaning (Csikszentmihalyi, 1998). More specifically,
each individual scenario portrays the future in a fundamentally different
way, allowing users to interpret the meaning of a given set of variables or
issues, and how they play out in the future in a variety of different ways.
Scenarios provide a scaffolding for making meaning out of a complex set of
forces and how they interact to form a unique future (Chermack & van der
Merwe, 2003).

THE SCENARIO QUALITY ASSESSMENT CHECKLIST

Using the senses as criteria for assessing scenarios results in a framework
that is easy to apply. Figure 7.16 presents the Scenario Quality Assessment
Checklist and illustrates the use of the senses as scenario assessment criteria.
Useful questions intended to prompt the judgment of the scenario team for
each criterion are provided.

Figure 7.17 is an example of using the Scenario Quality Assessment
Checklist for the Technology Corporation scenarios. The six senses are applied as snapshot indicators of criteria for compelling scenarios.

COMMUNICATING THE SCENARIOS

When the scenario planning team has settled on a set of scenarios believed
to be high in quality and utility, they must be communicated throughout

	Scenario A	Scenario B	Scenario C	Scenario D
Design Are the scenario titles clever and easy to remember? Is the presentation of the scenario workbook attractive and aesthetically pleasing?				
Story Is each scenario story *relevant*, *challenging*, and *plausible* to the intended audience? Is the story presented in each scenario compelling and interesting?				
Symphony Does each scenario present a consistent world in which the various elements relate? Does each scenario describe integrated events that can be presented as a whole?				
Empathy Do the scenarios evoke empathy? Are the characters and events in each scenario easy for managers to relate to, and do they draw on real issues?				
Play Does each scenario provide the background for managers to experiment with varying ideas? Does each scenario lend itself to creativity in answering the "what if" questions?				
Meaning Does each scenario provide a forum in which a management team can derive and create meaning? Do the scenarios incorporate events that are meaningful?				

FIGURE **7.16** The Scenario Quality Assessment Checklist

	Airbus	Concorde	Horse and Buggy	Titanic
Design Are the scenario titles clever and easy to remember? Is the presentation of the scenario workbook attractive and aesthetically pleasing?	Yes	Yes	Yes	Yes
Story Is each scenario story *relevant*, *challenging*, and *plausible* to the intended audience? Is the story presented in each scenario compelling and interesting?	Yes	Yes— but story needs more work	Yes	Yes
Symphony Does each scenario present a consistent world in which the various elements relate? Does each scenario describe integrated events that can be presented as a whole?	Yes	Yes	Needs more detail, fact, research— internal consistency is lacking	Yes
Empathy Do the scenarios evoke empathy? Are the characters and events in each scenario easy for managers to relate to, and do they draw on real issues?	No— revisit	No— revisit	Yes—good illustration of what happens when few people work hard and lead the organization	Yes
Play Does each scenario provide the background for managers to experiment with varying ideas? Does each scenario lend itself to creativity in answering the "what if" questions?	Fairly pre-scriptive as written—not a lot of room for creativity and play; open this one up more	OK	OK	OK
Meaning Does each scenario provide a forum in which a management team can derive and create mean-ing? Do the scenarios incorpor-ate events that are meaningful?	OK—could be improved	Good	OK	Good

FIGURE **7.17** The Scenario Quality Assessment Checklist—Technology Corporation the organization. Usually, the set of scenarios is captured in a document, but a document is not enough. The work of the scenario planning team is really only beginning. The use of websites, videos, and other technologies to disseminate and communicate scenarios is becoming common. The most successful scenario planners use multiple methods to communicate their ideas. Short but compelling presentations followed by extensive dialogue sessions were the preferred tools used by early scenario planning pioneers. Common techniques for communicating scenarios include these:

- Videos
- Websites
- Documents (workbook)
- Role-playing activities
- Audiotapes/podcasts
- Presentations
- Workshops

Disseminating the scenarios has two key components. The first is communicating the scenarios throughout the organization. The second is using the scenarios in a purposeful way to examine the initial issue, test the business idea, and explore other aspects of the organization in each of the alternative futures. The latter component is covered in detail in Chapter 9—the scenario consideration phase. Before moving into the consideration phase, decision makers should consider advantages of communicating the scenarios more generally, throughout the organization.

There are different strategies for accomplishing this, and some decision makers may have reason to avoid distributing the scenarios organization-wide. For example, scenarios may be built for a strategic business unit and may not be relevant across the organization. Again, the context should be the guide for how widely to communicate the scenarios. At a minimum, decision makers should distribute the scenarios to the people who were involved in their development, and follow up with an invitation to a forum in which they can ask questions and join the conversation.

A recent project I worked on featured a unique way of communicating the scenarios. The strategy generated excitement and buy-in. When the decision makers had finalized a set of scenarios they deemed high utility, they invited particular individuals to a meeting. These individuals were known for their positions as informal leaders and were well liked. They were also individuals known as key social information brokers throughout the organization. In the meeting, the scenarios were presented in concept and with just enough detail to whet their appetites. In the days and weeks after the meeting, these individuals could not help but tell their colleagues about the scenarios, and positive rumors spread quickly. Within a few weeks, an excitement and desire to know more about the scenarios had caught on like wildfire and spread rapidly throughout the organization. The decision makers created a mystique around the scenarios that compelled members of the organization to want to know more. The scenarios were then rolled out organization-wide in a series of meetings in various departments, locations, and branches. While perhaps somewhat manipulative, the effects of this strategy paid off, and the scenarios were well received, popular, embraced, and *used*.

However they are distributed, the scenarios must be used purposefully to explore the original question and beyond. If the project simply ends with the dissemination of the scenarios, the project will fail. Activities for using scenarios to explore the original question and purpose are presented in Chapter 9 on the scenario consideration phase. It is wise to dedicate significant resources in developing a strategy for implementing and using the scenarios. How scenarios are used is the crux of scenario planning.

Constructing and presenting the scenarios should be fun. Most of us are taught to stop being creative around grade 3. It is amazing how fast creativity skills return, and participants should be encouraged to let their creative insights flow. The point is, "If you're not having fun, you're not doing it right" (Ogilvy & Schwartz, 1998, p. 19).

CONCLUSION

This chapter has presented the activities and workshops used to construct scenarios. In addition, this chapter has suggested tools for writing scenarios including additional research, team structure, plots, time lines, titles, and others. A sample set of scenarios for Technology Corporation has also been provided. Finally, this chapter has described a comprehensive set of assessment criteria for increasing the scenarios' effectiveness and the likelihood they will shift the thinking inside the organization.

This phase of the scenario system is lengthy and requires a great deal of work. The goal of this phase is to have developed four scenarios that are deemed high quality and high utility. The scenarios can then be disseminated as the context suggests and used for the specific purposes described in the next chapter.

Phase 4—Scenario Implementation: Putting Scenarios to Use

Chapter 7 presented the tools and processes for constructing scenarios. This chapter describes how to use the scenarios to accomplish the objectives of the project—the scenario implementation phase (Figure 8.1). In other words, this chapter describes how to use the scenarios once they have been developed. Common general objectives are to provoke strategic insights, expand the assumptions of decision makers, and develop the capacity to see major discontinuities before it's too late. However, the specific objectives that were defined in the project preparation phase drive the scenario implementation phase of the project. This chapter explains how to design a set of workshops for using the scenarios to assess the organization in a variety of alternative futures.

This phase involves returning to the original question or issue and using the scenarios to develop multiple ways of answering the question and addressing the issue. These strategies include using the scenarios to examine the initial question, test the current theory of the business/business idea, analyze current strategies, and develop strategic resilience and robustness. However, the toolbox for using scenarios can be quite extensive. Several methods are available for facilitating change and communicating the content of the scenario in participatory and creative ways. The discipline of organization development specializes in a variety of activities and change interventions that can be used in the presentation and consideration of scenarios. A short list of change models that may be useful in the scenario implementation phase is as follows:

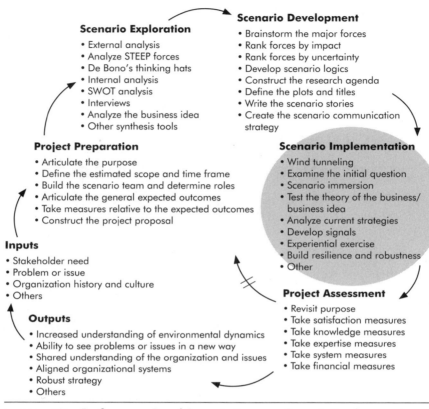

Scenario Exploration

- External analysis
- Analyze STEEP forces
- De Bono's thinking hats
- Internal analysis
- SWOT analysis
- Interviews
- Analyze the business idea
- Other synthesis tools

Scenario Development

- Brainstorm the major forces
- Rank forces by impact
- Rank forces by uncertainty
- Develop scenario logics
- Construct the research agenda
- Define the plots and titles
- Write the scenario stories
- Create the scenario communication strategy

Project Preparation

- Articulate the purpose
- Define the estimated scope and time frame
- Build the scenario team and determine roles
- Articulate the general expected outcomes
- Take measures relative to the expected outcomes
- Construct the project proposal

Scenario Implementation

- Wind tunneling
- Examine the initial question
- Scenario immersion
- Test the theory of the business/ business idea
- Analyze current strategies
- Develop signals
- Experiential exercise
- Build resilience and robustness
- Other

Inputs

- Stakeholder need
- Problem or issue
- Organization history and culture
- Others

Project Assessment

- Revisit purpose
- Take satisfaction measures
- Take knowledge measures
- Take expertise measures
- Take system measures
- Take financial measures

Outputs

- Increased understanding of environmental dynamics
- Ability to see problems or issues in a new way
- Shared understanding of the organization and issues
- Aligned organizational systems
- Robust strategy
- Others

FIGURE 8.1   Performance-Based Scenario System—Scenario Implementation Phase

- Lewin's force field analysis
- Nominal group technique
- Team building
- Value voting
- Simulations
- Visioning

All of these approaches to change management can be useful in considering the implications of scenarios, and all of them can be incorporated into workshops using scenarios to leverage change in organizations. The critical tip for focusing scenario use, however, is that the initial issue must drive any method. This approach will keep the project from slipping onto other issues.

Each scenario planning project is a customized learning project. Therefore, there are few specific outcomes that will be common to all scenario projects. Returning to the original purpose, issue, or question, and looking at the business model in each scenario are critical requirements of nearly all scenario projects. The suggestions in this chapter are a framework aimed at getting the most out of scenarios. Experienced change consultants may want to add to and modify the workshops listed here and create other ways of using scenarios. The goal is to make sure the scenarios are used to think critically about various aspects of the organization. Scenario use is intended to shift the thinking inside the organization, so the fun and creativity that emerge in developing scenarios should be carried through into the scenario implementation phase.

Scenarios must be presented to participants in ways that provoke learning that leads to strategic insight. Many participants will have insights and communication breakthroughs during some of the scenario construction workshops described in the previous chapter. Research shows that a great deal of learning happens throughout the scenario construction and implementation phases (Chermack, Lynham, & van der Merwe, 2006; Chermack & van der Merwe, 2003). Thus, the likelihood of provoking strategic insights increases by involving people in the whole scenario planning system. This is another argument for deductive scenario building.

USING SCENARIOS PURPOSEFULLY

Roger Penrose (2004), a professor of mathematics at Oxford, wrote that when two people successfully communicate, the words most often used are "Oh, I see!" A logical question is "What is it that is seen?" What is the substance of a strategic insight (frequently called an "aha" moment)? This ability to see anew or to develop joint understanding via conversation and dialogue is a key intention of most scenario projects.

The specific activities using scenarios to build toward achieving this sense of sight are the focus of this chapter. Revisiting the initial problem and question begins the process of developing insights and creates a basis for the strategic conversation described by van der Heijden (1997, 2005a). The most critical strategic learning happens from the synthesis of using scenarios to examine strategic issues and various aspects of the organization.

WIND TUNNELING

The basic idea behind scenario implementation is the concept of wind tunneling. Wind tunneling first appeared in aerodynamics research to test airplanes and simulate the environment of free flight. Eventually, wind tunnels were used to test buildings and automobiles and examine a variety of structural properties. The concept is the same with scenarios. Scenarios function as conceptual wind tunnels in which to measure a variety of organizational characteristics.

This book—and many others—have highlighted the high degree of change in the external environment, describing things as turbulent. Turbulence occurs when there are sudden changes in the environment and the structural properties of objects begin to show their inadequacies. The objects can be airplane wings in aerodynamic wind tunnels, or organizations in conceptual wind tunnels. Either way, turbulence is an environmental characteristic that puts stress on the object in question, be it an airplane or an organization. Usually, pilots change altitude—they seek a different environment. Because such an option is not readily available for organizational decision makers, they are forced to think about how to build an organization that can withstand the stresses imposed on it. Scenarios are tools for building such a resilient organization.

Scenarios create a way to analyze the organization in a variety of conditions. Remember that a basic premise of scenario planning is that the environment changes too rapidly for most strategic planning models to be useful. Scenario planning is built on the assumption that the environment changes constantly. By building uncertainty into the environment as a basic structural feature, scenarios vary the environment in which the organization is operating. Learning scenarios are specifically used to present a range of possible external contextual conditions (Wack, 1984). With scenarios serving as varying contextual conditions, critical aspects of the organization are examined carefully.

> Scenarios represent the different future conditions within which the strategy, business model or other decisions must fit. Wind tunneling is used to test decisions for robustness and for exposing opportunities and risks. An important additional benefit of wind tunneling is that the leadership engaged in wind tunneling are continually adjusting their assumptions as they enter the different worlds described in each scenario.

As leaders check their decisions or business models in the various scenarios they are often required to adjust their thinking based on evidence of flawed assumptions. This process is filled with critical learning opportunities in the scenario-based strategy framework, and draws highly on constructivist learning principles (for a detailed description of the cognitive processes at work in scenario planning and wind-tunneling, see Chermack & van der Merwe, 2003). (van der Merwe, 2008, p. 233)

Each of the suggested workshops in this chapter are variations on the wind tunneling implementation strategy. To clarify, the workshops described here are all based on throwing ideas, strategies, plans, questions, and projects into the scenarios, asking questions, and finding out what more can be learned.

OVERVIEW OF THE SCENARIO IMPLEMENTATION WORKSHOPS

Like the scenario development phase, a series of workshops must be designed to use the scenarios and maximize their benefit. This chapter presents five recommended workshops for using scenarios, with the following focuses:

- Examining the initial question
- Testing the theory of the business/business idea
- Analyzing current strategies
- Developing "signals"
- Creating an experiential learning exercise

The first two workshops should be required; the others are optional. Again, experienced consultants may want to integrate scenarios into other processes with which they are familiar.

Examining the Initial Question—Workshop 1

The first step in putting the scenarios to use is to return to the initial purpose, problem, and question. After all, the priority of the project is to develop a variety of different ways to explore the problem and answer the question. This workshop can be informal and needs only to bring the team and decision makers back together in a room suitable for brainstorming. Again, whiteboards or newsprint on the walls, room to move around, comfortable chairs, and plenty of paper, pencils, and markers will work nicely.

The scenario project leader can present all of the scenarios, or, if appropriate, individuals who wrote the specific scenarios can present them. The presentations should be short, involve the essence of the stories, and use colorful pictures or slides to describe each scenario. The project leader then facilitates a dialogue relating back to the initial question. The following questions may be useful in starting the conversation:

- What have we learned throughout the scenario development process that relates to our initial question?
- How would we answer the initial question in each scenario? Are the answers different in each scenario?
- What additional information would we want to know?
- What different ways of solving our strategic dilemma are suggested by entertaining these scenarios?
- What are the clear strategic opportunities that can be seen in each scenario?
- What general actions would we recommend around the initial problem, question, or issue, having considered each of these scenarios and their implications?

The goal of this workshop is to begin a genuine conversation about the potential issues decision makers may face and to provide a mechanism to wonder about the future. Research indicates that executives spend less than 10 percent of their time on strategic issues (Nash, 2007). Providing a space to think and reflect on strategic issues on its own is a valuable contribution. Depending on the size of the organization and the reaction to once again thinking strategically, more than one scenario presentation around the initial issue may be necessary.

Often, additional workshops to simply reflect on the project and explore insights that have come up are requested. I have found that almost anyone who participates in a scenario project develops a clear desire to reflect; and once given the time and space to think in this way, they seem to want more of it. This was certainly the case with Technology Corporation. Corporate leaders initially agreed to three half-day workshops to implement scenarios. Based on the participant interactions, and insightful dialogue that was coming out of the first two workshops, leaders asked to extend the conversation with two additional workshops beyond the initial three. They specifically asked that the additional time not be structured but, rather, left open to continue dialogue on deep issues that had arisen.

Tips for Presentations

Presentations are an effective way to communicate scenarios. Wack's presentations at Shell are legendary, and he traveled throughout the world delivering compelling sets of scenarios. By all accounts, he was a gifted communicator. Honing communications skills is an evolutionary process, and a few basic understandings will increase the effectiveness of any presentation.

The surest way to void a presentation of meaning and put the audience to sleep is to read the presentation slides. This is an unacceptable practice, yet many presenters fall into this habit. A few tips to consider in sharing a presentation are as follows:

- *Rehearse.* Great presenters rehearse for each slide of their presentations. They plan the core message that goes along with each of the slides and create innovative ways to deliver that message.
- *Use visuals.* Slides should offer minimal text. Instead, incorporate images that are aesthetically pleasing. These make it impossible to read the slides, and they provide the viewer with something more interesting to look at than bulleted text.
- *Be enthusiastic.* If you don't have passion for your topic, neither will your audience. Great speakers get excited about what they are talking about because they have to. Presentations given by Pierre Wack and Peter Schwartz are legendary for their passion and enthusiasm.

For more useful information about delivering effective presentations, consider Garr Reynolds's (2010) book *Presentation Zen*, or visit his website at www.garrreynolds.com.

SCENARIO IMMERSION: A VARIATION ON EXAMINING THE INITIAL QUESTION—WORKSHOP 2

A similar approach to considering the scenarios is called "scenario immersion" (Wilson & Ralston, 2006). Participants develop their thoughts about the opportunities and threats as well as possible actions and strategies for each scenario. The facilitator explains that the goal of the workshop is to develop as many ideas as possible about how the organization should proceed, and participants are encouraged to think broadly to capture a wide range of possible actions for decision makers to take. The process unfolds as each scenario is presented, and participants are asked to assume the role of a decision maker. Each participant is asked to identify three to five opportunities and three to five threats. Each of these is recorded on a single note card. Participants are then asked to develop a strategy they believe could be effective in that scenario.

Once these exercises are complete, the process moves into a voting round. Each participant is asked to nominate one threat and one opportunity he or she believes to be critical in that scenario. The idea is to leverage the collective capital of the participants in the room to distill a core set of opportunities and threats. This part of the process is completed for each scenario.

When critical opportunities and threats have been identified, the process turns to strategies. The group is asked to consider all of the strategies that have been brainstormed, and to look for the strategies that appear in more than one scenario. The goal is to identify two or three strategies that can be viable across all or multiple scenarios. This is perhaps the most useful outcome of any scenario project.

TESTING THE THEORY OF THE BUSINESS/BUSINESS IDEA— WORKSHOP 3

Another effective exercise is to examine the theory of the business/business idea in each scenario. Using the same brainstorming space set up described in earlier chapters, the team can take the theory of the business and business idea developed in the scenario exploration phase (see Chapter 6) and wind-tunnel them through each of the scenarios.

The process of testing the theory of the business in the context provided by each scenario should take about a half day. The scenario team presents a scenario to decision makers, and a dialogue is initiated about how the theory of the business may need to change in order to be viable in a given scenario. Key questions for exploring the theory of the business include these:

- Do our assumptions about the environment, mission, and core competencies fit or enable us to take action within the futures presented in each of the scenarios?
- Do our assumptions about the environment, mission, and core competencies fit each other in each of the scenarios?
- Is our theory of the business known and understood throughout the organization?
- How can we continuously test our theory of the business?

These questions should be posed for each scenario. These conversations can become quite diverse and reach into unexpected areas. It is OK to continue to explore ideas during these conversations, but keep in mind the goal is to work toward how the theory of the business may need to change to suit a variety of potential futures.

A similar process can be used to explore the business idea. One workshop described in the scenario exploration phase is to ask decision makers to draw or write out a model of how they interpret the business idea. Then, facilitators attempt to synthesize the various models, capturing the variety in interpretation. The synthesized model can then be considered in each scenario. Here are key questions for the business idea:

- Are we continuing to serve a business need with our products/services in each scenario?
- Would our distinctive competencies still be distinctive in each of the scenarios?
- Would we lose our competitive advantage in any of the scenarios? How would it change?

Revised Theory of the Business/Business Idea for Technology Corporation

As a result of a workshop to test the theory of the business/business idea in Technology Corporation, the team decided their business idea needed to change if they were to move beyond their current single source of funding. The resulting revised business idea is captured in Figure 8.2.

Technology Corporation's revised business idea clearly includes moving beyond the production of intellectual property and into the production of new, useful technology products. The new business idea includes increased contracting with R&D partners, the licensing and selling of new technology, and cross-functional collaboration. These additions will be critical in moving Technology Corporation forward, beyond its current situation.

The response to the revised business idea in Technology Corporation was overwhelming. Many expressed surprise that such a simple exercise could have such profound results. Managers expressed a greater understanding of what was going on in the minds of decision makers and leaders after conversations about the core purpose of the organization. Executives expressed a sense of unity in knowing and understanding what their colleagues thought and their rationale for taking certain stances.

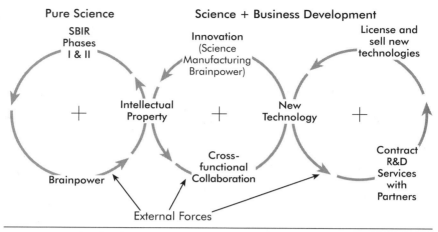

Pure Science   Science + Business Development

SBIR Phases I & II

Innovation (Science Manufacturing Brainpower)

License and sell new technologies

Intellectual Property

New Technology

Brainpower

Cross-functional Collaboration

Contract R&D Services with Partners

External Forces

FIGURE **8.2** Technology Corporation's Revised Business Idea

ANALYZING CURRENT STRATEGIES—WORKSHOP 4

Most decision makers operate under a set of strategic goals whether they have used scenario planning or not. These goals and strategies can be viewed through the "lens" of each scenario to see where they may or may not make sense. In this optional workshop, participants come together to consider the organization's strategy, current strategic initiatives, risky potential projects, and other organizational goals in the context of each scenario. The purpose of this workshop is to assess current organizational goals and their viability in each scenario. Ultimately, a manageable set of strategies that contribute to the advancement of the organization is sought. Goals and strategies that are found to distract from the core purpose of the organization (the theory of the business/business idea) can be considered further and potentially removed from the strategic agenda.

For example, a major corporation I worked with had a set of eleven strategic goals. We designed a workshop in which we asked participants to rank their eleven strategic goals in each of the scenarios. Participants saw that their priorities shifted in each scenario. After working through the exercise, decision makers saw that four of their strategic goals were generally irrelevant in all four scenarios. They saw that elements of the four strategic goals that were low in utility could be absorbed as components of other goals. With some modification, shifting, and rewriting, decision makers collectively decided to collapse their goals into a more efficient list of seven strategic goals.

The point is not necessarily to have fewer strategies or goals. Instead, the goal is to learn to see redundancies or initiatives that are not useful in moving the organization forward, or to discover activities that do not contribute to the long-term sustainability of the company. Activities that are not seen to contribute should be examined closely and abandoned if they don't offer at least potential utility in sustaining the organization and contributing to growth over the long term.

Developing "Signals"—Workshop 5

Signals are sometimes referred to as "leading indicators" or "signposts." Signals are the events in a given scenario that may indicate its story is beginning to unfold. In other words, they are things to pay attention to that could indicate the future is beginning to happen as it is described in one of the scenarios. Developing signals is a highly undervalued part of the scenario planning system. It is worth spending time thinking about the things that will indicate major shifts in the external environment. Using the same workshop format as described earlier, the team should spend a few hours going over each scenario and identifying the events that can be viewed as triggers of larger change tendencies.

In another recent scenario project I facilitated, these signals were the primary output sought by the CEO. She was very interested in these events that signaled major changes on the horizon. Therefore, we spent extra time on these elements and found it to be highly worthwhile. We designed a presentation that focused solely on the signals. The conversation that formed around the signals led to several other insights, and those insights served to bolster the decision makers' "anticipatory capacity" in that they left that presentation knowing what to look for in the following eighteen months.

"Signals" for Technology Corporation

Figure 8.3 presents the signals for Technology Corporation's scenarios. These signals are general indicators that a given scenario may be starting to unfold. As such, these are the items that should be on decision makers' "radar screens."

Concorde

- Technology Corporation successfully recruits world-renowned energy research scientists
- Technology Corporation's reputation in energy research grows as its world-renowned energy research scientists enable research partnerships with national laboratories and major research universities
- Lucrative energy research partnerships create pressure to sustain that portion of the enterprise to the detriment of development activities
- Lack of collaboration from the scientists create a dysfunctional siloed organization with each division operating as functionally separate enterprises
- A funnelling effect over the years transforms Technology Corporation into a contract, narrowly focused, energy research laboratory
- "Brain-Drain" as scientists and engineers leave or are recruited to more stable environments
- Unable to turn Technology Corporation into the entrepreneurial enterprise originally envisioned, its owner decides to sell

Talent Management

Primarily R&D Contract Based

Airbus

- Existing employees transition from old framework to new innovated/market-driven consciousness
- 2012 Obama reelected and funding increased for energy immovation—vision, goals aligned
- Proprietary Foundation interested in partnering with Technology Corporation because of new success with partners
- 10-year turn-around for innovations from conception to market
- With a new election approaching in 2016, Technology Corporation has protected itself against threat of SBIR funding cut by securing primarily R&D contracts
- Two key innovations take off
- Demand for clean coal and other green technology increases—gain more R&D contracts
- Diversification in new market pays off
- Propiertary Foundation provides continued funding for Technology Corporation—sparks interest from other organization for R&D contracts
- Top industry competitors were not prepared for the cut of SBIR funding and fold or merge
- Significant increase in employees
- 2-year turn-around for innovations from conception to market

---

Neglected, Siloed, Individually Innovative

Titanic

- Decrease in SBIR funding
- Siloed mind-set
- Increase in activities with cross-functional teams
- Growth in alternative energy government funding
- Stronger global protections on IP
- Long-term R&D partnerships
- Decrease in collaboration with outside partners
- Increased interest in water technologies
- Technologies do not advance beyond phase 2
- Inability to identify investors for technologies
- Technology development expenses outweigh the revenues generated from the technology over time
- Significant, sharp decline in R&D services and customer base

 Cohesive, Cross-functional, Collaboratively Innovative

Horse and Buggy

- Congress will vote to reauthorize the SBIR program prior to March 20, 2009
- Monitor **http://www.zyn.com/** for increased chatter regarding SBIR funding. Monitor number of SBIR training seminars for increased attendance. Monitor statistics regarding application and awards of SBIR projects
- Technology Corporation is successful at retrieving, retaining, and disseminating knowledge from not only its workforce, but the industry as well. Technology Corporation Knows (TC-Knows) is an example of a "system" that conceptually explores the possibilities of harnessing the power of knowledge
- The request for "bailouts" and "loans" continue to cause friction
- Monitor national debt annual increases. Current estimates are $2–3 trillion per year
- Monitor national savings rate in U.S. provided by the Bureau of Economic Analyst (**http://www.bea.gov/briefrm/saving.htm**)
- Monitor AARP research for indicators of current issues affecting the older generation. Monitor GDP for China and U.S.: IMF (**http://www.imf.org/external/index.htm**); World Bank (**http://www.worldbank.org**); CIA World Factbook (**https://www.cia.gov/publications/the-world-factbook/index.htm**)
- Monitor congressional hearings related to SBIR funding

Primarily SBIR Based

 Funding Sources

FIGURE **8.3** Signals for Technology Corporation Scenarios

CREATING AN EXPERIENTIAL LEARNING EXERCISE— WORKSHOP 6

One of the most profound scenario planning experiences I have had was at a large international organization. Members of the scenario planning team suggested we build four rooms, each reflecting one of the scenarios. The rooms had walls that were plastered with artifacts, posters, banners, and newspaper articles that characterized the scenarios. To the extent possible, material artifacts (in this case, it was a computer company, so the team brought in early computer logic boards) for participants to "play" with will immediately capture participant attention. Executives were put into cross-organizational teams, and each team was assigned to a room. One of the members of the scenario planning team presented the scenario and explained that the task for the group was to tell the story of how the scenario came to unfold. The "aha" moments and critical learning points were observable in participant behavior. For some, it was a highly emotional experience because the scenarios came alive in such profound ways.

Activities that attempt to bring the imagination into reality, like those in this suggested workshop, have been shown to increase learning (Manning, 2002). The military has used simulations and virtual reality technologies for decades because of their learning benefits. The idea is similar with experiential learning workshops. Anything that can be done to get the scenarios "off the page" and into the microcosms of the decision makers will increase their potential effects. Writers and filmmakers talk about the "suspension of disbelief," and this is a central concept in scenario planning as well. Sometimes, scenarios will no doubt be met with disbelief, and it is in the presentation, communication, and consideration of scenarios that disbelief can be handled. Of course, scenarios must be well researched, so that their potentially unbelievable stories can be told with data establishing their legitimacy.

Experiential learning workshops require a great deal of time and effort to design, but their payoff can be high. Keep in mind, too, that some organizational cultures will be less open to this kind of exercise than others. For example, engineers are not likely to go for creative exercises like this one, but designers, sociologists, and industries or organizations with close working teams are likely to benefit.

OTHER WIND-TUNNELING STRATEGIES

Decision makers can use the scenarios to examine their strategy, goals, human resource capacity, specific decisions and outcomes, business model, and a variety of other items (see Figure 8.4).

Figure 8.4 is a basic structure for wind-tunneling various organizational elements through each scenario. At its most simple, this framework suggests some very basic questions that get to the heart of scenario planning. For example, logical questions that fall out of this framework include the following:

- Do we have a viable strategy in each of the scenarios? In which scenarios does our strategy fall apart?
- Does our organization structure support the kind of organization we might be in each of the scenarios?
- Is our organizational culture an asset or liability in each scenario? Why? What implications does our current organizational culture carry for our strategic options in each scenario?
- Do we have the necessary human resource capabilities to maintain our business idea in each scenario? Do we have the leadership capacity to manage the challenges evident in each scenario?

WIND TUNNELING FOR TECHNOLOGY CORPORATION

A wind-tunneling workshop was done with Technology Corporation, and various organization elements were explored in each scenario. The results

		Scenarios			
		A	B	C	D
Organizational Elements	The Business Idea				
	Strategy				
	Structure				
	Culture				
	Capabilities				

FIGURE 8.4 Using Scenarios to Examine Organizational Elements (based on van der Merwe)

revealed a need for several critical internal changes so that the organization could be better positioned to handle a variety of potential futures. The workshop results are summarized in Figure 8.5.

RESILIENCE AND ROBUSTNESS

Additional or substitute workshops can be designed around any one, all, or other organizational elements. The workshops need only to inform the initial purpose of the project. Beyond that, the scenarios should be used to explore. The more creatively they are used, the further the thinking inside the organization can potentially be shifted.

| | | Scenarios | | | |
		Concorde	*Airbus*	*Horse and Buggy*	*Titanic*
Organization Elements	Theory of the business/ business idea	Requires changes	Requires changes	Requires changes	OK (this is what happens if we continue on as we are)
	Strategy	(No clearly articulated strategy or specific goals)	(No clearly articulated strategy or specific goals)	(No clearly articulated strategy or specific goals)	(No clearly articulated strategy or specific goals)
	Structure	No implications for structure	No implications for structure	No implications for structure	No implications for structure
	Culture	No implications for culture	Requires a significant shift toward team/collaboration	Requires a significant shift toward team/collaboration	No implications for culture
	Capabilities	Requires some growth— hiring of designers and scientists	Requires some growth— hiring of designers and scientists		Reduction of workforce (can't support it)

FIGURE **8.5**   Wind-Tunneling Summary for Technology Corporation

The collective use of workshops designed in the scenario implementation phase is generally thought to build organizational resilience and robustness. For example, the scenario immersion activity described in this chapter asked participants to identify strategies that work in all scenarios. The purpose of this is to build a strategy that can handle the stresses of all of the scenarios—a robust strategy. Scenario planning is not a magic bullet and is not intended to gather up *all* of the potential futures. Rather, the purpose is to pose a variety of alternatives to decision makers such that they will be more prepared for anything that might come to pass. Resilient organizations are those that find ways to survive in rapidly changing environmental conditions. The activities suggested in this chapter are all aimed at developing the ability to respond quickly to major shifts in the environment.

Resilience can be defined as "the ability to recover readily from illness, depression, adversity, or the like" (*Merriam-Webster's Dictionary and Thesaurus*, 2006, p. 677). Some of the purposes of scenario planning are to learn about the possible futures, prepare for them, and avoid catastrophe, but equally important is the ability to recover quickly from challenging situations. Thus, for many organization leaders, simply thinking through the options can decrease the response time to challenging events. A reduced response time can give some companies an edge over their competition.

THE STRATEGIC CONVERSATION

The other general outcome of the scenario implementation phase is to begin or sustain an ongoing conversation about strategy and alternatives—the strategic conversation. If the organization is not currently using any structured approach to strategy, this will be revolutionary. The simple idea is that strategy must be more than an annual retreat-style event. Strategy must become a part of the daily conversation that takes place within the organization. Scenarios are tools for having this conversation, but it is the informal parts of the conversation—in the hallways, when colleagues just "stop by" each other's offices, or conversations that happen over lunch—that use the scenario planning process as a foundation from which to leap forward to other insight and creativity.

The crux of the institutional aspects of the processual paradigm is conversation. The learning loop model shows the interwovenness of thinking and action. If action is based on planning on the basis of a mental model, then institutional action must be based on a shared mental model. Only through a process of conversation can elements of observation and thought be structured and embedded in the accepted and shared organizational theories-in-use. (van der Heijden, 1997, p. 41)

An effective strategic conversation requires (1) a common language, (2) alignment of ideas, (3) willingness to engage in rational argumentation, and (4) the evolution of ideas inside the organization (van der Heijden 1997).

Common Language

The requirement for common language is logical and not complex. Stated simply, organization members participating in any process need a common understanding of the process to be used and some way to define and sort through the jargon that has invaded today's business world.

Alignment of Ideas

Strategy literature increasingly includes reference to the notion of alignment (Manning, 2002; Mintzberg, Ahlstrand, & Lampel, 1999). While most of the strategy literature refers to alignment among organization, process, and individual goals, the strategic conversation aims to produce alignment among ideas. The strategic conversation stresses the importance of revealing and analyzing mental models in scenario planning and in this context, the notion of idea alignment can be considered as an output of building a collective mental model (Wack, 1985b). Sharing assumptions, values, and the basic scaffolding of a unified purpose are critical to establishing this kind of alignment (Manning, 2002).

Willingness to Engage in Rational Argumentation

The scenario planning process is one of dialogue, challenge, and willingness to critique ideas. Thus, participants must be comfortable engaging in conversation and must be open to having their ideas challenged by other participants. By definition, learning happens when people begin to see things in a new way. Without this critical piece, the strategic conversation becomes lip service, and none of its implications are taken seriously as nothing is learned.

EVOLUTION OF IDEAS INSIDE THE ORGANIZATION

This final requirement can be thought of as the result of the previous three. Evolution of ideas in the organization is the goal of the strategic conversation. The stage for the evolution of ideas within an organization is set through a common language, working toward aligning ideas, and through a willingness to critique and be critiqued by the majority of people in an organization. Often, scenarios are just a starting point for ideas to be sparked, which leads to revision of the scenarios and further debate and dialogue until assumptions are shattered.

DIALOGUE

Although not one of van der Heijden's initial components of the strategic conversation, the notion of dialogue as developed by Bohm (1989, 2002, 2004) is an additional critical component that cannot be ignored in considering the strategic conversation. Given the positioning of communication in this article and in the larger context of scenario planning, it is useful to consider the nature of communication.

The requirements of strategic conversation are intended to clarify the essence of strategic conversation itself. All of these elements are integrated in the scenario planning system. Thus, it is a means by which to have strategic conversations. The distinction is that the scenario planning system features the formal part of the conversation. Decision makers would be wise to find ways to support the informal part of the conversation as well.

CONCLUSION

To reiterate, there is a lot of freedom in finding the most useful ways to implement and apply scenarios. The goal of this chapter has been to provide a framework for using scenarios. Consultants should feel free to be creative in designing a set of workshops for scenario implementation. However, keeping in line with the project proposal is critical, and therefore, returning to the initial purpose, question, or issue is required for each project. In addition, the business model should be tested in each scenario. These two workshops are a minimum, in my view, and they will provoke strategic thinking in virtually any circumstances.

This chapter has presented and described additional workshops that focus on analyzing current strategies, developing signals, and facilitating experiential exercises. These are all useful approaches to applying scenarios and should also be considered. These workshops demonstrate the use of wind-tunneling various organizational elements to ensure the development of resilient and robust strategies.

9

Phase 5—
Project Assessment:
Documenting Results

Assessing scenario projects is critical. Most texts on scenario planning do not include methods for documenting or assessing the outcomes of scenario planning. Pick up any of the popular scenario planning books, and check the index for *assessment*, *evaluation*, or *results*. I predict that you will not find these entries. The lack of effort invested to understand the outcomes of scenario projects is a serious shortcoming. The dearth of evidence demonstrating that scenario planning is an effective investment makes it difficult to argue for the proposed benefits. Most seasoned practitioners and users of scenario planning know through their own experience that scenarios create value in numerous ways. However, scenario planning should be more than a strategic management tool falling in and out of favor depending on the stability of the global business environment. To establish the true contribution of scenario planning, projects must be assessed to build a suite of evidence supporting scenario planning and its utility. Minimally, "if the scenario process does not bring out strategic options previously unconsidered by managers, then it has been sterile" (Wack, 1985c, p. 10).

The efforts described in this project assessment chapter are aimed at understanding and documenting the strategic options that can be attributed to scenario projects (Figure 9.1). Sadly, in my own experiences (including research projects with senior executives and several prominent scenario planning professionals), I have heard numerous times that there is simply no way to measure the success of scenario projects. One premise of this

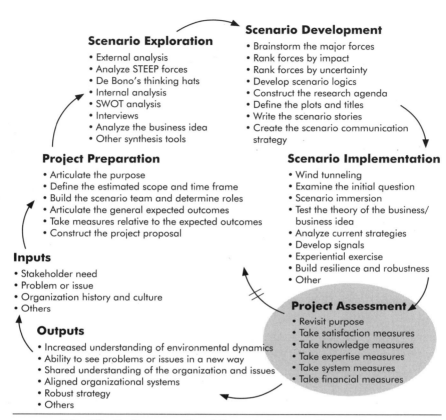

Scenario Exploration
- External analysis
- Analyze STEEP forces
- De Bono's thinking hats
- Internal analysis
- SWOT analysis
- Interviews
- Analyze the business idea
- Other synthesis tools

Scenario Development
- Brainstorm the major forces
- Rank forces by impact
- Rank forces by uncertainty
- Develop scenario logics
- Construct the research agenda
- Define the plots and titles
- Write the scenario stories
- Create the scenario communication strategy

Project Preparation
- Articulate the purpose
- Define the estimated scope and time frame
- Build the scenario team and determine roles
- Articulate the general expected outcomes
- Take measures relative to the expected outcomes
- Construct the project proposal

Scenario Implementation
- Wind tunneling
- Examine the initial question
- Scenario immersion
- Test the theory of the business/business idea
- Analyze current strategies
- Develop signals
- Experiential exercise
- Build resilience and robustness
- Other

Inputs
- Stakeholder need
- Problem or issue
- Organization history and culture
- Others

Outputs
- Increased understanding of environmental dynamics
- Ability to see problems or issues in a new way
- Shared understanding of the organization and issues
- Aligned organizational systems
- Robust strategy
- Others

Project Assessment
- Revisit purpose
- Take satisfaction measures
- Take knowledge measures
- Take expertise measures
- Take system measures
- Take financial measures

FIGURE 9.1   The Performance-Based Scenario System—Project Assessment Phase

chapter is to disagree, and another is to present a comprehensive approach to documenting the benefits of scenario projects.

Scenario projects are not that different from what we do every day in our personal lives. We consider a variety of possibilities in our future and then plan accordingly, often investing in insurance policies to prepare for an occurrence that may never happen, but, should it happen, we have thoughtfully considered it and planned for its possibility (Harper, 2010). An important outcome of scenario work is a clear sense of choices, implications, and costs and benefits associated with a variety of possibilities. Thinking through options—even unlikely (or undesirable) options—and giving them equal attention and consideration is what leads to robust thinking about the future. This is just what an insurance provider does.

Scenario projects, by their very nature, deal with the world of perceptions as well as knowledge and performance. Therefore, some traditional approaches to assessment may not be appropriate. This chapter provides strategies for assessing scenario projects. The foundation for project assessment is set in the project preparation phase at the start of the project. The desired outcomes of the project, set forth in the earlier scenario project proposal, are what is measured once the project is complete. The assessment strategy proposed in this chapter is a modified version of the results assessment system (Swanson & Holton, 1999). The results assessment system can be applied to any organizational intervention. An overview of the system is described, and then specific examples are used to illustrate the implementation of this assessment system for scenario projects.

OVERVIEW OF THE RESULTS ASSESSMENT SYSTEM

Swanson and Holton (1999) proposed a general assessment system for organization improvement efforts. Their system was designed to be practical, usable, and easy to implement. They were quick to point out that the majority of assessments in organizations (if any is done at all) focus on perceptions of satisfaction (Swanson & Holton, 1999). In other words, most change efforts are assessed on the basis of whether participants perceived the project to be useful and enjoyable. To move beyond this level, a more comprehensive approach is required. Consequently, the results assessment system has three domains: satisfaction, learning, and performance (Swanson & Holton, 1999). All three of these domains should be included in a responsible assessment effort.

SATISFACTION RESULTS

Satisfaction results measure opinions about the utility of the change intervention. Usually, short surveys are distributed, and participants rate their perceptions of the event. Often, these are the only assessment measures used at all. Responsible assessment must include other measures, but perceptions matter, and they are an important part of estimating the success of any project. The key is to obtain the data, use what is pertinent, and prevent overanalysis of satisfaction results. Satisfaction results should be obtained from both participants and stakeholders.

Participants

Participant perceptions can provide valuable information for making subtle adjustments to any change project. Participant perceptions should not overtake the project and become the primary, or most important, measure of success. These results can be used to improve practical issues related to the experience of the project.

Stakeholders

Several categories of stakeholders are possible, and each should be included in a measure of satisfaction. Stakeholders are leaders of divisions or systems within the organization, or anyone with a vested interest in the organization. Stakeholders can be internal or external, such as board members, producers or consumers of company products, or anyone with a primary or secondary investment in the organization (Swanson & Holton, 1999). A short survey should be designed and sent to representatives from each stakeholder group. The purpose of these surveys is to take a quick measure of whether the project has met stakeholder expectations.

LEARNING RESULTS

Measures of learning are critical to organizational change efforts, as learning is a prerequisite to change. People cannot change their behaviors, have strategic insights, or create a novel way of seeing a situation if they have not learned. Learning begins in the mind, and neuroscience is increasingly able to explain, physiologically, how learning happens (see Dispenza, 2007). For assessment purposes, it is important to find out whether participants have learned during the course of the project. Because learning is required for action, the logical other component in this domain is new expertise. In other words, the aim of this domain is to assess what it is that participants know and can do differently as a result of their engagement in the project.

Knowledge

Knowledge assessments involve having participants demonstrate the knowledge they gained through the course of the change project (Swanson & Holton, 1999). Knowledge gains are usually measured with tests. However, other techniques for analyzing knowledge gained, discussed later, are more appropriate in the scenario planning context. The general idea is to find a way to determine what participants know after the project that they did not know before the project.

Expertise

Expertise refers to action and doing. That is, participants should also be able to do something differently based on knowledge they have gained throughout the project. The goal of assessing expertise is to find a way for participants to demonstrate how what they have learned has changed their behaviors.

PERFORMANCE RESULTS

Performance results are the most difficult part of assessment for scenario projects given the timeline of events. Performance results rest in two key areas: system and financial. System results generally refer to the product, good, or service that can be increased or maximized through the change intervention. The financial results refer to the conversion of system result gains into a financial measure.

System

System results can be the general performance indicators of the organization as a whole. These are the products produced, contracts sold, hours billed, and services provided. They are defined as "the units of mission-related outputs in the form of goods and/or services having value to the customer and that are related to the core organizational, work process, and group or individual contributors in the organization" (Swanson & Holton, 1999, p. 14).

Financial

Financial results are "[t]he conversion of the output units of goods and or services attributable to the intervention into financial interpretation" (Swanson & Holton, 1999, p. 16). Financial results convert any increases in system results into a monetary measure (see Swanson, 2001a).

SUMMARY

This short overview of the results assessment system is intended to orient readers to a comprehensive approach to assessment. Most organizations stop at satisfaction surveys, if they assess anything at all. Responsible performance improvement efforts must apply these concepts to specific organizational interventions. The following section refines the system for use in the context of scenario planning.

ADAPTING THE RESULTS ASSESSMENT SYSTEM TO SCENARIO PLANNING

Some aspects of scenario projects are difficult to assess, particularly when they are successful. For example, how does the team know that they have helped to avoid a catastrophe if they have, indeed, avoided it? How can innovative ideas and strategic insights be attributed directly to the scenario planning project? Because of these difficulties, most authors have chosen to avoid dealing with how to assess scenario projects entirely. Given the costs associated with most scenario planning projects, it is responsible to spend time thinking about how the project has benefitted the organization. That is the purpose of adjusting the results assessment system for use in looking at the effectiveness of scenario planning projects.

To reiterate, many of the important and expected outcomes of the project were described and defined in the project reparation phase. This, once again, highlights the importance of the preparation phase in that the attention given to outcomes and expectation at the start of the project influences the ease and elegance of the project assessment. Spend time up-front defining the outcomes of the project, and keep the expectations and goals in mind throughout.

USING A VARIETY OF MEASURES IN EACH DOMAIN

Because the assessment of scenario projects is not well documented and can be difficult, scenario project leaders should consider a variety of tools and approaches. These can include both quantitative and qualitative strategies for gathering and analyzing information. I suggest using the results assessment system as a framework and trying out a variety of specific tools within each domain. For example, using surveys to gather satisfaction results from participants and stakeholders is relatively straightforward. However, tests to assess knowledge gained from scenario planning projects require a closer attention. One way is to directly ask participants what they learned throughout the project. The same skills used for interviews at the start of the scenario project can be used to inquire into its results. This section describes how the satisfaction, learning, and performance domains of the results assessment system can be adjusted to form a comprehensive assessment strategy for scenario projects.

Satisfaction Results in Scenario Projects

There is little need to adjust the method for assessing satisfaction results in the results assessment system. The method uses short surveys designed to capture basic opinions and reactions to the scenario project.

Participants. The recommended approach is to design a simple survey with ten or fewer questions plus room for comments and distribute it to participants at the conclusion of the project. Data can be entered into a basic software program and analyzed quickly. For example, Microsoft Excel can be used to compute mean scores for each item. A sample participant survey is provided in Figure 9.2.

Stakeholders. Stakeholder satisfaction surveys are also simple and effective. Again, a short survey should be sent to project stakeholders after the conclusion of the project. The purpose is to gather stakeholder perceptions of the usefulness of the project. A sample stakeholder satisfaction survey is in Figure 9.3.

Learning Results in Scenario Projects

Unless the manager's thinking changes, there will be no behavior changes (Wack, 1985b). Results in the learning domain are intended to capture whether, and to what degree, the thinking may have changed. Learning results may require some adjustment from the original results assessment system given the context of scenario planning and the fact that there is no prescribed content to be learned in scenario projects. For example, traditionally, paper-and-pencil tests are used to assess content mastery, and some form of observation is used to determine the improved expertise. These approaches are not always appropriate in scenario projects, but that does not mean the domain should be neglected. The solution is in using other strategies that fit the purpose of scenario projects.

Knowledge. Clearly, the intention is that participants learn during the scenario project process. Because what is learned can vary significantly among participants in a group, a useful strategy is to look for patterns or themes that connect the learning experience to the participants. For example, instead of looking at individual decisions per person, decision-making

FIGURE 9.2 Participant Satisfaction Survey

SCENARIO PLANNING PROJECT

Project Title _____   Date _____

Project Leader _____   Code _____

Please answer the following questions. Your responses will help us improve future programs. Circle the response that best represents your opinion.

	Strongly agree	Agree	No opinion	Disagree	Strongly disagree
1. This project was useful for me in my role in the organization.	1	2	3	4	5
2. I was motivated to participate in this project.	1	2	3	4	5
3. The project made me think differently about the organization.	1	2	3	4	5
4. I learned about the industry and external environment in this project.	1	2	3	4	5
5. I expect that I will use what I learned in this project.	1	2	3	4	5
6. My colleagues were motivated to participate in this project.	1	2	3	4	5
7. I have a better understanding of challenges facing the organization.	1	2	3	4	5
8. I will encourage others to participate in these projects in the future.	1	2	3	4	5
9. I will make decisions differently based on what I learned.	1	2	3	4	5
10. This project will benefit the organization as a whole.	1	2	3	4	5

What was the most valuable part of this project for you?

_____

_____

What was the least valuable part of this project for you?

_____

_____

Additional comments are appreciated.

_____

_____

FIGURE **9.3**   Stakeholder Satisfaction Survey

SCENARIO PLANNING PROJECT

Project Title _____   Date _____

Project Leader _____   Code _____

Please answer the following questions. Your responses will help us improve future programs. Circle the response that best represents your opinion.

	Strongly agree	Agree	No opinion	Disagree	Strongly disagree
1. This project has shown benefits for the organization.	1	2	3	4	5
2. I was motivated to support the purpose of this project.	1	2	3	4	5
3. The project has shown results.	1	2	3	4	5
4. I can see evidence that participants learned about the industry.	1	2	3	4	5
5. I expect that our employees will use what was learned in this project.	1	2	3	4	5
6. My colleagues were motivated to participate in this project.	1	2	3	4	5
7. I have a better understanding of challenges facing the organization.	1	2	3	4	5
8. I will encourage others to participate in these projects in the future.	1	2	3	4	5
9. I will make decisions differently based on results of this project.	1	2	3	4	5
10. This project has possible long-term benefits for the organization.	1	2	3	4	5

What was the most valuable part of this project for you?

_____

_____

What was the least valuable part of this project for you?

_____

_____

Additional comments are appreciated.

_____

_____

patterns or tendencies may be more appropriate. Useful tools for assessing these patterns include van der Merwe's Conversation Quality and Engagement Checklist (2007), Watkins and Marsick's Dimensions of the Learning Organization Questionnaire (1995), and Scott and Bruce's General Decision Making Style Survey (1994).

The Conversation Quality and Engagement Checklist (CQEC) was developed by Louis van der Merwe at the Centre for Innovative Leadership (www.cil.net). CIL specializes in capacity-building scale in (1) scenario-based strategy, (2) leadership development, (3) systems thinking, (4) organization effectiveness, and (5) executive coaching. The CQEC has been used in practice for over twenty years as a metric for conversation quality in scenario work. It is divided into two categories: Level I skills and Level II skills. Level I skills assess how individuals perceive their personal communication capabilities. Level II skills assess individual perceptions of interpersonal communication skills. The CQEC has also been used and validated in a variety of organizations, industries, and contexts (van der Merwe, Chermack, Kulikowich, & Yang, 2007). The Conversation Quality and Engagement Checklist is provided in Figure 9.4 as an example of the kinds of surveys and instruments that can be useful in scenario projects.

The CQEC was used with Technology Corporation in a pretest/posttest design. Participants assessed their own skill levels before and after the scenario project. Again, mean scores for Level I and Level II skills were computed, and a t-test was conducted between pre- and posttest scores. Results showed that participants perceived improvement in their individual and interpersonal dialogue, conversation quality, and engagement skills over the course of the project.

The Dimensions of Learning Organization Questionnaire (DLOQ) is an instrument designed to assess perceptions of an organization's learning culture. In scenario projects, the DLOQ can be used to assess participant perceptions of the organization's orientation toward learning as a critical function. The instrument has been heavily validated (Yang, 2003; Yang, Watkins, & Marsick, 2004) and has been shown as a proxy for firm financial performance (Ellinger, Ellinger, Yang, & Howton, 2002). The DLOQ measures seven factors: (1) creating continuous learning opportunities, (2) promoting inquiry and dialogue, (3) encouraging collaboration and team learning, (4) creating systems to capture and share learning, (5) empowering people toward a collective vision, (6) connecting the organization to its environment, and (7) providing strategic leadership for learning.

FIGURE **9.4**   The Conversation Quality and Engagement Checklist

Please assess your conversation and engagement skills and score yourself. Ask somebody else to also score your skills, and compare both scores. Use this checklist both in the work setting as well as other settings such as any leadership, social and family settings to keep practicing and improving your skills. Work on improving Level 1 Skills first.

Name _____

FEEDBACK—LEADERSHIP, AND MANAGING ACCOUNTABILITY AND PERFORMANCE

Complete the following statements by indicating which level of frequency most accurately reflects your conduct in conversations and engagement in a team and one-to-one setting. Each score should be accompanied by concrete feedback support by describing specific behavior in specific situations. Start the assessment process by asking: **During leadership and performance conversations, . . .** **(follow the items below)**	Never	Sometimes	Often	Usually	Always
LEVEL I SKILLS					
1. I use active listening to understand another person's point of view.	1	2	3	4	5
2. I paraphrase what is said to ensure deeper understanding.	1	2	3	4	5
3. I take responsibility for myself by choosing language that indicates this.	1	2	3	4	5
4. I listen to what is being said and am self-aware when judging.	1	2	3	4	5
5. I maintain balance between asking questions and stating my opinions.	1	2	3	4	5
6. I do my best to be explicit about the assumptions under my opinions.	1	2	3	4	5
7. I constantly question my opinions with intent of reaching observable data.	1	2	3	4	5
8. I use concrete examples to describe behavior, sensing, feelings, and impact.	1	2	3	4	5
9. I stay engaged to identify events that could assist in understanding underlying patterns of behavior and structural aspects.	1	2	3	4	5
10. I use open-ended questions to clarify the patterns and structures.	1	2	3	4	5
LEVEL II SKILLS					
11. I avoid third party involvement (triangulation) by dealing directly with others with the issues at hand.	1	2	3	4	5
12. I confront others constructively when I disagree with their opinions.	1	2	3	4	5
13. I take a stand and express outcomes while remaining engaged with the conversation at hand.	1	2	3	4	5
14. I make informed choices about personal behavior by balancing the purpose of the conversation, its desired results, and current reality.	1	2	3	4	5
15. I encourage others to make choices that support engagement in the conversation.	1	2	3	4	5
16. I define personal and organizational boundaries and review them when necessary.	1	2	3	4	5

(continued)

FIGURE **9.4** The Conversation Quality and Engagement Checklist *(continued)*

	Never	Sometimes	Often	Usually	Always
LEVEL II SKILLS *(continued)*					
17. I know my personal patterns of behavior and "hot buttons" and can intervene effectively and make choices.	1	2	3	4	5
18. I understand the origins of my behavioral patterns and "hot buttons."	1	2	3	4	5
19. I apply conflict resolution skills as required.	1	2	3	4	5
20. I use applicable coaching skills such as deep listening, empathy, respect, concreteness, and genuineness as appropriate.	1	2	3	4	5
SUB TOTAL					
TOTAL SCORE					

DEVELOPING CONVERSATION QUALITY AND ENGAGEMENT SKILLS—SCORES

Conversation quality and engagement skills can improve the quality of your relationships both at work and at home. These essential life skills are the foundation to learning and leadership.

Score	Description and Interpretation Guidelines
0–25	Low potential for leadership. Others feel out of touch, and no effort is made to be in touch; even disrespect. Conversations easily escalate into conflict and leave feelings of frustration. General lack of trust and alignment. Low morale and commitment is common. Open, authentic conversations are difficult and seldom happen. Teams and individuals don't know what their priorities and roles are, and results are unclear.
26–50	Medium potential for leadership. Others feel that you are somewhat distant. Conversations are often unsatisfactory, and people don't know where they stand. Trust is at a low level. Open and authentic conversations sometimes happen and when they do the contrast is immediately noticed. Indirect behavior with third parties is commonplace, and many areas of undiscussability develop. Priorities are often unclear, and choices are difficult to make; boundaries are also unclear and easily violated.
51–75	Average to above-average potential for leadership. Trust levels are building. Practicing conversation and engagement skills in real time is accepted and encouraged. Regular feedback and coaching for the purposes of learning is commonplace. Priorities are clear and tough choices are made and adhered to. Boundaries are often the focus of conversations. Systems thinking is a way of looking at the world and influencing it, and this informs many choices at interpersonal and intrapersonal levels.
76–100	High potential for leadership. Priorities are clear and there is continuous improvement with little wastage. Raising of performance standards and changes in direction are both easily executed. Others experience openness and authenticity in the leadership process. Confidence, humility, courage, firmness, vulnerability, and openness characterizes relationships. Confronting in a tough yet compassionate and constructive way occurs frequently and is skillfully executed using conversation and engagement skills naturally, and sometimes intuitively. Thinking and actions are informed by a systems perspective and self-knowledge. Trust is continuously being built and the team performs at a high level and in alignment with the overall goals and with each other.

(continued)

FIGURE **9.4**   The Conversation Quality and Engagement Checklist *(continued)*

Leadership is defined as influence potential. Leadership is executed through the capacity to take a stand and then skillfully, in a nonanxious way, holding this stand while staying in touch with the system you lead, until the followers align themselves with your stand.

Competent conversation and engagement consists of frequent face-to-face communications one on one as well as one on many, which are characterized by openness and authenticity, together with a tough-minded focus on agreed purpose and results. This enables high performance through robust, trusting relationships and a learning climate. In this approach, individuals and teams are taking personal responsibility and are accountable, which enables rapid self-correcting, which in turn supports the capacity for self-organizing at individual, team, and organizational levels.

Select one or two of the skills that you would like to improve and include them in your Personal Development Plan (PDP). Create practice areas in different settings where you can raise your level of competence, including contracting for regular structured feedback processes.

The DLOQ was used with Technology Corporation in a pretest/ posttest design. Measures of participant perceptions were taken using the DLOQ at the start of the scenario project and again at its conclusion. Pre- and posttest scores were then compared. The mean scores for each of the seven factors were considered, and then a *t*-test was conducted. The results indicated participants perceived improvements in how their organization created learning opportunities, promoted inquiry and dialogue, encouraged team learning, connected the organization to its environment, and provided strategic leadership for learning.

The General Decision Making Style Survey (GDMS) is another tool for assessing knowledge results. The GDMS includes five decision-making styles, and individuals will tend to favor one of these styles. The five styles are (1) rational decision making, (2) intuitive decision making, (3) dependent decision making, (4) spontaneous decision making, and (5) avoidant decision making.

The GDMS was also used to assess changes in decision-making styles in Technology Corporation. Again, using a pretest/posttest design, participants took the survey before and after the scenario project. Results indicated significant shifts in participant decision-making styles. Of particular interest is that participants who scored high on rational decision making in the pretest, tended to shift into other decision-making styles through the scenario project. Intuitive and dependent decision-making categories showed significant increases in posttest scores. Overall, the results suggested that the scenario project promoted intuitive and dependent approaches to decision making.

These instruments captured participant perceptions of the organization's learning capabilities, individual communication skills, and individual decision-making styles. These surveys and instruments are best used when a measure is taken at the beginning of the project and again at its conclusion so that change comparisons can be made. A variety of tools can be used to assess cognitive changes, and facilitators should use tools related to the goals and purpose of the scenario project. Any surveys used for project assessment should, however, be directly related to the expected outcomes defined in the project preparation phase. The instruments listed here are examples that are related to common general objectives of scenario projects.

Another effective strategy for understanding what participants learned during the scenario project is to simply ask them. This approach will provide details and anecdotes that are missed by the survey technique. At times, it is more powerful to hear participant stories of their "aha" moments and strategic insights. A few simple questions can launch a useful conversation about what was learned and how it may affect the ways in which participants go about their work. Suggested questions are as follows:

- What have you learned as a result of participating in this project?
- Did you have any major strategic insights or "aha" moments? If so, can you describe them?

Expertise. As with assessing knowledge, assessing expertise gained from a scenario planning project is tricky. Typically, expertise is observed. Changed behaviors and the application of expertise can be demonstrated in the performance of specific work tasks. In the context of scenario planning, expertise is more difficult to assess. Where appropriate, the observation method of participants "doing" may still be used. For example, if an individual usually makes decisions independently, without the review of external information and without conversations including colleagues and other experts prior to the scenario project, changes in how that individual approaches decision making may be quite obvious afterward. It is common for people to rely on conversations, colleagues, and further information gathering in making decisions after participating in scenario planning projects (Chermack & Nimon, 2008). Behavioral changes can be observed. The key is to create time and space in which the behaviors can be seen and discussed openly.

The knowledge assessment instruments can be used as proxies for behaviors and converted into an expert observation checklist. Using expert observations to assess behavior change moves the assessment beyond self-reported data and gains a level of objectivity. The knowledge assessment tools described here informed the construction of an expert observation worksheet. These items are combined in the scenario expertise audit (see Figure 9.5). The audit is aimed at gathering evidence of performed behaviors that contribute to a valued service or product (Swanson & Holton, 1999). It is based on expertise observation templates provided by Swanson and Holton (1999).

The scenario expertise audit should be used for expert ratings of project participants. The audit can be used to randomly observe individual participants after the project has concluded. The goal is to find evidence for changed observable behaviors when participants have returned to their normal work functions. The audit combines elements from each of the knowledge assessment instruments outlined earlier.

Interview techniques can be an additional proxy for assessing expertise gains. It is revealing to simply ask participants or fellow participants how they or others function differently after participating in scenario planning. Questions like this will prompt participants to reflect about their learning experience. At times, a useful strategy is to send the questions a few days prior to the interview so that participants can think through how their behaviors may have changed as a result of the scenario planning experience. Alternatively, sometimes immediate reactions are more useful. Other relevant questions can include the following:

- How has your learning affected your behavior as a result of participating in this scenario project?
- How has learning of others affected the behavior as a result of participating in this scenario project?
- How do you function differently in your work that you would attribute to participating in the scenario project?

FIGURE **9.5**   The Scenario Expertise Audit

Project Title _____   Date _____

Participant Being Observed _____   Code _____

Experts should use the following items to rate participant performance in normal work activities.

0 **Unable to observe** No opportunity to observe	1 **Not evident** Does not demonstrate	2 **Functional** Applies skills; requires some guidance	3 **Proficient** Uses skills in complex situations; minimal guidance	4 **Expert** Coaches and supports others

Behaviors Ratings*	0	1	2	3	4
In conversations, the participant:					
1. Uses active listening to understand another person's point of view.					
2. Maintains balance between asking questions and stating opinions.					
3. Questions his or her opinions with intent of reaching observable data.					
4. Uses concrete examples to describe behavior, sensing, feelings, and impact.					
5. Confronts others constructively when opinions differ.					
In decision making the participant:					
6. Plans important decisions carefully.					
7. Relies on instincts.					
8. Relies on intuition.					
9. Uses the assistance of other people when making important decisions.					
10. Uses the advice of other people in making important decisions.					
Regarding learning culture, the participant:					
11. Extends effort to share and distribute learning/knowledge.					
12. Continuously looks for opportunities to learn.					
13. Helps other people learn.					
14. Rewards people for learning.					
15. Gives honest feedback for development.					

*For any rating of 2 or lower, attach development recommendations and explanations.

- How do others function differently in their work that you would attribute to participating in the scenario project?

PERFORMANCE RESULTS IN SCENARIO PROJECTS

Performance measures in scenario planning projects are necessarily estimates. Purposes of scenarios are either to "avoid regret or to generate insights that were previously beyond the mind's reach" (Wack, 1985b, p. 87). But how can these be valued? In fact, the entire insurance industry is based on assigning values to things that have not happened yet. While there is no standard formula for valuing strategic insights or avoiding catastrophes, estimates are a useful way of suggesting the utility of scenario planning. Assessing performance results is absolutely dependent on the purpose of the scenario project. Logically, the more specific the purpose, the easier it will be to estimate the performance results. For example, a project in which focused scenarios are used to examine the uncertainties around building a new oil-drilling platform in a remote location is much easier to evaluate than general global scenarios used to explore the technology environment for a cell-phone company. The more narrow the scope of the project, the more defined the estimates of system results can be. Scenario project system results and financial results are directly linked. Time spent carefully defining and estimating the system results will make for an easier assessment because the financial results merely required the conversion of system results to a monetary value.

System

At their most general level, system results are indicated by the fact that the organization is still viable and operating. This point may seem obvious, but most organizations have an average life span of forty to fifty years (de Geus, 1997). The ability to stay a viable, profitable organization is the primary measure of system performance. More specific system results include ways in which the scenario project is perceived to influence the productivity of the organization. For example, Shell's scenarios that explored whether to construct an oil-drilling rig in Siberia included estimates of how that drilling rig would increase its oil supply, thus adding value to the company. Similarly, scenario projects that reveal opportunities or foster innovative product ideas may carry an estimate of how that idea can lead to results. For example, if an engineering organization is the first to achieve a technological breakthrough and develop a new flow technology that is superior to Coriolis (a current standard in material flow technology), there would be positive implications for the organization's system results. Conversely, heading off a catastrophe or loss has its own positive result.

For example, Toyota has long boasted its product quality. Toyota was under strong fire for not following its own famous quality management principles (Liker, 2010). Error rates and defective products are system results that may be useful in scenario projects. Error rate and defective product numbers can be gathered before the scenario planning project and again afterward. Assuming that the strategic issue is focused on resolving error issues, the number of errors or defective products can be compared before and after scenario planning to establish improvement. Furthermore, error rates and defective products can easily be converted into financial data. So, resolving quality problems has direct implications for financial performance.

In another case, leaders in BP Amoco didn't explore the "what ifs" associated with the risks of drilling for oil five thousand feet below the surface of the ocean at all. Fumbling around with what to do after over two million gallons of oil flowed into the ocean, while the whole world watched, had serious implications for the oil giant. The complete lack of considering the possible outcomes of a high-risk activity could have been the demise of the organization.

Financial

Fear and greed are effective motivators for organizational decision makers—fear of the regrets, and motivators toward the strategic insights referred to by Wack (1984). And few things inspire fear and greed better than dollar signs. In looking at the financial results of a scenario planning project, the task is to convert system results into a dollar value. If we use the same examples just cited, increasing oil reserves would have a dollar value attached to it that would be relatively easy to compute. Likewise, developing a new flow technology before competitors would provide strategic marketing opportunities and sales that could be estimated as a financial return to the organization. Other examples are as follows:

- Apple Computer's iPad is a significant technological development. Using this as an example (and speculating that Apple developed a scenario project around such a tablet), estimates would have been made that quantified the system results (projected demand and production numbers of the tablet computer) and financial results (sales and profits) based on previous successes with the iTunes music (now media) store and the iPhone.

(Note that this example positions scenario planning as an activity that could generate ideas for the innovative, new product.)

- A research and development company using scenarios to explore the viability of several projects may find that focusing on fewer projects could leverage greater human capital. One possible outcome is that one specific project becomes a marketable new technology. If we assume the scenarios included this possibility, estimates of sales and production quantities could be generated based on perceived demand for the product.

Another effective question is what discontinuities have been avoided due to anticipatory thinking? Using a financial savings approach, each scenario can be approached from the mind-set of financial resources saved if things that may change the nature of our business are anticipated.

Sound financial data on projected or estimated costs and benefits from an internal organizational financial expert can also be used in assessing system and financial results (see Swanson, 2001a, 2001b). Data gathering should be designed to spark conversations about how estimates of savings or profits can be made due to avoiding major discontinuities or realizing innovative opportunities. Suggested thinking with which to begin this data gathering with experts includes the following:

- What if scenario A happens and we are not prepared? What kind of losses would we be looking at?
- Alternatively, what if scenario A happens and we are well prepared? What gains can we imagine due to strategic insights that lead to innovative products? (See Figure 9.6—the strategic gains and losses matrix.)

In Technology Corporation, we estimated costs and potential benefits based on assumptions that led to either significant strategic gains or losses within each scenario. For each scenario, we brainstormed what the implications of the story line could be. There was a logical consistency that flowed

Scenario A	Scenario B
• If we are not prepared, what kind of losses would we be looking at? • If we generate strategic insights, what estimates of sales and profits can be made?	• If we are not prepared, what kind of losses would we be looking at? • If we generate strategic insights, what estimates of sales and profits can be made?
Scenario C	Scenario D
• If we are not prepared, what kind of losses would we be looking at? • If we generate strategic insights, what estimates of sales and profits can be made?	• If we are not prepared, what kind of losses would we be looking at? • If we generate strategic insights, what estimates of sales and profits can be made?

FIGURE 9.6   The Strategic Gains and Losses Matrix

from the stories that were told in each scenario. The estimated financial implications for each case are summarized in Figure 9.7.

Cost/Benefit Models and Return on Investment

Finally, there is high utility in considering cost/benefit and return-on-investment models. In the project preparation phase, I suggested using a simple financial forecast model—the financial assessment benefit model (Swanson, 2004):

Performance Value – Cost = Benefit

At this point in the project, the costs are known. The exercises in defining system and financial results are aimed at estimating the performance value of the project. These values can then be inserted into the simple equation, and the benefit of the scenario planning project can be estimated. Of course, the goal is that the performance value exceeds the costs. In my experience, using even modest estimates of performance value produces some amount of benefit. This model essentially produces the return on investment. While other, more complex models can be used, this simple model is usually effective in demonstrating the estimated benefits of scenario planning.

Concorde *Strategic Losses*	Airbus *Strategic Gains*
Relying on the expertise of a few, losses could be significant from inability to leverage collective human capital. Major project lost due to lack of collaboration could potentially cost up to $1 million.	Collective collaboration could bring about new projects and more efficient development of those projects. Major project leading to innovative technology that can be taken to market (e.g., mobile phone) could be worth $5 million or more.
Titanic Potentially facing bankruptcy if nothing changes. Little opportunity for strategic gains in this situation.	**Horse and Buggy** *Strategic Losses* Collaborative efforts without new funding sources allow for sustained business, but minimal development. Potential losses are considerable for high numbers of missed opportunities. Potentially $10 million or more in losses. *Strategic Gains* It is still possible that a novel insight could produce a marketable product.

FIGURE **9.7**   The Strategic Gains and Losses Matrix for Technology Corporation

The scenario project proposal in Chapter 5 demonstrates how the estimation of financial benefits begins at the start of the project. While costs of scenario projects can seem high at first, consider the implications of saving from one major catastrophe or one major strategic insight. For example, if Toyota had done some scenario planning, not around brake pedals or floor mats, but around the managed response to quality defects, executives might have avoided a very costly and damaging sequence of events. The same could be said for BP Amoco. Oil cleanup in the Gulf of Mexico, drilling moratoriums, lawsuits for oil workers, compensating states with affected tourism industries, and many other related costs rose to potentially devastating heights after the oil spill in the summer of 2010. The costs to the natural ecosystem in the Gulf of Mexico and, by its integrated nature, the world will not be realized for years, maybe decades.

A COMPREHENSIVE PLAN FOR ASSESSING SCENARIO PROJECTS

The information relevant to assessing a scenario project can be put into a table as a comprehensive plan for assessing scenario projects. Figure 9.8 is an example of how this information can be synthesized. The earlier these elements are considered in the project, the more relevant the measures will be. If possible, these items should be considered as part of the project preparation phase, and measurements of expected outcomes can be documented in the scenario project proposal. The scenario assessment plan is a road map for documenting the results of a scenario project. Using a comprehensive assessment plan ensures the ability to discuss results and track the contribution of the scenario project to individual, process, and organization performance.

The elements of the project come together for Technology Corporation in Figure 9.9. The major assessment elements are taken directly from the

FIGURE **9.8** A Comprehensive Plan for Assessing Scenario Projects

	Quantitative	Qualitative
Satisfaction Results		
Participant	Survey (10 items, strongly agree to strongly disagree)	Interview questions:
Stakeholder	Survey (10 items, strongly agree to strongly disagree)	Interview questions:
Learning Results		
Knowledge	Surveys/instruments that measure aspects of the organization related to the purpose of the project	Interview questions:
Expertise	Observations of behaviors where appropriate using the Scenario Expertise Audit	Interview questions:
Performance Results		
System	Estimates of system results based on the initial purpose of the project.	Interview questions:
Financial	Performance Value – Cost = Benefit Estimates of discontinuities avoided Estimates of profits due to strategic insights	Interview questions:

FIGURE 9.9 Comprehensive Scenario Project Assessment for Technology Corporation

	Quantitative	Qualitative
Satisfaction Results		
Participant	Survey (10 items, strongly agree to strongly disagree)	Interview questions: 1. Are you satisfied or dissatisfied with the scenario planning project? Why? 2. What things contributed most to the utility (or lack of utility) of the project?
Stakeholder	Survey (10 items, strongly agree to strongly disagree)	Interview questions: 1. Describe your level of satisfaction with the scenario planning project. 2. What things contributed most to the utility (or lack of utility) of the project?
Learning Results		
Knowledge	Surveys/instruments that measure: • Decision making • Learning organization • Characteristics • Mental models • Conversation quality and engagement *Note:* Use instruments pre– and post–scenario planning to measure change.	Interview questions: 1. What have you learned as a result of participating in this project? 2. Did you have any major strategic insights, or "aha" moments? If so, can you describe them?
Expertise	Observations of behaviors where appropriate using the Scenario Expertise Audit	Interview questions: 1. How has your learning affected your behavior as a result of participating in this project? 2. What things do you do differently in your work that you would attribute to participating in the scenario planning project?

(continued)

FIGURE **9.9** Comprehensive Scenario Project Assessment for Technology Corporation (*continued*)

	Quantitative	Qualitative
Performance Results		
System	Estimates of system results based on the initial purpose of the project	Interview questions: 1. Has the scenario planning project helped the organization be more productive? 2. If so, how? In what ways? 3. Have there been strategic insights, creative leaps, or other innovations you feel are attributable to the scenario planning project? Please describe them.
Financial	Performance Value – Cost = Benefit Estimates of discontinuities avoided Estimates of profits due to strategic insights	Interview questions: 1. How has the scenario planning project contributed to the financial stability of the organization?

proposal outlined at the start of the project. The project assessment phase features the actual measures taken that can then be compared to create an overall picture of the project's success and influence.

CONCLUSION

Assessing scenario planning projects is critical to understanding and documenting their effects. Furthermore, establishing evidence of the contributions of scenario projects lends credibility to strategic activities in general. This chapter has presented a comprehensive approach to assessing scenario planning projects. The goal has been to present a method for estimating the benefits of scenario planning, and making the case that scenario planning can result in a variety of benefits. Among these benefits are participant and stakeholder satisfaction, participant knowledge and expertise, and system and financial improvements.

The literature on scenario planning generally does not include methods or approaches to assessing the outcomes of scenario planning projects. This chapter has acknowledged the difficulties in such an assessment and provided a framework for synthesizing the results of scenario projects. The elements of this approach form a complete and theoretically sound approach to assessing scenario projects that moves beyond simple reaction forms and into observable, objective results. Using the tools and techniques provided in this chapter creates a mechanism for clearly understanding and documenting the impact of scenario projects.

P A R T

T H R E E

LEADING SCENARIO PROJECTS

CHAPTERS

10 Managing Scenario Projects

11 Human Perceptions in the Scenario System

12 Initiating Your First Scenario Project

SCENARIO PLANNING is a complex organizational activity, with many barriers and nuances that are often skimmed over or receive little attention. Some dilemmas are not easily solved. Part Three of Scenario Planning in Organizations explores some cutting-edge thinking that can suggest ways of overcoming common barriers in scenario planning.

The following chapters make up this part:

- Chapter 10, "Managing Scenario Projects"
- Chapter 11, "Human Perceptions in Scenario Planning"
- Chapter 12, "Initiating Your First Scenario Project."

Chapter 10 describes several common pitfalls in scenario planning. A scenario project worksheet is also provided to help structure the entire scenario project, as well as avoid the pitfalls. This chapter will help keep the project on track, and its tools are useful in overall project management.

Chapter 11 reviews some recent neurology research and suggests how several barriers to human creativity can be overcome. This chapter also speculates on some techniques from brain research that may improve the effectiveness of scenario planning and certainly form the foundation for interesting research questions in future scenario planning research.

Chapter 12 summarizes the key points of *Scenario Planning in Organizations* and offers some tips for how to get started on your own scenario projects.

Managing
Scenario Projects

The purpose of this chapter is to provide recommendations for helping you manage scenario projects. The skills and abilities required to make scenario projects work are diverse, and they improve over time and experience. The nature of scenario work avoids specific procedures that are repeated in each project. However, scenario projects do lend themselves to frameworks (such as the phases presented in this book). In addition, there are several strategies I have learned from making my own mistakes and from hearing about others. These insights are followed by twenty scenario pitfalls presented in the scenario planning literature (Schoemaker, 2005), including their solutions. This chapter can thus serve as a guide providing a few key leverage points for getting the most out of scenario projects.

STRATEGIES TO MANAGE SCENARIO PROJECTS

Scenario projects have many dimensions and need to be thoughtfully managed. Important strategies for managing scenario projects include the following:

- Spending time on the problem, issue, or question
- Recognizing the importance of the team
- Spending time on analysis
- Defining important outcomes
- Putting your scenarios to use
- Assessing your impact
- Recognizing an evolving context

.es are suggested as important pieces of the scenario system, ,aid attention to, they can help your scenario project stay on deliver results. Each is described in detail.

SPENJING TIME ON THE PROBLEM, QUESTION, OR ISSUE

How the scenario project is framed influences everything. The initial problem, question, or issue must be referenced repeatedly throughout the project. The more specific you can be about the issue at the outset, the easier it is to consistently address that issue throughout. However, it is useful to keep in mind that initial scenarios are usually general "learning" scenarios that explore the external environment. So, if your organization is new to scenario planning, it is very useful to design a first set of scenarios focused on a general understanding of the external environment. Using these scenarios as context, you can then move into a second set of scenarios focused on a specific issue. This approach will allow thinking to sharpen on a specific issue and design a set of scenarios specifically to illuminate the problem. Because this second set of scenarios is highly focused, the project will be easier to assess and likely to have a more lasting impact on decision making.

If an organization is already using general-level scenarios, a project team can jump directly into the "decision" scenarios, moving straight to the problem, question, or issue and working directly on it.

The importance of spending time on the problem, question, or issue cannot be overstated. Having a specific issue creates boundaries for the project. Given the volatility, uncertainty, complexity, and ambiguity of the business environment, there will be difficulties enough in steering a project designed to "promote organizational learning." Such a general focus is not easily assessed. The more specific the focus of the scenario project can be, the more easily it can be assessed. In addition, the pressure for specific assessment data can vary across organizations.

The importance of specifying a problem, question, or issue is intimately related to how decision makers view the utility of the project. Organizations using scenario planning as a one-time effort usually result in project failures. These failures are due to the generation of contextual learning scenarios that do not offer enough specifics for managers to exercise their judgment.

RECOGNIZING THE IMPORTANCE OF THE TEAM

The right team is critical to the success of any scenario project. Team members can provide valuable information about the history, context, issues, personalities, and politics. Therefore, teams must include members internal to the organization. Critical functions of the team include overseeing the administrative management of the project; keeping the initial problem, question, or issue central to the work done in the project; gathering relevant information; conducting research; and facilitating workshops. The team should also be multilevel and cross-functional.

My own failure to recognize the importance of the team in an early scenario project is an example. I did not assign anyone as the project coordinator. As a result, workshops and meetings were poorly attended because there was nobody internal to the organization coordinating the various events and communicating the details of the projects among team members.

Another example from my own projects involved having someone assigned to the team who turned out to be looking for ways to sabotage the project. Although such malintent does not happen often, organization politics can come into play. Team membership should be negotiated. The more committed, excited, and motivated the team members are, the more likely the outcomes will meet and even exceed the expectations of decision makers.

SPENDING TIME ON ANALYSIS

Chapter 6 was dedicated to analysis activity. The activities described allow the team to understand the problem, question, or issue in its context. Analysis activities should not be cut short or otherwise reduced to save project costs. This is a critical phase in the scenario system as it establishes what is known about the issue. Forecasts and trend reports can often be used as a substitute for thinking on the part of the user; therefore, the goal of analysis and the scenario exploration phase is to generate the team's own understanding and thinking about the problem, question, or issue.

Projects that reduce time and commitment to the exploration phase have little impact. This is because the workshops and subsequent phases are tailored to what is learned during analysis and scenario exploration. As is the case with any organizational improvement activity, everything rests on this foundational work. I have seen projects in which little time is given to understanding the issue, and these projects have generally lacked the momentum for significant impact.

DEFINING IMPORTANT OUTCOMES

One key to making scenarios work is having an idea of what the expectations are. While these expectations can become a moving target, the more that is known about what decision makers hope to get out of the project, the more the project can be tailored to address those expectations. Some managers and executives are comfortable with ambiguity and vague outcomes like "continuous learning about the industry," but the vast majority will have specific desired outcomes in mind. Ask for them.

My own experience has told me that the type of organization matters as well. For example, scenario projects I have worked on with engineering firms have had specific, targeted outcomes. These projects have also required more effort to stimulate strategic thinking than working with design teams in technology-driven industries. In other words, organizational culture and personality can drive an orientation toward more specific (or more ambiguous) outcomes.

PUTTING YOUR SCENARIOS TO USE

Perhaps the most common reason for disappointment in scenario projects is a lack of use. So many consulting companies now provide scenario planning interventions, yet few boast anything beyond developing scenarios for their client organizations. The development of scenarios can be highly creative and fun, but using them should be the most rewarding phase. The amount of time and effort spent on scenario development should be mirrored in scenario implementation.

This book provides a framework for using scenarios. Specific workshops have been described with guidance for making them work. Communicating and using the scenarios is the opportunity to begin an organization-wide strategic conversation. This conversation can be the catalyst for real change inside the organization. Do not let the delivery of three or four scenarios be the end of your project. You must use them to challenge thinking within and across the organization.

ASSESSING YOUR IMPACT

Most scenario projects lack assessment or evaluation. How do decision makers know they are getting anything for their investment? Some claim to simply "know." Particularly in lean economic times (although equally important anytime), organizational change interventions must have documentation of their delivered outcomes. Chapter 9 of this book has laid out a comprehensive approach to scenario project assessment. The proposed activities take time and resources. However, if carried out, these assessment techniques will make the case that scenario planning is easily worth every penny invested.

If you have experience with other assessment tools, use them. The purpose is to begin establishing evidence that scenario planning works. Scenario planning literature is full of claims about decision making, learning, and navigating the future, but little evidence is provided to support these claims. Most scenario planners could tell you stories of their successes or failures, which may constitute a form of evidence, but few people document these stories. Though helpful, these stories also are not always compelling to financially driven executives. Scenario projects should include a cost/benefit analysis. Even if the figures it contains are estimates or forecasts, they should be included. The scenario system presented in this book demands that you assess the projected financial benefits of the project at the outset. Following up at the conclusion of the project and beyond should be a simple exercise in collecting a few pieces of relevant data.

RECOGNIZING AN EVOLVING CONTEXT

A very exciting aspect of scenario planning is the increasing variety of contexts in which it is being used. The Mont Fleur Scenarios (Kahane, 1992) were the first example of using the scenario planning technique in a noncorporate context. The Mont Fleur Scenarios brought together a diverse group of business leaders, politicians, civil rights activists, artists, and others concerned with the future of South Africa. Their scenario efforts were aimed at building a community sharing a vision for a better South Africa. Adam Kahane, the primary facilitator, was previously a member of Shell's scenario team. Kahane has since focused his efforts more carefully in this area, moving on to scenarios for Colombia.

These projects (and particularly the Mont Fleur Scenarios) were a clear signal that scenarios could be useful beyond corporate planning. Part group decision-making process, part team building, part envisioning, part analysis, among others, it is easy to see that the scenario system can apply in a variety of contexts. The world in general features the same characteristics (e.g., volatility, uncertainty, complexity, and ambiguity) as the business environment, and tools for thinking differently about the future can be applied to problems related to global climate change, health care, water supply, ecology, and other natural resources.

ADDITIONAL PITFALLS AND ACCOMPANYING SOLUTIONS

Schoemaker (2005) has described twenty common pitfalls in scenario planning. These pitfalls are divided into ten process pitfalls and ten content pitfalls. Although there is some overlap with the strategies for managing scenario projects described earlier in this chapter, they will all be presented—along with proposed solutions—to keep the integrity of Schoemaker's list.

TEN PROCESS PITFALLS

The first ten pitfalls are specifically related to managing the scenario project process (Schoemaker, 2005). These pitfalls are results of an inability to understand the nuances related to facilitating scenario projects and the administrative side of directing and steering scenario projects.

- *Failure to ensure top leadership support.* Any organizational change intervention must have leadership support in order to be successful. Scenario planning is an executive-level activity, so if the executives are not involved, forget it!
- *Not enough contribution from outside.* The dangers of groupthink (too much homogeneity in the thinking) are ever present with scenario planning. Using outside sources—"remarkable people" or experts in a variety of disciplines—pays significant dividends (Wack, 1984). In my experience, each project should use a minimum of two external experts. The more participants involved in the project, the more external experts should be sought.
- *Lack of balance between line and staff people.* A basic feature of scenario planning is that it must involve a cross section of the organization. That includes levels and functions. If it doesn't, it's not scenario planning. Make sure each function in the organization is represented in the conversation.

- *Unrealistic expectations.* This pitfall is avoided by clarifying expectations and documenting them in the scenario project proposal. Expectations should be clarified before any exploration or development work is begun.
- *Poorly defined roles.* The scenario project proposal also demands the identification of team members and clarification of roles. The importance of this issue has been discussed thoroughly but cannot be overstated.
- *Failure to keep on track.* Again, the scenario project proposal demands the articulation of a strategic problem, issue, or question. Clearly defining this issue and consistently coming back to it are critical to success.
- *Too many scenarios.* Do not use more than four scenarios. The system presented in this book is designed to produce four useful scenarios. Having more than four scenarios is overwhelming for decision makers and complicates the project.
- *Not enough time allowed.* The scenario project proposal calls for an agreed-on time line. If decision makers expect to complete a scenario project with two workshops in two weeks, explain the consequences and conditions required for thinking strategically. If they insist, an alternative is to suggest a different facilitator. It is important to be ready to remove yourself from projects that are set up to fail. Short-cutting with an unrealistic time frame is a sure path to disappointing and low-utility outcomes.
- *Failure to link to existing processes.* The scenario system presented in this book connects scenario development to the organization through several workshops. Those workshops are specifically designed to link the scenario project to various existing processes inside the organization, including organization culture, structure, current strategies, human resources, design, and others.
- *Failure to link to our everyday world.* Scenarios have to be relevant for the managers who will use them. Projects that fail to capture the things that managers are concerned with in their everyday decision making will have little impact. An effective way to overcome this pitfall is to use information gathered in the interviews and make sure it appears in the scenarios. The interview questions described

in the scenario exploration phase are designed to draw out the things managers worry about in their roles as organizational leaders. If these items appear in the scenarios, relevance is increased that will catch the users' attention.

TEN CONTENT PITFALLS

The following ten pitfalls are related to the content in the scenarios them-selves (Schoemaker, 2005). Again, solutions are suggested based on the system provided in this book.

- *Failure to take the long view.* Scenario projects should look ahead five, ten, or twenty years to stimulate creative thinking. The goal is to get participants into a space that is truly unknown to them. Targeting scenarios within a year or two is often too close to managers' mind-sets, and their scenarios will often be extrapolations of their current thinking and their own understanding of trends.
- *Failure to take the wide view.* Scenarios have to expand beyond your own industry. Given the complexity of today's business environment, it is difficult to see how an honest look at any issue would fail to link it to numerous other issues in a variety of industries. Thus, the scenario exploration phase provides the tools for analyzing issues in their context, revealing their interdependencies.
- *Too much attention to trends.* Trends are often used as a substitute for real thinking. Trends are not a viable shortcut to deep analysis and the development of real knowledge. Trends are a part of the scenario exploration phase and should be considered. If allowed to dominate, however, trends can derail the development of understanding.
- *Too homogeneous a range of views.* Again, using "remarkable people," or experts outside the organization, from different industries can prevent this pitfall. Diversity of thinking is important, and one signal that views are too homogeneous is when meetings and workshops are completed quickly, with minimal dialogue or challenge. This can be an indicator of a very efficient team of people who work well together, but as the project leader, it may be a signal for you to bring in a different perspective.
- *Lack of internal logic.* Scenarios are not compelling when they are not based on facts and research. This is why "scenario light" projects,

based on concepts and ideas, without deep analysis, are so often useless.

- *Failure to look at deeper-level causes, failure to challenge mind-sets, and failure to make the scenarios dynamic.* These three scenario pitfalls are attributable to the fact that there are no methods or systems available for checking the utility of any given set of scenarios. This book presents a scenario quality checklist designed to promote deep analysis, optimize the likelihood of changing mind-sets, and ensure dynamic, compelling scenario stories. Using a checklist like this, or developing your own, and asking the input of the team to make sure these items are addressed will help you avoid these issues.

- *Irrelevance.* Again, using information from interviews with managers will immediately bring the scenarios to their doorstep. Obviously, having people for whom the scenarios must be relevant involved in the process is critical.

- *Failure to create a real breakthrough.* This pitfall signals an overarching problem with most scenario planning methods. What is a breakthrough? Existing methods don't push for a defined purpose, goals, or expected outcomes of the scenario project. So a breakthrough is a nebulous, undefined, and in most cases random event. True, there must be room in the scenario project for things unplanned to emerge (Mintzberg, Ahlstrand & Lampel, 2005). However, breakthroughs can also be outcomes of deep, disciplined thinking about and critical analysis of strategic issues. The system presented in this book is designed to optimize scenario projects toward articulated purposes, expected outcomes, and deep thinking.

CONCLUSION

Most of the pitfalls in scenario planning projects can be avoided by using the scenario system presented in this book. The scenario project management worksheet (Figure 10.1) is designed to make the scenario system immediately applicable and to help translate the concepts presented in this book to any organization. It will help plan, structure, and manage the phases of performance-based scenario planning, and it can be used as a guide throughout the project for avoiding the common problems in scenario projects that have been discussed.

This chapter has presented key issues in managing scenario projects, including the following:

- Spending time on the problem, issue, or question
- Recognizing the importance of the team
- Spending time on analysis
- Defining important outcomes
- Putting your scenarios to use
- Assessing your impact
- Recognizing an evolving context

The guidance provided to address these issues is largely a result of my own experience in designing, managing, and facilitating scenario projects.

This chapter has also presented the common pitfalls in scenario projects according to Schoemaker (2005). These descriptions and accompanying solutions are intended to help you manage and facilitate your own scenario projects and avoid some of the more common issues that come up. Tips for optimizing scenario projects will help project facilitators avoid common traps and barriers to generating successful, strategically insightful scenario projects. Finally, this chapter has shared the scenario project management worksheet, which will help you plan, structure, and facilitate a scenario project. This worksheet makes the concepts from this book immediately applicable in any organization.

FIGURE **10.1**   The Scenario Project Worksheet

SCENARIO PROJECT WORKSHEET

This sheet is a general guide for planning and managing scenario projects and can be used as an organizational guide and project management checklist. There is a total of five phases to the Performance-Based Scenario System.

Phase 1: Project Preparation
Defined Problem, Question, or Issue: _____
Stated Purpose of the Project: _____
Project Scope and Time Line: _____
Roles and People Assigned: _____
    Project Leader: _____   Coordinator: _____
    Remarkable People: _____
    Team Members: _____
    Other: _____
Expected Outcomes of the Project: _____
Measurement Tools: _____

Phase 1: Project Preparation Phase Pitfall Management   Yes   No
    Is top leadership participating in the project?   ____ ____
    Are remarkable people recruited to participate in the project?   ____ ____
    Is there a balance between line and staff participants?   ____ ____
    Is the time line realistic given the expectations?   ____ ____
    Does the project link to existing processes?   ____ ____
    Will the project address fundamental issues in organization
      management?   ____ ____

Phase 2: Scenario Exploration
A. External Analysis: ☐ STEEP forces
    (check those that   ☐ Thinking hats
    apply)   ☐ Trends and forecasts
        ☐ Other: _____

B. Internal Analysis: ☐ Interviews (list interview participants):

    _____   _____
    _____   _____
    _____   _____
    _____   _____
    _____   _____

        ☐ Analyze the business idea
        ☐ Analyze the theory of the business

(continued)

FIGURE **10.1**   The Scenario Project Worksheet *(continued)*

C. Analysis and Synthesis Tools Used:
- ☐ Questionnaires
- ☐ Observations
- ☐ Existing data: _____
- ☐ Swanson's Performance Diagnosis Matrix
- ☐ Rummler and Brache's Nine Performance Variables
- ☐ Other analysis and synthesis tools:

_____

_____

	Yes	No
D. Analysis is thorough and demonstrates our own understanding of the problem or issue.	____	____

Phase 2: Scenario Exploration Phase Pitfall Management

	Yes	No
Scenarios extend 5, 10, 15, or 20 years into the future?	____	____
Other industries included in the analysis and scenarios?	____	____
Trends are included but do not dominate?	____	____

Phase 3: Scenario Development

A. Workshop Planning (Dates):
   Brainstorming _____
   Ranking by impact _____
   Ranking by relative uncertainty _____

B. Two Critical Uncertainties (High Impact + High Uncertainty) for the Scenario Matrix:

   1. _____   2. _____

C. Draft Scenario Matrix:

(continued)

FIGURE **10.1**   The Scenario Project Worksheet *(continued)*

D. Research Agenda (elements that require more data gathering and investigation):

_____   _____
_____   _____
_____   _____
_____   _____
_____   _____

E. Draft Scenario Titles/Themes/Possibilities:

_____ _____ _____
_____ _____ _____
_____ _____ _____

F. Plots:
Suggestions: _____ Revolution   _____ Cycles   _____ Infinite Possibility
                 _____ Lone Ranger _____ My Generation
Other:

_____   _____
_____   _____

G. Story Writing (name[s] of individual[s] to write each scenario):
1. _____   2. _____
3. _____   4. _____

H. Communication Strategy:
☐ Workbook   ☐ Podcasts
☐ Website   ☐ Presentations
☐ Video   ☐ Workshops
☐ Activities: _____
☐ Other: _____

Phase 3: Scenario Development Phase Pitfall Management   Yes   No

Four scenarios (if other, check for novelty; avoid best/worst)?   _____ _____
Scenarios have input from external experts?   _____ _____
Scenarios are logical and well researched?   _____ _____
Scenarios include deep analysis and are data driven?   _____ _____

Phase 4: Scenario Implementation

A. Workshop Planning for Using the Scenarios (dates):
Revisit the initial problem/question _____
Theory of the business _____
Business idea _____

Analyze current strategies _____
Developing signals _____
Experiential exercise _____

(continued)

FIGURE 10.1   The Scenario Project Worksheet *(continued)*

B. Outcomes
- Key Strategies Useful in All Scenarios:
  1. _____   2. _____
  3. _____   4. _____
- Signals:

  _____   _____
  _____   _____
  _____   _____
  _____   _____
  _____   _____

Phase 4: Scenario Implementation Phase Pitfall Management   Yes   No

Scenarios are interesting and relevant for managers?   ____   ____
Scenario can create a real breakthrough?   ____   ____

Phase 5: Project Assessment Phase

	Quantitative	Qualitative
Satisfaction Results		
Participant	Survey (10 items, strongly agree to strongly disagree)	Interview questions:
Stakeholder	Survey (10 items, strongly agree to strongly disagree)	Interview questions:
Learning Results		
Knowledge	Surveys: 1. _____ 2. _____ 3. _____ 4. _____ 5. _____ 6. _____	Interview questions:

(continued)

FIGURE **10.1**   The Scenario Project Worksheet *(continued)*

	Quantitative	Qualitative
Learning Results *(continued)*		
Expertise	Observations of behaviors where appropriate using the Scenario Expertise Audit (who will be observed?) 1. _____ 2. _____ 3. _____ 4. _____ 5. _____ 6. _____	Interview questions:
Performance Results		
System	Estimates of system results based on the initial purpose of the project	Interview questions:
Financial	Performance Value Performance Value – Cost = Benefit Estimates of discontinuities avoided Estimates of profits due to strategic insights	Interview questions:

11

Human Perceptions in the Scenario System

Scenario planning is a social activity. It integrates learning, social interaction, dialogue, and human perceptions. These things come together in the form of a recalibrated view of the organization and its situation if the project has been successful.

Three critical barriers to optimal innovation and human creativity are (1) perception, (2) a natural fear response, and (3) social intelligence (Berns, 2008). Decision makers are limited by a brain that requires approximately forty watts—the amount needed to power a lightbulb (Berns, 2008). To perform its many complex functions, the brain must be efficient, and therefore it draws on past experiences and any other easily accessible information sources to make sense of its situation. Decision makers are limited by fear of uncertainty and the public consequences of decisions with unfavorable results. Many people become easily paralyzed by the prospect of being wrong. Finally, optimal human innovation requires the ability to convince other people that an idea has merit, and this requires social intelligence (Berns 2008). An analysis of highly innovative, creative thinkers revealed that these people found ways to overcome such barriers. The results are published in Berns's 2008 book *Iconoclast*.

This chapter examines these core barriers to optimal human innovation and potential. More specifically, it explores the role of scenario projects in overcoming these barriers. The barriers identified by Berns are intricately linked to strategic decision making—for which scenario planning has been positioned as a critical aid. This chapter uses examples from neurology research to make the case that scenario planning can address these barriers to innovative and creative human activity, and help people overcome problems of perception, fear, and social intelligence.

Additional research studies based on the thinking underlying quantum physics reveal the untapped potential of the human brain. These studies suggest a new take on the relationship between thought and action. Sample research studies that relate to the power of scenarios are presented and the implications considered.

THE NEUROLOGY OF LEARNING

Brain research suggests that by the time we are in our mid-thirties, we have literally "memorized" the majority of repeated activities in our lives (Dispenza, 2007). For example, the process of waking up, putting on clothing, brushing teeth, preparing the kids for school, and driving to work require minimal focused thought because we have literally memorized the necessary routines required to accomplish these activities. The brain is a relatively small organ given what it is responsible for, and one of its key features is efficiency (Berns, 2008). The brain must be efficient because it is trying to reduce the amount of energy it uses to accomplish its tasks (Berns, 2008). The way the brain accomplishes efficiency is by creating neural networks. These networks can consist of billions of neurons that learn to "fire" together when activities are repeated over and over again. There is a network of related neurons that fire together for each repeated activity in your life. For example, one group of neurons is responsible for brushing your teeth, and one for driving your car.

Learning can be described as the process developing neural networks that fire together and become habitual. When we first learn to drive a car, it seems exceedingly complex. But, in a relatively short period of time, driving seems to require little concentrated thought at all. Learning can also be described as the process of "unwiring" existing neural networks, and "rewiring" neurons in different ways (Dispenza, 2007). The accompanying "aha" experience is a result of neurons in the brain making new connections as new concepts are absorbed and linked to other concepts (Berns, 2008). The brain is far more complex than we have understood, and the potential for new discoveries is vast.

PERCEPTION

The problem of perception is not new, but the impact of problems of perception is often greater than we realize. According to the neuroscience view, imagination uses the same neurons as natural sight but works in reverse (Berns, 2008). As a result, imagination is an extension of past experience—what you are able to imagine is based on what you have experienced in the past. Again according to the neuroscience view, the way to increase your capacity to imagine is to continuously bombard your brain with new experiences (Dispenza, 2007).

Recurring experiences build neural networks, which eventually lead to the ability to perform a task expertly without directing much conscious thought toward that activity. In strategic and organizational contexts, neural networks can be equated with mental models—the buildup of past experiences, beliefs, assumptions, and expertise that tell us what to do. When these networks or mental models lead to successful results, there is little incentive to question them.

The description of the scenario system presented in this book makes a clear case for how perceptions can be shifted. However, the social approach to strategy required by scenario planning is not automatic. A secondary barrier to adjusting perceptions is simply arrogance. Participants must engage in the project with a willingness to question their knowledge and be faced with the possibility they might be wrong. People who are unwilling to consider that their knowledge or expertise may be wrong will get little out of scenario planning.

FEAR

Fear is usually what prevents participants from opening up enough to examine their assumptions and perceptions. Fear can be viewed as a driver of perceptions. There is risk associated with questioning the popular view—asking, "What if the experts are wrong?"—but there is also risk in ignoring the volatility, uncertainty, complexity, and ambiguity in the external environment. Which is a greater risk? Executives eventually find that ego does not have a useful place in solving difficult strategic dilemmas, and scenario planning does not require a "bet the farm" strategy as one of its outcomes. As a result, scenario planning seems a much less risky way of questioning conventional wisdom because it does not require commitment to a single strategy for moving ahead. It is actually a more natural approach to decision making.

Berns's (2008) research has shown that the most effective strategy for mitigating fear in group situations is to "recruit one like-minded individual" (p. 103). This makes it highly unlikely that any single individual will be up against the collective view of the group. Scenario planning has a built-in mechanism in using outside experts specifically designed to prevent group-think. However, many scenario projects do not make use of this critical resource, and the results show it. The barrier of fear is overcome in scenario planning by using its time-tested methods, including alternative voices, and making sure that views are diverse enough to prevent one-against-all situations.

SOCIAL INTELLIGENCE

Familiarity and reputation are two key aspects of social intelligence, and they go hand in hand (Berns, 2008). These aspects are important when attempting to communicate ideas. Though less relevant in scenario planning in terms of a barrier, these aspects become factors in considering who should be involved in the scenario project (team members and other outside experts) and in presenting ideas to decision makers. In scenario planning, the goal is less to convince others that your idea is correct or right, and more to convince people to entertain ideas contrary to their own.

However, there is a role for convincing other people in the organization that scenario planning is a useful, appropriate approach to strategy. This is why internal leaders should be recruited as participants and team members. Every organization has leaders who are not leaders in formal title. Participation of these informal leaders sends a signal to the rest of the organization that the project is useful and likely to produce results. Louis van der Merwe called these individuals "linking pins" throughout the organization because they connect people across the organization regardless of functional silos.

THREE STUDIES ON THE BRAIN AND PERCEPTIONS

The visual and creative nature of scenario planning carries additional implications. Recent neurology research suggests that the more deeply participants can be pushed into visualizing the scenarios, the more effective they will be. A review of these research studies provokes some exciting speculations about the potential results of participants who focus and concentrate deeply on the content and possible outcomes presented in each scenario. The next section reviews several research studies and speculates what these research studies could mean in the context of scenario planning.

The brain's capacity to imagine is particularly unique. Emerging research in this area is producing some startling discoveries with important implications. Research studies of note include work on visualized weightlifting versus actual weightlifting (Yue, 2001), work on visualized piano playing versus actual piano playing (Pascual-Leone, Dang, Cohen, Brasil-Neto, Cammorata, & Hallett, 1995), and work on comparing the effects of maximal voluntary and imagined muscle contractions (Yue & Cole, 1992). Each of these studies is summarized briefly.

VISUALIZED WEIGHTLIFTING VERSUS ACTUAL WEIGHTLIFTING

Research participants were asked to "imagine flexing one of their biceps as hard as possible in training sessions five times a week" (Yue, 2001, p. 1717). Researchers recorded brain activity and electrical impulses at the motor neurons of the biceps muscles. "The volunteers who thought about flexing their biceps showed a 13.5 per cent increase in strength after three weeks, and maintained that gain for three months after training stopped" (Yue, 2001, p. 1717).

VISUALIZED PIANO PLAYING VERSUS ACTUAL PIANO PLAYING

Researchers used cortical motor mapping on subjects learning a one-handed exercise on the piano (Pascual-Leone, Dang, Cohen, Brasil-Neto, Cammorata, & Hallett, 1995). Subjects were assigned to a physical practice group, a mental practice group, or a control group. Subjects in the physical practice group practiced the exercise for two hours daily, subjects in the mental practice group visualized the exercise for two hours daily, and the control group did not practice the exercise.

> Over the course of five days, mental practice alone led to significant improvement in the performance of the five-finger exercise, but the improvement was significantly less than that produced by physical practice alone. However, mental practice alone led to the same plastic changes in the motor system as those occurring in the acquisition of the skill by repeated physical exercise. (Pascual-Leone et al., 1995, p. 1037)

MAXIMAL VOLUNTARY AND IMAGINED MUSCLE CONTRACTIONS

Researchers compared the results between groups with maximal voluntary muscle contractions and imagined muscle contractions in the left fifth finger (Yue & Cole, 1992). A third group served as the control group. "Average abduction force of the left fifth digit increased 22 per cent for the imagining group, and 30 per cent for the actual contraction group" (Yue & Cole, 1992, p. 1114).

BRAIN STATES

These research studies show that imagined activities can cause similar results to actual activities. What is important about these findings is that they suggest we take the power of the brain and its capabilities for granted. Furthermore, the measurement of brain waves in all of these studies showed that participants in the visualization/imagination groups all had significant changes in the nature of their brain waves during the imagination exercises. Participants in these groups all transitioned from beta brain waves to alpha brain waves, indicating a mental state of relaxed focus and concentration.

These research studies suggest that profound changes can be realized when the brain transitions from beta waves to alpha waves (i.e., from the hurried, hectic pace of everyday life to relaxation and calm). Some have called this state meditation, and Csikszentmihalyi (1998) would call it "flow." There need be nothing mysterious about achieving a state of total concentration and focus. Most people have experienced a time of such absorption in an activity that they lost a sense of time and space. This state is measurable in functional MRI brain scans. Participants in these research studies achieve such a mental state according to their brain wave scans.

THE BRAIN IN SCENARIOS

Whereas traditional approaches to strategy and strategic planning focus on trend reports and updates of budget projections, scenario projects are designed to help decision makers understand the dynamics at play in uncertain environments. Scenarios helps decision makers uncover blind spots, the things they don't know they don't know, and reframe the strategy process as a learning activity.

VISUALIZATION IN SCENARIOS

The experience of visualization and "being in" a specific scenario and then being asked to explain how it came to be has been a profound tool, but brain activity during scenario immersion has not yet been studied. An early hypothesis based on neurology research would be that participants who achieve beta brain waves and get "lost" in the scenarios are more likely to have strategic insights. If confirmed, there would be implications for facilitating scenario projects. How can scenarios be presented such that the likelihood of provoking focused concentration is maximized? What is the best format for presenting scenarios with a goal of capturing the full attention of participants? I would love to see functional MRI scans of various participants in scenario projects. Of course, it is not quite that simple!

SEEING

Scenario planning literature frequently uses a metaphor of seeing, as in the sense that scenarios allow the participant to "see" the same situation in a different way. Every way of seeing is based on a certain set of assumptions, and if those assumptions or mental models can be changed, there is the potential for new learning, cognitive shift, new understanding, and, concomitantly, new and most desirable outcomes.

Additional neurological research suggests that the human brain cannot tell the difference between what it experiences through the known five senses and what it imagines (Le Doux, 2000; Schwartz, Stapp, & Beauregard, 2005). In a recent research, scientists monitored neurological activity in subjects and found the same activities in exactly the same areas of the brain when subjects were seeing and when they were remembering (Schwartz et al., 2005).

MEMORIES OF THE FUTURE

This finding is significant in the context of scenario planning because it blurs the lines between reflection and action—between thinking and doing. More specifically, this research suggests that scenario planning is a means for creating a memory that can serve as actual experience.

High-utility scenario planning creates memories of the future (Ingvar, 1985). However, by definition, these are memories of things that have not actually occurred. Scenario planning helps participants to make sense of their experience, linking the past to the present and future, and creating alternative future end states (Burt, 2006). The extent to which these future states create memories could be largely dependent on the extent to which each participant is engaged in the project—often a function of facilitation, relevance, and learning.

MAXIMIZING THE EFFECTIVENESS OF SCENARIOS

Other chapters in this book have presented criteria for assessing the quality of scenarios. This chapter has briefly described some provocative ideas that speculate on human perceptions and brain activity during the scenario project. Neurology research confirms that people learn more when they concentrate and focus on the task at hand. This book has argued that in many organizations, strategy has become an automated activity consisting of updating budget projections and injecting popular trends as priority activities. Largely, thinking and learning have become lost as important parts of the planning process. Scenario planning puts thinking and learning at the forefront of strategy, which has implications for, yet is influenced by, human perceptions and brain activity.

Emerging research on human perceptions provokes questions about how to most effectively engage participants. Choosing participants who are motivated to learn is always helpful. However, the mode in which scenarios are presented can make or break the deal for participants as well. Scenario planning, therefore, becomes a delicate balance between the learning orientation of participants and the skills of facilitators. Both work together to create a focused, deliberate effort at studying and understanding the dynamics at play in a specific situation.

CONCLUSION

The goal of this chapter has been to consider some stimulating ideas on the horizon for facilitators and participants in scenario projects. Three barriers to optimal human perception and innovation have been presented. It has been suggested that scenario planning is a natural system for dealing with these barriers. Related neurology research was briefly discussed to show that the human brain functions differently when its attention is directed and focused. These research studies are intended to provoke new ideas regarding the format, presentation, and engagement of participants in scenario projects.

12

Initiating Your First Scenario Project

Many scenario projects are glorified brainstorming sessions with little connection to critical organization inputs and outputs. The most difficult yet most compelling use of scenarios will connect innovative thinking to everyday work. Participants should approach their work differently as a result of working on scenario projects. Sustaining these changes requires attention to detail, accountability, and general management skills—and, leadership is really management done well (Mintzberg, 2009).

Stressing the importance of up-front analysis and project assessment adds considerably to the robustness of a scenario project. Most currently available methods do not require these analysis and assessment components, and as a result, using the system presented in this book may seem daunting. The added activities are designed to feed directly into, and out of, the scenario construction phase. The nuts and bolts of scenario projects as presented in this book require time spent understanding the issue, approximately six days of workshops over two to three months, and assessment activities. These bookend activities will be the biggest shift for users of other scenario methods. However, these components are critical and require statements of expectations up-front and evidence of value at the project's conclusion. To help get a handle on the flow of a scenario project, the scenario project management worksheet was presented in Chapter 10. The worksheet is intended to be used as a guide for structuring and managing a scenario project in any organization, and to make the concepts described in this book immediately useful.

Essentially, the activities in the preparation and assessment phases are aimed at connecting the scenario project to performance improvement. Given a tendency to dismiss strategic initiatives as "too difficult" or "impossible" to evaluate, responsible facilitators of scenario projects will find a way to show the value of what they do. The phases in this book provide a clear approach to all the elements required for successful scenario planning.

Frustration with planning methods that simply do not work are what usually initiates a first scenario project. Perhaps your organization is stuck in the once-a-year planning retreat, or maybe your current approach to planning takes last year's financial data, adds a percentage, and rolls out new goals and growth targets, and that's called strategy. Whatever the case, the premise of this book is that the majority of planning methods cannot account for uncertainty, and they are generally unsuitable for dealing with the nature of today's strategic dilemmas. So, if you have read this book, you are probably ready to try something else.

HOW TO GET STARTED

Users of this book are likely to fall into one of two categories: (1) those wanting to carry out a scenario project for the first time or (2) those who have tried scenarios before but were disappointed with the outcome. No matter which category you are in, initiating your scenario project rests on two key items: (1) finding out whether decision makers understand what scenario planning is really about and (2) developing commitment and support for the project. These two items lay the foundation for beginning the scenario project proposal.

If decision makers are not familiar with scenario planning, there is some educating to do. A short presentation can easily cover the benefits of scenario planning and what differentiates it from other approaches to planning. The first two chapters of this book provide the relevant material and explain the benefits and general process of scenario planning. Part of any briefing on scenario planning should emphasize involvement as critical to the success of the project and that support on its own is not enough.

The second task is to develop support and commitment. It should be clear that scenario projects are not individual-driven projects. They require support and involvement from senior decision makers, colleagues, managers, line workers, and outside experts. They require a substantial amount of coordination and resources—the most important of which are people who are ready to think deeply and critically about the organization and its environment.

Sometimes the excitement about scenario projects can catch on like wildfire. The prospect of time to reflect and think is appealing to many decision makers, and some will jump at the chance. Scenario projects are also appealing because they blend creativity, analysis, thinking, and action. The biggest struggle can involve economic conditions and time commitments. These challenges can be overcome by presenting the potential benefits of a single strategic insight. Scenario projects may appear expensive when costs are viewed alone, but once the financial implications of ideas that lead to innovative products or save the organization from a serious shift are realized, these costs seem to shrink in the larger perspective.

Once you have developed an understanding of the scenario planning system and support for the project has been cultivated, you can consider the logistics of the project preparation phase. Starting with the steps described in the project preparation phase will lead you through the critical elements that go into the project proposal. The following phases (and their corresponding chapters in this book) lead you through the rest.

Again, the scenario project management worksheet (Figure 10.1) should not be missed by anyone planning to take this book and its concepts into action. The worksheet synthesizes the phases of the performance-based scenario system and translates the content of this book into clear activities.

THE PERFORMANCE-BASED SCENARIO SYSTEM IN REVIEW

The performance-based scenario system is presented again in Figure 12.1, complete with each of its phases and their major components.

Following the systematic framework provided here will lead to successful and innovative scenario project results. The scenario system was designed to avoid the major pitfalls in the scenario literature and is a practical system.

Experts in planning will tell you that using a systematic approach will relieve some of the headaches associated with vague, uncertain, complex and ambiguous problems. Working through the preparation, exploration, construction, implementation, and assessment phases connects the scenario project to organizational inputs and outputs. In particular, the project

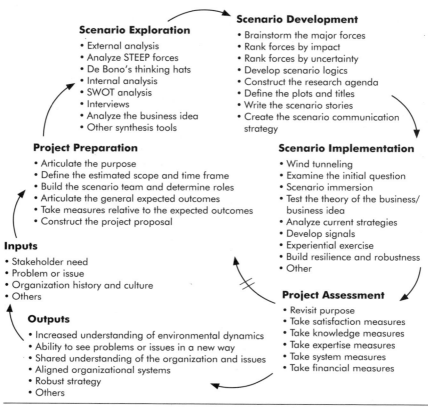

Scenario Exploration

• External analysis
• Analyze STEEP forces
• De Bono's thinking hats
• Internal analysis
• SWOT analysis
• Interviews
• Analyze the business idea
• Other synthesis tools

Scenario Development

• Brainstorm the major forces
• Rank forces by impact
• Rank forces by uncertainty
• Develop scenario logics
• Construct the research agenda
• Define the plots and titles
• Write the scenario stories
• Create the scenario communication strategy

Project Preparation

• Articulate the purpose
• Define the estimated scope and time frame
• Build the scenario team and determine roles
• Articulate the general expected outcomes
• Take measures relative to the expected outcomes
• Construct the project proposal

Scenario Implementation

• Wind tunneling
• Examine the initial question
• Scenario immersion
• Test the theory of the business/business idea
• Analyze current strategies
• Develop signals
• Experiential exercise
• Build resilience and robustness
• Other

Inputs

• Stakeholder need
• Problem or issue
• Organization history and culture
• Others

Outputs

• Increased understanding of environmental dynamics
• Ability to see problems or issues in a new way
• Shared understanding of the organization and issues
• Aligned organizational systems
• Robust strategy
• Others

Project Assessment

• Revisit purpose
• Take satisfaction measures
• Take knowledge measures
• Take expertise measures
• Take system measures
• Take financial measures

FIGURE 12.1   The Performance-Based Scenario System

preparation and project assessment phases work directly with measures of performance.

The preparation and exploration phases form the foundation of the problem and its nuances. As a result, these phases provide the outputs on which the rest of the scenario project is based. Therefore, shortcut or sloppy work in the preparation and exploration phases can easily lead to scenarios that have no utility. Examples of such projects are those that simply quantify different outcomes of obvious variables. For example, scenarios inside Shell that simply showed oil prices going up, down, or remaining the same were hardly insightful or innovative. That is because they are based on such obvious information. Deep analysis reveals critical variables hiding underneath the system, and it takes hard thinking and a lot of time to find them. But the rewards are seen in compelling scenarios that provoke strategic insights.

The scenario development phase presents materials found in other scenario publications. However, this book presents a case to illustrate each phase and each step of the scenario system. Thus, examples and relevant materials are provided along the way. The result is a clearer explanation of the workshops and suggested activities that can be abstract and hard to grasp otherwise.

The scenario implementation and project assessment phases are two of the book's unique contributions. Few sources on scenario planning suggest methods for using the scenarios to provoke strategic insights, and even fewer provide examples. Scenarios fail to live up to expectations unless they are used to examine and further analyze parts of the organization and, ultimately, to take action. This book shows a clear path for putting scenarios to use. In addition, it provides an assessment strategy that, when used, will produce a complete picture of the scenario project's impact. While not easy work, these phases bring the scenario project out of the abstract and conceptual realm, and put them into practice.

CONCLUSION

The goal of scenario planning in organizations is to avoid the crises associated with fundamental shifts in the organizational environment and to take advantage of opportunities that may not be obvious. It means being prepared for an uncertain future. Therefore, scenario planning is a system designed to heighten the overall awareness of decision makers. The processes within the scenario system are designed to put decision makers in touch with the realities of their industries and organizations. Following the scenario system in this book gives them the "pulse" of the organization. In the end, the purpose of scenarios is to help individuals and teams contribute to the organization's ability to outperform a volatile, uncertain, complex, and ambiguous environment. This book demonstrates the utility of using scenarios in organizations.

Scenario work is challenging and should be very stimulating. Strategic problems or dilemmas are complex and ambiguous, with unknown solutions. These issues can become frustrating to work on without a sound set of tools for analyzing and understanding them. This book provides a system for tackling these difficult issues and working through the phases in an orderly manner so as to produce results.

References

Ackoff, R. L. (1970). *A concept of corporate planning.* New York: Wiley.

Ackoff, R. L. (1978). *Creating the corporate future.* New York: Wiley.

Ackoff, R. L. (1981). *The art of problem solving.* New York: Wiley.

Alexander, W., & Serfass, R. (1998). Creating and analyzing your organization's quality future. *Quality Progress, 31*(7), 31–36.

Allee, V. (1997). *The knowledge evolution: Expanding organizational intelligence.* Newton, MA: Focal Press.

Amara, R., & Lipinski, A. J. (1983). *Business planning for an uncertain future: Scenarios and strategies.* New York: Pergamon.

Argyris, C., & Schon, D. A. (1996). *Organizational learning II. Theory, method, and practice.*

Bauden, R. (1998, March). The Leadership Revolution. Keynote address to AUSTAFE Regional Conference, Ballarat, Victoria.

Bechtel, W. (1998). Representations and cognitive explanations: Assessing the dynamicist's challenge in cognitive science. *Cognitive Science, 22*(3), pp. 295–318.

Berger, P. L., & Luckmann T. (1966). *The social construction of reality: A treatise in the sociology of knowledge.* New York: Doubleday.

Berns, G. (2008). *Iconoclast: A neuroscientist reveals how to think differently.* Cambridge, MA: Harvard Business School Press.

Bloom, M., & Menefee M. L. (1994). Scenario Planning and Contingency Planning. *Public Productivity & Management Review, 17*(3), 223–230.

Bohm, D. (1989). *Quantum theory.* London: Dover.

Bohm, D. (2002). *Wholeness and the implicate order.* London: Routledge.

Bohm, D. (2004). *On dialogue.* London: Routledge.

Brauers, J. L., & Weber, M. (1988). A new method of scenario analysis for strategic planning. *Journal of Forecasting, 7*(1), 31–47.

Brehmer, B. (1990). Strategies in real-time, dynamic decision making. In R. Hogarth (Ed.), *Insights in decision making* (pp. 262–291). Chicago: University of Chicago Press.

Brehmer, B. (1992). Dynamic decision making: Human control of complex systems. *Acta Psychological, 81,* 211–241.

Burt, G. (2006). Pre-determined elements in the business environment: Reflecting on the legacy of Pierre Wack. *Futures, 38*(7), 830–840.

Burt, G., & van der Heijden, K. (2002). Reframing industry boundaries for structural advantage: The role of scenario planning. In G. Ringland (Ed.), *Scenarios in business* (pp. 223–232). New York: Wiley.

Burt, G., & van der Heijden, K. (2003). First steps: Towards purposeful activities in scenario thinking and future studies. *Futures, 35*(10), 1011–1026.

Cascio, J. (2009, October 19). Futures thinking: Asking the question. *Fast Company.*

Chandler, J., & Cockle, P. (1982). *Techniques of scenario planning.* London: McGraw-Hill.

Charon, R. (2001). Narrative medicine: A model for empathy, reflection, profession and trust. *Journal of the American Medical Association, 286,* 1897–1902.

Chermack, T. J. (2002). The mandate for theory in scenario planning. *Futures Research Quarterly, 18*(2), 25–28.

Chermack, T. J. (2004). A theoretical model of scenario planning. *Human Resource Development Review, 3*(4), 301–325.

Chermack, T. J. (2005). Studying scenario planning: Theory, research suggestions and hypotheses. *Technological Forecasting and Social Change, 72*(1), 59–73.

Chermack, T. J., & Kasshanna, B. (2007). SWOT analysis: Reviewing uses, misuses and implications for HRD professionals. *Human Resource Development International, 10*(4), 383–399.

Chermack, T. J., Lynham, S. A., & Ruona, W. E. A. (2001). A review of scenario planning literature. *Futures Research Quarterly, 17*(2), 7–31.

Chermack, T. J., Lynham, S. A., & van der Merwe, L. (2006). Exploring the relationship between scenario planning and perceptions of learning organization characteristics. *Futures, 38*(7), 767–777.

Chermack, T. J., & Nimon, K. (2008). The effects of scenario planning on participant decision-making style. *Human Resource Development Quarterly, 19*(4), 351–372.

Chermack, T. J., & van der Merwe, L. (2003). The role of constructivist learning in scenario planning. *Futures, 35*(5), 445–460.

Chermack, T. J., van der Merwe, L., & Lynham, S. A. (2007). Exploring the relationship between scenario planning and strategic conversation quality. *Technological Forecasting and Social Change, 74*(3), 379–390.

Cleary, T. (1988). *The art of war.* Boston: Shambhala.

Collins, J. (2001). *Good to great: Why some companies make the leap . . . and others don't.* New York: HarperCollins.

Csikszentmihalyi, M. (1996). *Creativity: Flow and the psychology of discovery and invention.* New York: HarperCollins.

Csikszentmihalyi, M. (1998). *Flow: The psychology of happiness.* London: Rider Publications.

D'arcy, M., M. O'Hanlong, P. Orszag, J. Shapiro, & J. Steinberg. (2006). *Protecting the homeland*. New York: Brookings Institution Press.

De Bono, E. (1990). *Six thinking hats*. New York: Penguin.

De Geus, A. (1988). Planning as learning. *Harvard Business Review, 66* (2), 70–74.

De Geus, A. (1997). *The living company*. Boston: Harvard Business School Press.

Delbecq, A., & Van de Ven, A. (1971). A group process model for problem identification and program planning. *Journal of Applied Behavioral Science, 7*(4), 466–492.

Denzin, N. K., & Lincoln, Y. S. (2000). *Handbook of qualitative research* (2nd ed.). Thousand Oaks, CA: Sage.

Dispenza, J. (2007). *Evolve your brain: The science of changing your mind*. Deerfield Beach, FL: Health Communications Books.

Dorner, D. (1996). *The logic of failure*. New York: Metropolitan Books/Holt.

Doyle, J. K., & Ford, D. N. (1999). Mental models concepts revisited: Some clarifications and a reply to Lane. *Systems Dynamics Review, 15*(4), 411–415.

Dreyfus, H. L., & Dreyfus, S. E. (1998). Frictionless forecasting is a fiction. In N. Akerman (Ed.), *The necessity of friction* (pp. 267–284). Boulder, CO: Westview.

Drucker, P. (1994). The theory of the business. *Harvard Business Review, 72*(5), 95–104.

Economist. (2008, September). Scenario planning. Available: www.economist.com/node/12000755.

Ellinger, A. D., Ellinger, A. E., Yang, B., & Howton, S. W. (2002). The relationship between the learning organization concept and firms' financial performance: An empirical assessment. *Human Resource Development Quarterly, 13*(1), 5–21.

Emery, F. E., & Trist, E. L. (1965). The causal texture of organisational environments. *Human Relations, 18,* 21–32.

Fahey, L., & Randall, R. M. (1998). What is scenario learning? In L. Fahey & R. Randall (Eds.), *Learning from the future: Competitive foresight scenarios* (pp. 3–21). New York: Wiley.

Flowers, B. S. (2003). The art and strategy of scenario writing. *Strategy & Leadership, 31*(2), 29–33.

Ford, D. N., & Sterman, J. D. (1998). Expert knowledge elicitation to improve formal and mental models. *Systems Dynamics Review, 14*(4), 309–340.

Forrester, J. W. (1961). *Industrial dynamics*. Cambridge, MA: MIT Press.

Forrester, J. W. (1994). Policies, decisions, and information sources for modeling. In J. Morecroft & J. Sterman (Eds.), *Modeling for learning organizations* (pp. 51–84). Portland, OR: Productivity Press.

Fosnot, C. T. (1996). Constructivism: A psychological theory of learning. In C. T. Fosnot (Ed.), *Constructivism: Theory, perspectives and practice* (pp. 31–49). New York: Teachers College Press.

Frentzel, W. Y., Bryson, J. M., & Crosby, B. C. (2000). Strategic planning in the military. *Long Range Planning, 33*(1), 402–429.

Freyd, J. J. (1987). Dynamic mental representations. *Psychological Review, 94*(4), 427–438.

Georgantzas, N. C., & Acar, W. (1995). *Scenario-driven planning: Learning to manage strategic uncertainty.* Westport, CT: Quorum.

Gladwell, M. (2007). *Blink: The power of thinking without thinking.* San Francisco: Back Bay Books.

Global Business Network. (2003). www.gbn.com/about/scenario_planning.php. Accessed September 14, 2010.

Godet, M. (1987). *Scenarios and strategic management: Prospective et planification strategique.* (D. Green & A. Rodney, Trans.). London: Butterworths.

Godet, M. (2000). The art of scenarios and strategic planning: Tools and pitfalls. *Technological Forecasting and Social Change, 65,* 3–22.

Godet, M., & Roubelat, F. (1996). Creating the future: The use and misuse of scenarios. *Long Range Planning, 29*(2), 164–171.

Greene, R. (1998). *The 48 laws of power.* New York: Penguin.

Hampden-Turner, C. (1990). *Charting the corporate mind: From dilemma to strategy.* Oxford: Blackwell.

Harper, C. (2010). *An alternative approach to marketing scenario planning.* Retrieved from Colorado State University, Organizational Performance and Change Program website: www.scenarioplanning.colostate.edu/researchinprogress.htm.

Hitt, M. A., Hoskisson, R. E., & Ireland, R. D. (1990). Mergers and acquisitions and managerial commitment to innovation in M-form firms. *Strategic Management Journal, 11*(3), 29–47.

Hoffman, B. (2002). *Lessons of 9/11: Testimony before the United States Joint September 11, 2001 Inquiry Staff of the House and Senate Select Committees on Intelligence on October 8, 2002.* Arlington, VA: RAND Corporation. (RAND Corporation Document Number CT-201)

Holton, E. F., III. (1999). Performance domains and their boundaries. In R. J. Torraco (Ed.), *Performance improvement theory and practice* (pp. 26–46). Advances in Developing Human Resources, 1. San Francisco: Berrett-Koehler.

Huss, W. R., & Honton, E. J. (1987). Scenario planning: What style should you use? *Long Range Planning, 20*(4), 21–29.

Ingvar, D. H. (1985). Memory of the future: An essay on the temporal organization of conscious awareness. *Human Neurobiology 4*(1), 127–136.

Johansen, B. (2007). *Get there early: Sensing the future to compete in the present*. San Francisco: Berrett-Koehler.

Johnson-Laird, P. M. (1983). *Mental models*. Cambridge, MA: Harvard University Press.

Kahane, A. (1992). The Mont Fleur Scenarios: What will South Africa be like in the year 2002? Supplement to *Weekly Mail* and *The Guardian Weekly*, Bellville, South Africa.

Kahane, A. (2004). *Solving tough problems*. San Francisco: Berrett-Koehler.

Kahn, H., & Weiner, A. J. (1967). *The year 2000: A framework for speculation on the next thirty-three years*. New York: Macmillan.

Karlgaard, R. (2004, April 26). The age of meaning. *Forbes, 35*.

Kleiner, A. (1996). *The age of heretics*. New York: Doubleday.

Kleiner, A. (2008). *The age of heretics: A history of the radical thinkers who reinvented corporate management* (J-B Warren Bennis Series) (2nd ed.). San Francisco: Jossey-Bass.

Kleiner, A., & Roth, G. (2000). *Oil change: Perspectives on corporate transformation*. London: Oxford University Press.

Kloss, L. (1999). The suitability and application of scenario planning for national professional associations. *Nonprofit Management & Leadership, 10*(1), 71–83.

Koenig, H. G. (2001). *Spirituality in patient care: Why, how, when and what*. San Francisco: Templeton Foundation Press.

Kolb, D., & Rubin, I. M. (1991). *Organizational behavior: An experimental approach*. Englewood Cliffs, NJ: Prentice Hall.

LeDoux, J. E. (2000). Emotion circuits in the brain. *Annual Review of Neuroscience, 23*(3), 155–184.

LeGault, M. E. (2007). *Think: Why crucial decisions can't be made in the blink of an eye*. New York: Threshold.

Lewin, K. (1948). *Resolving social conflicts: Selected papers on group dynamics*. New York: Harper & Row.

Lewin, K. (1951). *Field theory in social science: Selected theoretical papers*. (D. Cartwright, Ed.). New York: Harper & Row.

Liker, J. (2010, February 9). What should Toyota do now? *Business Week*. Retrieved September 14, 2010, from www.businessweek.com/bwdaily/dnflash/content/feb2010/db2010029_723140.htm.

Lindgren, M., & Bandhold, H. (2003). *Scenario planning: The link between future and strategy*. New York: Palgrave Macmillan.

Linneman, R. E., & Klein, H. E. (1979). The use of multiple scenarios by U.S. industrial companies. *Long Range Planning, 12*(1), 83–95.

Linneman, R. E., & Klein, H. E. (1983). The use of multiple scenarios by U.S. industrial companies: A comparison study, 1977–1981. *Long Range Planning, 16*(6), 94–101.

Lynch, M. D. (2005). Developing a scenario-based training program. *FBI Law Enforcement Bulletin, 74*(10), 1–8.

Lynham, S. A. (1998). The development and evaluation of a model of responsible leadership for performance: Beginning the journey. *Human Resource Development International, 1*(2), 207–220.

Lynham, S. A. (2000a). *The development of a theory of responsible leadership for performance.* Unpublished doctoral dissertation, University of Minnesota, St. Paul.

Lynham, S. A. (2000b). Leadership development: A review of the theory and literature. In K. P. Kuchinke (Ed.), *Academy of Human Resource Development conference proceedings* (pp. 285–292). Baton Rouge, LA: Academy of Human Resource Development.

Lynham, S. A. (2002a). The general method of theory-building in applied disciplines. In S. A. Lynham (Ed.), *Advances in Developing Human Resources, 4*(3), 221–241. Thousand Oaks, CA: Sage.

Lynham, S. A. (2002b). Quantitative research and theory building: Dubin's method. In S. A. Lynham (Ed.), *Advances in Developing Human Resources, 4*(3), 242–276. Thousand Oaks, CA: Sage.

Lynham, S. A., Provo, J. M., & Ruona, W. E. A. (1998). The role of scenarios in business strategy and human resource development. In R. J. Torraco (Ed.), *Academy of Human Resource Development conference proceedings* (pp. 169–178). Baton Rouge, LA: AHRD.

Manning, T. (2002). Strategic conversation as a tool for change. *Strategy & Leadership, 35*(5), 35–38.

Martin, J. (1982). Stories and scripts in organizational settings. In A. Hastorf & A. Isen (Eds.), *Cognitive social psychology* (pp. 255–305). New York: Elsevier.

Marx, K. (1953). *Karl Marx and Frederick Engels on Britain.* Moscow: Foreign Languages Publication House.

McWhorter, R., Lynham, S. A., & Porter, D. (2008). Scenario planning as developing leadership capability and capacity. *Advances in Developing Human Resources, 10*(2), 258–284.

Meadows, D. H., Meadows, D. L., & Randers, J. (1992). *Beyond the limits.* White River Junction, VT: Chelsea Green.

Merriam-Webster's Dictionary and Thesaurus. (2006). Springfield, MA: Merriam-Webster.

Michael, D. N. (1973). *Learning to plan and planning to learn.* Alexandria, VA: Miles River Press.

Michael, D. N. (1995). Barriers and bridges to learning in a turbulent human economy. In L. Gunderson, C. Holling, & S. Light (Eds.), *Barriers and bridges to the renewal of ecosystems and institutions* (pp. 461–485). New York: Columbia University Press.

Micklethwait, J., & Woolridge, A. (1996). *The witch doctors: Making sense of the management gurus.* New York: Times Books.

Miller, S. L. (1971). The effects of communication training in small groups upon self-disclosure and openness in engaged couples' systems of interaction: A field experiment. Unpublished doctoral dissertation, University of Minnesota, St. Paul. *Dissertation Abstracts International, 32,* 2819A–2820A. (University Microfilms No. 71-28, 263)

Miller, S. L., Nunnally, E. W., & Wackman, D. B. (1976). A communication training program for couples. *Social Casework, 57,* 9–18.

Miller, S., Wackman, D. & Nunnally, E. W. (1982). *Straight talk: A new way to get closer to others by saying what you really mean.* New York: Signet.

Mintzberg, H. (1990). The design school: Reconsidering the basic premises of strategic management. *Strategic Management Journal, 11*(3), 171–195.

Mintzberg, H. (1994). *The rise and fall of strategic planning.* London: Prentice-Hall.

Mintzberg, H. (2005). *Managers, not MBA's: A hard look at the soft practice of managing and management development.* San Francisco: Berrett-Koehler.

Mintzberg, H. (2009). *Managing.* San Francisco: Berrett-Koehler.

Mintzberg, H., Ahlstrand, B. W., & Lampel, J. (2005). *Strategy safari: A guided tour through the wilds of strategic management.* New York: Simon & Schuster.

Mintzberg, H., & Lampel, J. (1999). Reflecting on the strategy process. *Sloan Management Review, 40*(3), 21–32.

Morecroft, J. D. W. (1983). System dynamics: Portraying bounded rationality. *OMEGA: The International Journal of Management Science, 11*(2), 131–142.

Morecroft, J. D. W. (1985). Rationality in the analysis of behavioral simulation models. *Management Science, 31*(7), 900–916.

Morecroft, J. D. W. (1990). Strategy support models. In R. G. Dyson (Ed.), *Strategic planning: Models and analytical techniques.* Chichester, UK: Wiley.

Morecroft, J. D. W. (1992). Executive knowledge, models and learning. *European Journal of Operational Research, 59*(1), 102–122.

Moyer, K. (1996). Scenario planning at British Airways: A case study. *Long Range Planning, 29*(2), 172–181.

Nash, H. (2007). *2007 strategic leadership survey: A retail boardroom perspective.* London: Nash.

Nunnally, E. W. (1971). *Effects of communication training upon interaction awareness and empathic accuracy of engaged couples: A field experiment.* Unpublished doctoral dissertation, University of Minnesota, St. Paul. *Dissertation Abstracts International, 32,* 4736A. (University Microfilms No. 72-05, 561)

Nunnally, J. C. (1970). *Introduction to psychological measurement.* New York: McGraw-Hill.

Nunnnaly, E. W., & Moy, C. (1989). Communication basics for human service professionals. New York: Sage.

Nutt, P. C. (2002). *Why decisions fail: Avoiding the blunders and traps that lead to debacles.* San Francisco: Berrett-Koehler.

Ogilvy, J. (1995). *Living without a Goal.* New York: Doubleday.

Ogilvy, J. (2002). *Creating Better Futures: Scenario Planning as a Tool for a Better Tomorrow.* Oxford: Oxford University Press.

Ogilvy, J., & Schwartz, P. (1998). Plotting your scenarios. In L. Fahey & R. Randall (Eds.), *Learning from the future* (pp. 1–19). Hoboken, NJ: Wiley.

Ogilvy, J., & Schwartz, P. (2000). *China's Futures.* San Francisco: Jossey-Bass.

Oxford English Dictionary. (2001). Oxford: Oxford University Press.

Oxford English Dictionary. (2006). Oxford: Oxford University Press.

Pascual-Leone, A., Dang, N., Cohen, L. G., Brasil-Neto, J. P., Cammorata, A., & Hallett, M. (1995). Modulation of muscle responses evoked by transcranial magnetic stimulation during the acquisition of new fine motor skills. *Journal of Neurophysiology, 74*(3), 1037–1045.

Penrose, R. (2004). *The road to reality: A complete guide to the laws of the universe.* New York: Vintage Books.

Phelps, R., Chan, C., & Kapsalis, S. C. (2001). Does scenario planning affect performance? Two exploratory studies. *Journal of Business Research, 5*(1), 223–232.

Piaget, J. (1977). *Equilibration of cognitive structures.* New York: Viking.

Pink, D. H. (2006). *A whole new mind: Why right-brainers will rule the future.* New York: Riverhead Books.

Porter, M. E. (1980). *Competitive strategy.* New York: Free Press.

Porter, M. E. (1985). *Competitive advantage.* New York: Free Press.

Provo, J., Lynham, S. A., Ruona, W. E. A., & Miller, R. (1998). Scenario building: An integral methodology for learning, decision-making, and human resource development. *Human Resource Development International, 1*(3), 327–340.

Ramirez, R., Selsky, J. W., & van der Heijden, K. (Eds.). (2008). *Business planning for turbulent times: New methods for applying scenarios.* London: Earthscan.

Reason, P., & Bradbury, H. (2001). *Handbook of action research, participative inquiry and practice.* Thousand Oaks, CA: Sage.

Reynolds, G. (2010). *Presentation Zen: Simple design principles and techniques to enhance your presentations.* Berkeley, CA: New Riders.

Ringland, G. (1998). *Scenario planning: Managing for the future.* New York: Wiley.

Ringland, G. (2002). *Scenarios in business.* New York: Wiley.

Rochlin, G. I. (1998). Essential friction: Error-control in organizational behavior. In N. Akerman (Ed.), *The necessity of friction.* Boulder, CO: Westview.

Rochlin, G. I., La Porte, T. R., & Roberts, K. H. (1987). The self designing high-reliability organization: Aircraft carrier flight operations at sea. *Naval War College Review, 40*(4), 76–90.

Rogers, C. (1957). The necessary and sufficient conditions of therapeutic personality change. *Journal of Consulting Psychology 21*(2), 95–103.

Rogers, C. (1961). *On becoming a person.* Boston: Houghton Mifflin.

Rogers, C., & Skinner, B. F. (1956). Some issues concerning the control of human behavior. *Science 124*(2), 1057–1065.

Rummler, G. A., & Brache, A. P. (1995). *Improving performance: How to manage the white space on the organization chart.* San Francisco: Jossey-Bass.

Schoemaker, P. J. H. (1993). Multiple scenario development: Its conceptual and behavioral foundation. *Strategic Management Journal, 14,* 193–213.

Schoemaker, P. J. H. (1995). Scenario planning: A tool for strategic thinking. *Sloan Management Review, 37*(2), 25–40.

Schoemaker, P. J. H. (2005). Navigating uncertainty: From scenarios to flexible options. In M. A. Hitt & R. D. Ireland (Eds.), *The Blackwell encyclopedia of management* (Vol. 3, pp. 190–193). Malden, MA: Blackwell.

Schwartz, J. M., Stapp, H. P., & Beauregard, M. (2005). Quantum physics in neuroscience and psychology: A neurophysical model of mind-brain interaction. *Biological Sciences, 360*(1458), 1309–1327.

Schwartz, P. (1991). *The art of the long view.* New York: Doubleday.

Schwartz, P. (1996). *The art of the long view: Planning for the future in an uncertain world.* New York: Doubleday.

Scnaars, S. P. (1989). *Megamistakes: Forecasting and the myth of rapid technological change.* New York: Free Press.

Scott, S. G., & Bruce, R. A. (1994). Decision-making style: The development and assessment of a new measure. *Educational and Psychological Measurement, 55*(5), 818–831.

Selin, C. (2007). Professional dreamers: The future in the past of scenario planning. In B. Sharpe & K. van der Heijden (Eds.), *Scenarios for Success* (p. 27–51). New York: Wiley.

Senge, P. (1990). *The fifth discipline.* New York: Doubleday.

Senge, P. (1994). Learning to alter mental models. *Executive Excellence, 11*(3), 16–17.

Senge, P. M., Kleiner, A., Roberts, C., Ross, R. B., & Smith, B. J. (1994). *The fifth discipline fieldbook: Strategies and tools for building a learning organization.* New York: Doubleday.

Sharpe, B. (2007). Conversations with Peter Schwartz and Napier Collyns. In B. Sharpe and K. van der Heijden (Eds.), *Scenarios for Success* (pp. 13–26). New York: Wiley.

Shaw, G., Brown, R., & Bromiley, P. (1998, May–June). Strategic stories: How 3M is rewriting business planning. *Harvard Business Review, 76*(3), 41–50.

Simon, H. A. (1957). *Administrative behavior.* New York: Macmillan.

Simpson, D. G. (1992). Key lessons for adopting scenario planning in diversified companies. *Planning Review, 20*(3), 11–18.

Swanson, R. A. (1994). *Analysis for improving performance: Tools for diagnosing organizations and documenting workplace expertise.* San Francisco: Berrett-Koehler.

Swanson, R. A. (1999). The foundations of performance improvement and implications for practice. In R. J. Torraco (Ed.), *Performance improvement theory and practice* (pp. 1–25). Advances in Developing Human Resources, 1. San Francisco: Berrett-Koehler.

Swanson, R. A. (2001a). *Assessing financial benefits of human resource development.* Cambridge, MA: Perseus.

Swanson, R. A. (2001b). Human resource development and its underlying theory. *Human Resource Development International, 4*(3), 1–14.

Swanson, R. A. (2007). *Analysis for improving performance: Tools for diagnosing organizations and documenting workplace expertise* (2nd ed.). San Francisco: Berrett-Koehler.

Swanson, R. A., & Holton, E. F., III. (1999). *Results: How to assess performance, learning and perceptions in organizations.* San Francisco: Berrett-Koehler.

Swanson, R. A., & Holton, E. F., III. (2001). *Foundations of human resource development.* San Francisco: Berrett-Koehler.

Swanson, R. A., & Holton, E. F., III. (Eds.). (2005). *Research in organizations: Foundations and methods of inquiry.* San Francisco: Berrett-Koehler.

Swanson, R. A., Lynham, S. A., Ruona, W., & Provo, J. (1998). Human resource development's role in supporting and shaping strategic organizational planning. In P. K. Kuchinke (Ed.), *Proceedings of the Academy of Human Resource Development conference* (pp. 589–594). Baton Rouge, LA: Academy of Human Resource Development.

Tessum, F. (1997). Scenario analysis and early warning systems at Daimler-Benz Aerospace. *Competitive Intelligence Review, 8*(4), 30–40.

Thomas, C. W. (1994). Learning from imagining the years ahead. *Planning Review, 22*(3), 6–10.

Thomas, C. W. (1997). Scenarios applied. In *Implementing and applying scenario planning.* New York: Doubleday.

Torraco, R. J. (1997). Theory-building research methods. In R. A. Swanson & E. F. Holton III (Eds.), *Human resource development research handbook: Linking research and practice* (p. 114–137). San Francisco: Berrett-Koehler.

Tucker, K. (1999). *Scenario planning. Association Management, 51*(4), 70–75.

Van der Heijden, K. (1997). *Scenarios: The art of strategic conversation.* New York: Wiley.

Van der Heijden, K. (2000). Scenarios and forecasting: Two perspectives. *Techno-logical Forecasting and Social Change, 65,* 31–36.

Van der Heijden, K. (2005a). Can internally generated futures accelerate organiza-tional learning? *Futures, 36*(3), 145–159.

Van der Heijden, (2005b). *Scenarios: The Art of Strategic Conversation* (2nd ed.). New York: Wiley.

Van der Heijden, K., Bradfield, R., Burt, G., Cairns, G., & Wright, G. (2002). *The sixth sense: Accelerating organizational learning with scenarios.* New York: Wiley.

Van der Merwe, L. (1994). Bringing diverse people to common purpose. In P. M. Senge, A. Kleiner, C. Roberts, R. B. Ross, & B. J. Smith (Eds.), *The fifth dis-cipline fieldbook: Strategies and tools for building a learning organization.* New York: Doubleday.

Van der Merwe, L. (2002). Utilizing scenarios for sustainable organizational re-newal and transformation. In *Corporate Sustainability 2002, Rotterdam School of Management, Erasmus University, The Netherlands, June 6–7.* Rotterdam: Erasmus University Press.

Van der Merwe, L. (2005). *Planning for certainty in uncertain times: Strategic con-versation, scenario based planning, and developing a sustainable business model.* Amsterdam: Centre for Innovative Leadership.

Van der Merwe, L. (2007). *Conversation Quality and Engagement Checklist.* Am-sterdam: Centre for Innovative Leadership.

Van der Merwe, L. (2008). Scenario-based strategy in practice: A framework. *Ad-vances in Developing Human Resources, 10*(2), 216–239.

Van der Merwe, L., Chermack, T. J., Kulikowich, J., & Yang, B. (2007). Strategic conversation quality and engagement skills: Assessment of a new measure. *International Journal of Training and Development, 11*(3), 214–221.

Visser, M. P., & Chermack, T. J. (2009). Perceptions of the relationship between scenario planning and firm performance: A qualitative study. *Futures, 41*(3), 581–592.

Von Hippel, E. (1998). Economics of product development by users: The impact of sticky local information. *Management Science, 44*(5), 629–644.

Vygotsky, L. S. (1978). *Mind in society.* Cambridge, MA: Harvard University Press.

Vygotsky, L. S. (1986). *Thought and language.* Cambridge, MA: MIT Press. (Orig-inal work published 1962)

Wack, P. (1984). *Scenarios: The gentle art of re-perceiving.* Unpublished manuscript, Harvard Business School.

Wack, P. (1985a). Scenarios: Shooting the rapids. *Harvard Business Review, 63* (6), 139–150.

Wack, P. (1985b). Scenarios: Uncharted waters ahead. *Harvard Business Review, 63* (5), 73–89.

Ward, E. W., & Schreifer, A. E. (1998). Dynamic scenarios: System thinking meets scenario planning. In L. Fahey & R. Randall (Eds.), *Learning from the future: Competitive foresight scenarios* (pp. 140–156). New York: Wiley.

Watkins, K. E., & Marsick, V. J. (1995). *Sculpting the learning organization: Lessons in the art and science of systematic change.* San Francisco: Jossey-Bass.

Weick, K. E. (1979). *The social psychology of organizing.* Reading, MA: Addison-Wesley.

Weick, K. E. (1985). Sources of order in underorganized systems: Themes in recent organizational theory. In Y. S. Lincoln (Ed.), *Organizational theory and inquiry* (pp. 106–136). Beverly Hills, CA: Sage.

Weick, K. E. (1990). Introduction: Cartographic myths in organizations. In A. S. Huff (Ed.), *Mapping strategic thought* (pp. 1–10). New York: Wiley.

Wilson, I. (1992). Teaching decision makers to learn from scenarios: A blueprint for implementation. *Planning Review, 20*(3), 18–22.

Wilson, I. (2000). From scenario thinking to strategic action. *Technological Forecasting and Social Change, 65,* 23–29.

Wilson, I., & Ralston, B. (2006). *Scenario Planning Handbook: Developing Strategies in Uncertain Times.* Mason, OH: South-Western.

Wright, G., Cairns, G., & Goodwin, P. (2009). Teaching scenario planning: Lessons from practice in academe and business. *European Journal of Operational Research, 194,* 323–335.

Wright, G., & Goodwin, P. (1999). Future-focused thinking: Combining scenario planning with decision analysis. *Journal of Multi-Criteria Decision Analysis, 8,* 311–321.

Wright, G., & Goodwin, P. (2009). Decision making and planning under low levels of predictability: Enhancing the scenario method. *International Journal of Forecasting, 25*(4), 813–825.

Wright, G., van der Heijden, K., Burt, G., Bradfield, R., & Cairns, G. (2008). Scenario planning interventions in organizations: An analysis of the causes of success and failure. *Futures, 40*(2), 218–236.

Yang, B. (2003). Identifying valid and reliable measures for dimensions of a learning culture. *Advances in Developing Human Resources, 5*(2), 152–162.

Yang, B., Watkins, K. E., & Marsick, V. J. (2004). The construct of the learning organization: Dimensions, measurement and validation. *Human Resource Development Quarterly, 15*(1), 31–55.

Yue, G. (2001, November 21). Mental gymnastics. *New Scientist,* 19.

Yue, G., & Cole, K. J. (1992). Strength increases from the motor program: Comparison of training with maximal voluntary and imagined muscle contractions. *Journal of Neurophysiology, 67*(5), 1114–1123.

Index

About the Author

THOMAS J. CHERMACK has studied and practiced scenario planning for over 15 years. His initial interest in scenario planning was due its unique combination of analysis and creativity in exploring difficult and complex issues. Tom is motivated to challenge status quo thinking and help people see things differently.

Tom consults on scenario projects through his company Chermack Scenarios (www.thomaschermack.com) with organizations worldwide, including Saudi Aramco, Motorola, Directlink Technologies, Cargill, Emerson Process, General Mills, Centura Health, and others. Many of these projects have yielded profound insights for their organization leaders resulting in significant re-perceptions of their organizations, environments, and capabilities. In consulting with world-class organizations, Tom has seen the utility and effectiveness of scenario planning firsthand.

An assistant professor in organizational performance and change at Colorado State University, Tom teaches courses on scenario planning, human expertise, analysis in organizations, change management, and organization development. With a focus on the theoretical foundations and outcomes of scenario planning, Tom's research has won awards of excellence from the Academy of Human Resource Development and has appeared in scholarly journals as well as books and magazines. Much of his published work on the theory and practice of scenario planning includes numerous studies that document its benefits.

Tom is also the founder and director of the Scenario Planning Institute at Colorado State University (www.scenarioplanning.colostate.edu). The Scenario Planning Institute (the first of its kind in the United States) is a hub of activity related to scenario planning, including research, consulting with organizations worldwide, a program for certifying scenario planning facilitators, seminars, and other activities that link Colorado State

University to organizations and members of the community, both locally and internationally.

Applied disciplines like scenario planning require both reflection and action—reflection, for understanding how scenario planning works and how it can be improved, and action, for putting new knowledge to use. Tom has made it a point of his career to study and apply scenario planning. An emphasis on both inquiry and application has provided a unique perspective, and a wealth of experiences that come together in this book.

Tom's experiences with the research and practice of scenario planning have yielded invitations to speak at organizations around the world, as well as present seminars, workshops, and keynote addresses.

Tom lives in Fort Collins, Colorado.

Berrett–Koehler
Publishers

Berrett-Koehler is an independent publisher dedicated to an ambitious mission: *Creating a World That Works for All*.

We believe that to truly create a better world, action is needed at all levels—individual, organizational, and societal. At the individual level, our publications help people align their lives with their values and with their aspirations for a better world. At the organizational level, our publications promote progressive leadership and management practices, socially responsible approaches to business, and humane and effective organizations. At the societal level, our publications advance social and economic justice, shared prosperity, sustainability, and new solutions to national and global issues.

A major theme of our publications is "Opening Up New Space." Berrett-Koehler titles challenge conventional thinking, introduce new ideas, and foster positive change. Their common quest is changing the underlying beliefs, mindsets, institutions, and structures that keep generating the same cycles of problems, no matter who our leaders are or what improvement programs we adopt.

We strive to practice what we preach—to operate our publishing company in line with the ideas in our books. At the core of our approach is stewardship, which we define as a deep sense of responsibility to administer the company for the benefit of all of our "stakeholder" groups: authors, customers, employees, investors, service providers, and the communities and environment around us.

We are grateful to the thousands of readers, authors, and other friends of the company who consider themselves to be part of the "BK Community." We hope that you, too, will join us in our mission.

A BK Business Book

This book is part of our BK Business series. BK Business titles pioneer new and progressive leadership and management practices in all types of public, private, and nonprofit organizations. They promote socially responsible approaches to business, innovative organizational change methods, and more humane and effective organizations.

Berrett–Koehler
Publishers

A community dedicated to creating
a world that works for all

Visit Our Website: www.bkconnection.com

Read book excerpts, see author videos and Internet movies, read our authors' blogs, join discussion groups, download book apps, find out about the BK Affiliate Network, browse subject-area libraries of books, get special discounts, and more!

Subscribe to Our Free E-Newsletter, the *BK Communiqué*

Be the first to hear about new publications, special discount offers, exclusive articles, news about bestsellers, and more! Get on the list for our free e-newsletter by going to **www.bkconnection.com**.

Get Quantity Discounts

Berrett-Koehler books are available at quantity discounts for orders of ten or more copies. Please call us toll-free at (800) 929-2929 or email us at **bkp** .orders@aidcvt.com.

Join the BK Community

BKcommunity.com is a virtual meeting place where people from around the world can engage with kindred spirits to create a world that works for all. BKcommunity.com members may create their own profiles, blog, start and participate in forums and discussion groups, post photos and videos, answer surveys, announce and register for upcoming events, and chat with others online in real time. Please join the conversation!